IMAGES
of America

SHARPSBURG

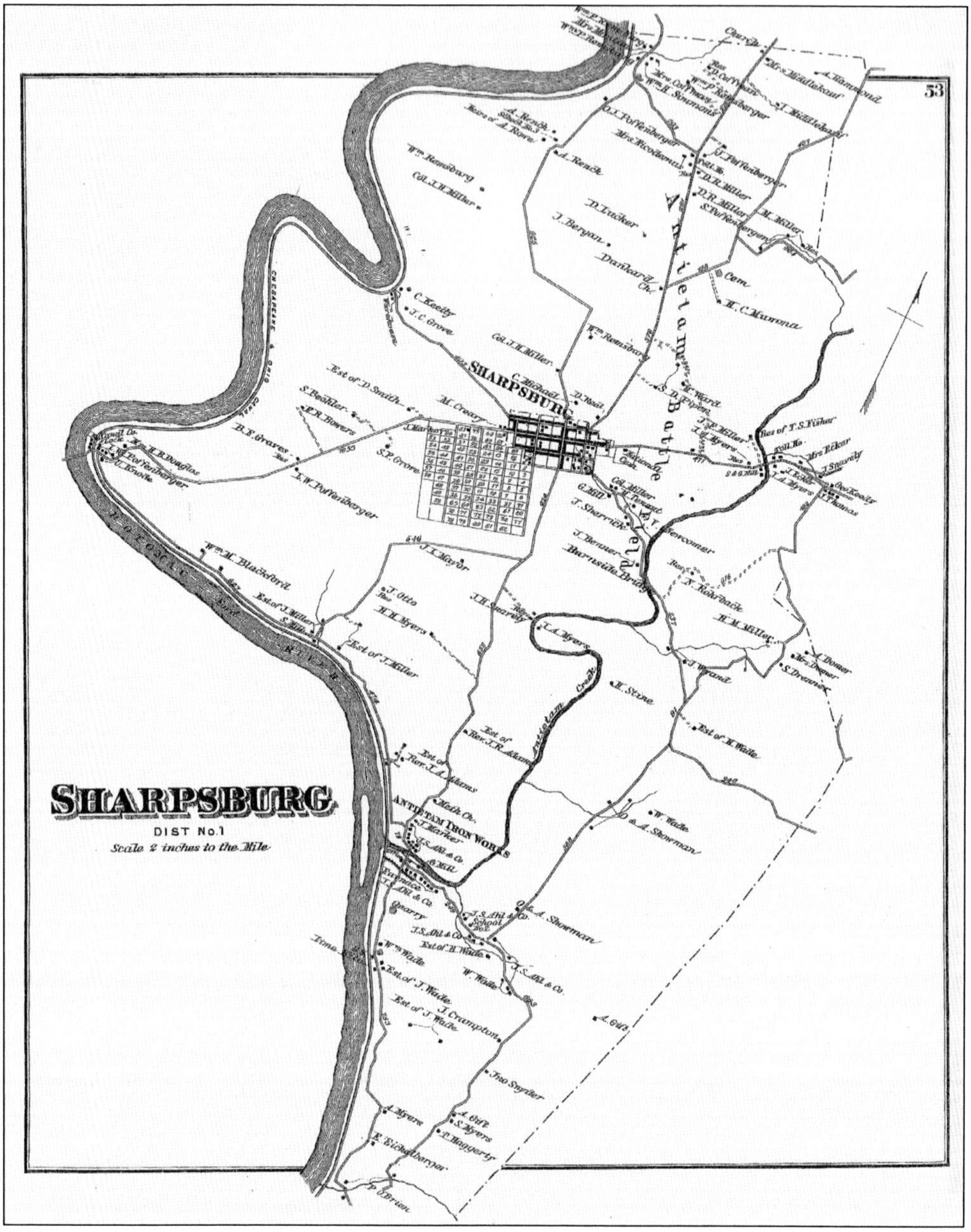

This 1877 map appeared in *An Illustrated Atlas of Washington County, Maryland*. It shows names of land holders, the numbered "out lots," and the sites featured in this book: Burnside Bridge, the National Cemetery, Dunkard church, toll houses, the Antietam Iron Works, Schools No. 2 and No. 3, sawmills and gristmills, Snyder's (Sharpsburg) Landing, and Town Run flowing from Sharpsburg's Big Spring to the Antietam Creek. (Courtesy Washington County Free Library, Western Maryland Room.)

ON THE COVER: Josiah Hammond stands in August 1932 among the items for sale in his J. Hammond General Merchandise store at 115 East Main Street in Sharpsburg. Over the years, as many as six general stores served a town population that has never climbed above 2,000 residents. (Courtesy Frank Hammond.)

IMAGES
of America

SHARPSBURG

Vernell Doyle and Tim Doyle

ARCADIA
PUBLISHING

ISBN 978-0-7385-6805-8

Published by Arcadia Publishing
Charleston, South Carolina

Printed in the United States of America

Library of Congress Control Number: 2009933394

For all general information contact Arcadia Publishing at:
Telephone 843-853-2070
Fax 843-853-0044
E-mail sales@arcadiapublishing.com
For customer service and orders:
Toll-Free 1-888-313-2665

Visit us on the Internet at www.arcadiapublishing.com

To all who look to the past to enrich the present and to inform the future

Contents

ACKNOWLEDGMENTS

We are deeply indebted to current and former residents of Sharpsburg and their families who shared time, suggestions, stories, and photographs. Of this group, we particularly thank Frank Hammond; Rosita Ray; Bonnard J. Morgan Sr.; William Poffenberger; Robert Brooks, M.D.; and Annabelle and the late Robert Earl Roulette.

This book would have been impossible to complete without help from the following: Sharpsburg Historical Society (SHS), Brad Toole; Washington County Historical Society (WCHS), James D. Neville; National Park Service, Antietam National Battlefield (NPS/ANB), Ted Alexander; National Park Service, Chesapeake and Ohio Canal National Historical Park (NPS/C&O Canal NHP), Sam Tamburro and Karen M. Gray, Ph.D.; Washington County Free Library, Western Maryland Room (WCFL/WMR), John Frye and Elizabeth Howe; *Maryland Cracker Barrel*, Suanne and Frank Woodring; Sharpsburg Town Council, Jeffrey Saylor; Sharpsburg Public Library, Betty Holtz; Sharpsburg Elementary School, Vickie Winston; Sharpsburg Volunteer Fire Company, Shawn McCoy; St. Paul's Episcopal Church, Rev. Mark Michael; Christ Reformed United Church of Christ, Rev. Delancy Catlett; and Holy Trinity Memorial Evangelical Lutheran Church, Judy Walkly.

We have, in many cases relied on previously published material. We apologize for any inaccuracies and mistakes we might have included. We welcome your correspondence; write to us at Antietamhouse111@aol.com.

Introduction

A man, a plan, a canal, and a pivotal Civil War battle shaped Sharpsburg, Maryland, Washington County's oldest town. Containing 321 properties with 515 contributing resources, Sharpsburg was added to the National Register of Historic Places as a Historic District on December 24, 2008.

Almost 250 years ago, Joseph Chapline Sr. laid out the town's plan and began selling lots. He was a landholder, a lawyer, a soldier, an assemblyman, a justice of the peace, and the father of nine children. As was customary, he and his wife, Ruhama (Williams), were first buried near their homesite, which was near the Potomac River about halfway between Shepherdstown, West Virginia, and Snyder's Landing on the Chesapeake and Ohio (C&O) Canal. A February 10, 1893, newspaper article reports that a Mrs. Dare of Washington, D.C., sent money to John P. Smith of Sharpsburg to pay for reinterring in Mountain View Cemetery "the remains of seven of the Chaplain [*sic*] family now buried on the Neikirk farm along the Potomac river about two miles west of Sharpsburg."

Joseph Chapline Jr., who inherited the town, built the country estate called Mount Pleasant near Snyder's Landing on the C&O Canal. Jeremiah Chapline inherited the original homesite after the death of his father, Joseph Sr., in 1769.

Until the 1830s, most residents were small-time farmers, merchants, or tradesmen. The C&O Canal brought a new means of livelihood to Sharpsburg families, and many became "canallers." At one time, 49 canal captains called Sharpsburg their home base.

The future of the town and surrounding farms forever changed when the Army of Northern Virginia met the Army of the Potomac outside Sharpsburg near Antietam Creek. Citizens found themselves after September 17, 1862, in a despoiled landscape with churches and homes turned into hospitals and fields into burial grounds.

The town eventually returned to a state of normalcy, and after the C&O Canal ceased operation in 1924, Sharpsburg evolved into a quiet community that was bypassed by major highways and development. The town plan and many of the homes and outbuildings are in 2009 as they were in the middle of the 19th century. The town's small log homes, now mostly covered with siding, still line the town's eight streets. Larger stone homes and brick structures on Main Street look much as they did on period postcards. Churches and schools may have been moved, but they are still vital community centers.

Veterans and other visitors have traveled to the town, to the National Cemetery, and to Antietam National Battlefield since that September day's battle left a record of 23,110 casualties. Today (2009) Sharpsburg embodies small-town America with the look and feel of the past, except for the traffic on Main Street.

This book about Sharpsburg, a town created by both great and ordinary people and one unforgettable event, will have fulfilled its purpose if it contributes both understanding and pleasure to its readers.

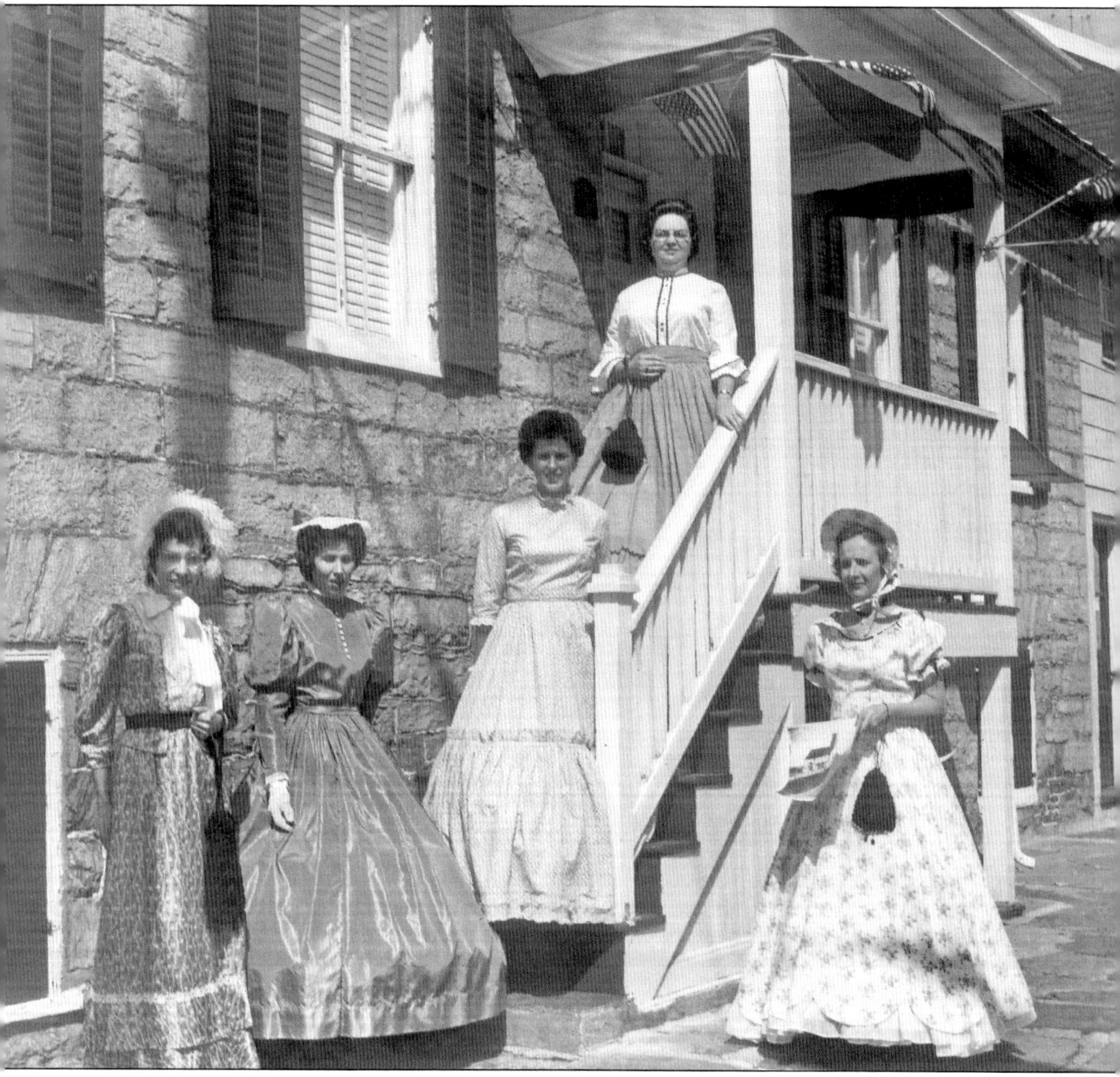

In 1962, Sharpsburg celebrated its bicentennial. These five women in period costumes were responsible for promoting a walking tour of the town. They are in front of the Good-Reilly House, perhaps the oldest house in Sharpsburg. William Good, Joseph Chapline's attorney, bought Lot 50 on Main Street in 1764. After 1811, Jeremiah Chapline's widow, Elizabeth, bought the house. In 1815, she sold it to her brother Gabriel Nourse, Sharpsburg's postmaster. Oliver T. Reilly, a leading battlefield guide, bought the house in 1894. He added a little store and operated a souvenir and relics shop in the basement. The woman at the top of the steps is unidentified; the others are, from left to right, Kathleen Boyer, Barbara Highbarger Leatherman, Mary Margaret Swain Poffenberger, and Mary Grove, who is holding a flyer that shows the Alexander Gardner photograph of the battle-damaged Lutheran church. The spirit of a walking tour infuses this book. (Courtesy authors' collection.)

One

The Town

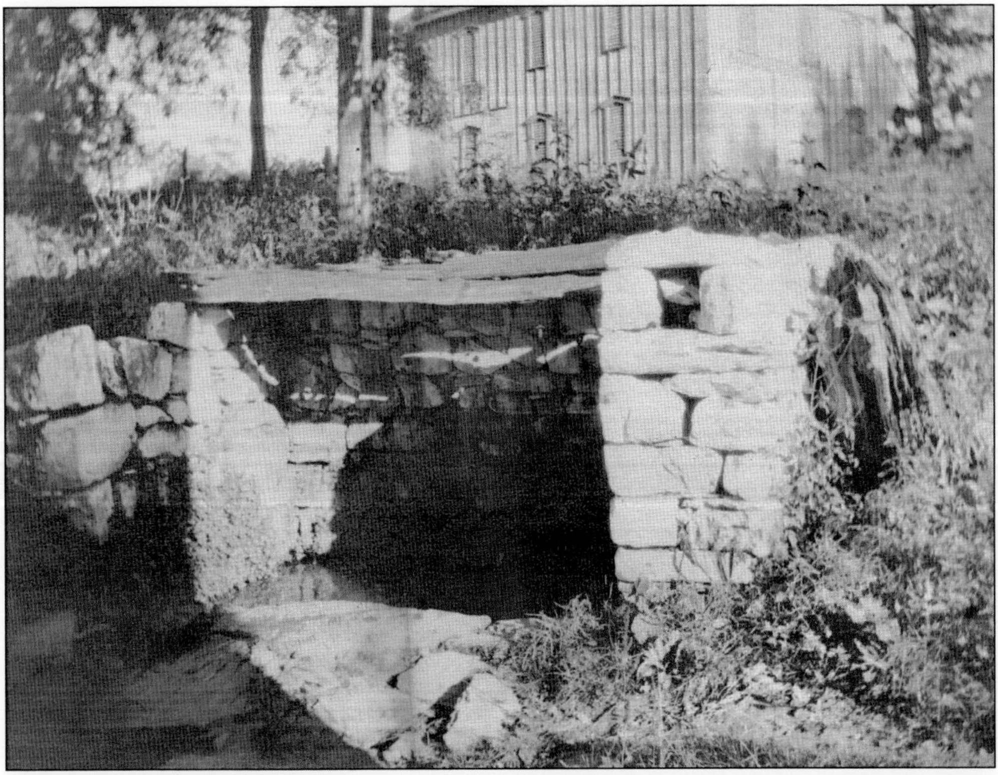

This is the Great Spring or Big Spring, which helped Joseph Chapline Sr. determine the placement of the town of Sharpsburg. Before 1763, a nearby settlement of four houses was called Great Spring. Before then, the Shawnee, Delaware, and Catawba Indians followed trails to this unfailing source of fresh water. At some point, protective stone walls and a plank roof were set around the town's main water source. (Courtesy Frank Hammond.)

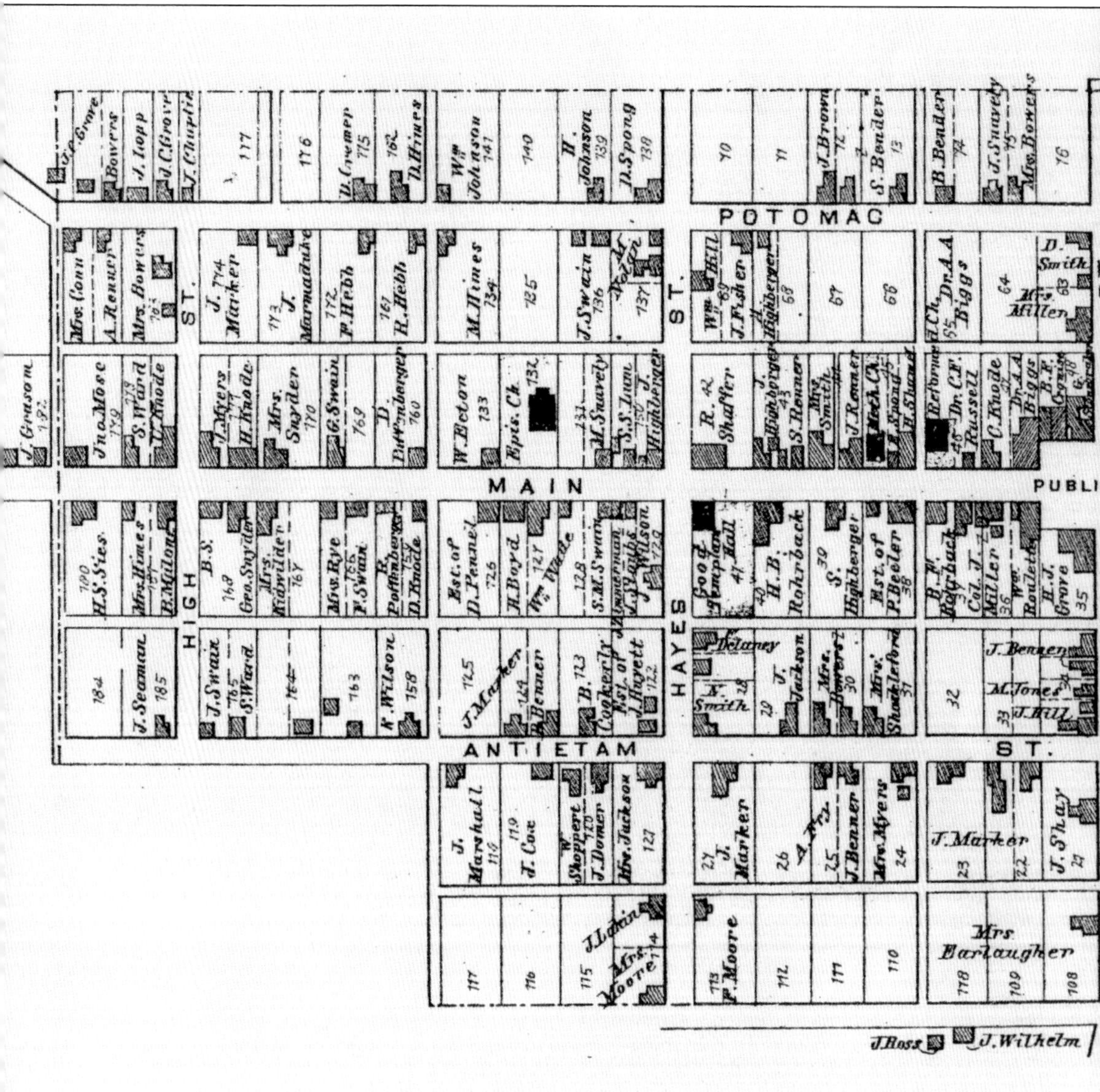

Reflecting few changes from founder Joseph Chapline's 1763 town design, this 1877 map shows Sharpsburg's eight streets and alleys. It also shows who owned the town's lots in 1877. Potomac Street is now Chapline Street, and High Street is Potomac Street. Hays Street is Hall Street. Miller Street is Church Street, and the unnamed last east-west street on the south side of town is now named High Street. Only Main, Mechanic, and Antietam Streets have retained their

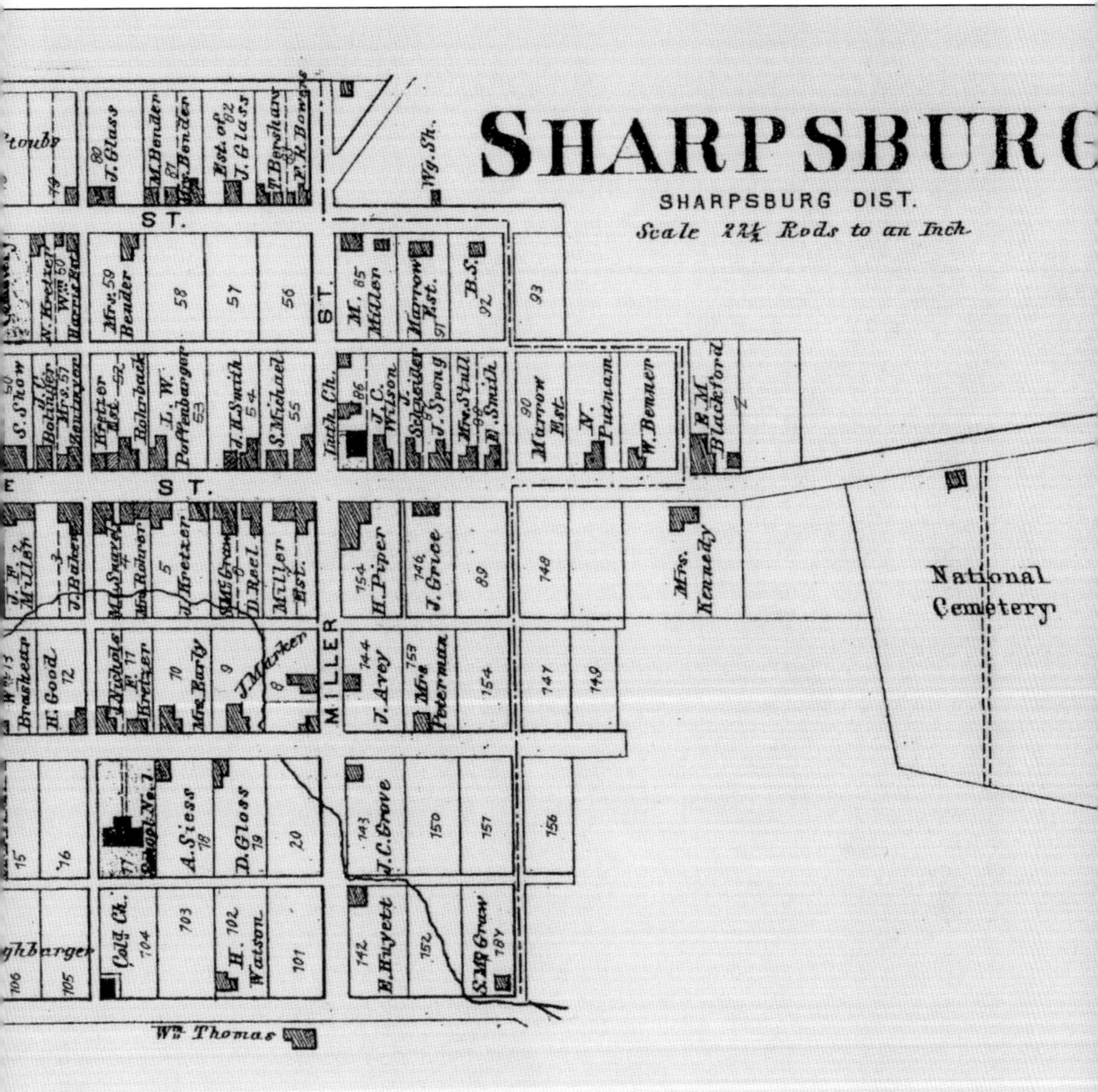

original street names. Joseph Chapline Sr. died in 1769 and, according to his will, seven of his children each received one town lot. James received Lot 76; Jeremiah, Lot 84; Deborah, Lot 43; Ruhannah, Lot 41; Sarah, Lot 130; Jean, Lot 16; and Theodosha, Lot 15. Joseph Chapline Jr. inherited the rest of the town. (Courtesy WCFL/WMR.)

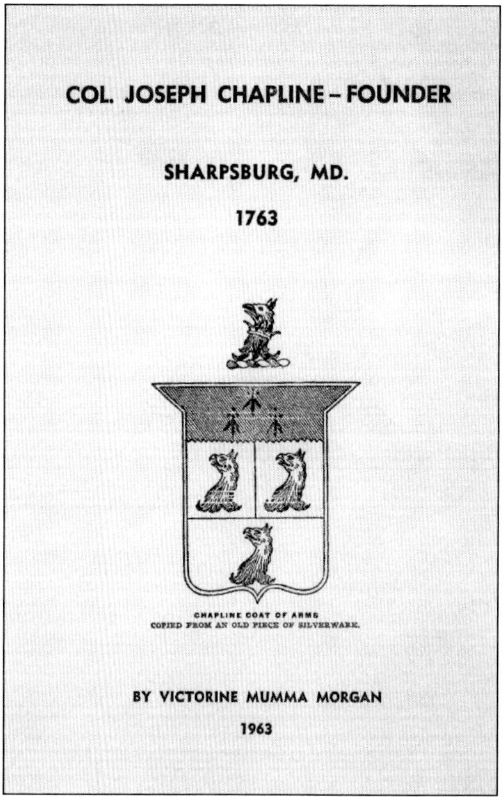

The framed original of Sharpsburg's official seal, designed by Dieter Protsch in 1986, hangs in town hall. The founding date surrounds a griffin's head. Griffins are on the coats of arms of Horatio Sharpe and Joseph Chapline. The banner on the seal refers to the town's great spring, symbolized by the horn of plenty pouring water, which flows into the Antietam Creek. The town's association with the Civil War is represented by the cannon, the Union and Confederate flags, and Burnside Bridge. The Latin word for governor identifies Horatio Sharpe, friend of Chapline, and the crosses signify the town's Christian heritage. The coat of arms shown here with four griffin heads, copied from an old piece of silverware, is on the cover of a biography of Chapline, founder of Sharpsburg. (At left, courtesy Bonnard J. Morgan Sr.; below, courtesy Jeffrey Saylor.)

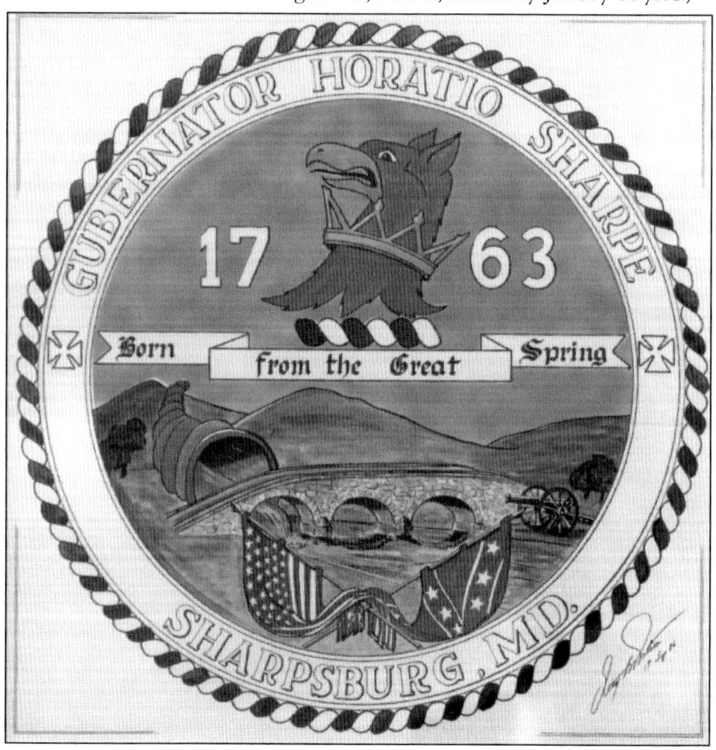

In his will dated January 27, 1768, Joseph Chapline Sr. gave to his son Joseph "all that Tract of Land called 'Joe's Lott' that lies on the west side of Bigg Anteatum together with the town of Sharpsburgh." According to Lee and Barbara Barron's *History of Sharpsburg*, that was 2,100 acres. This portrait of Joseph Chapline Jr., preserved behind cracked glass, shows a successful, fashionable gentleman of the last half of the 18th century. (Courtesy Bonnard J. Morgan Sr.)

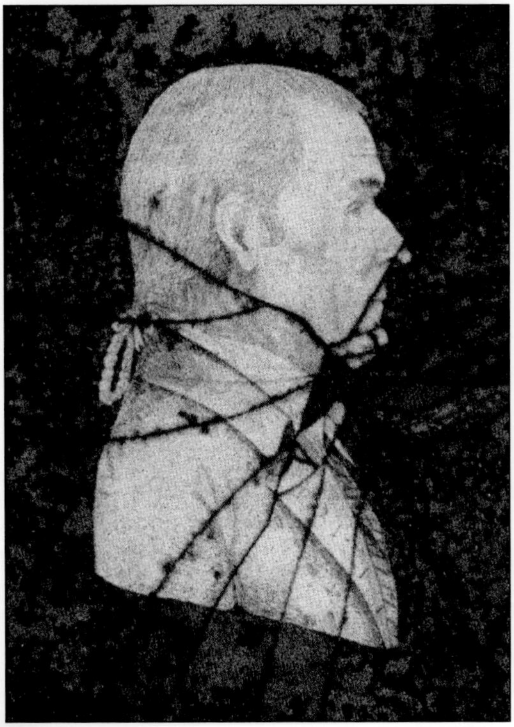

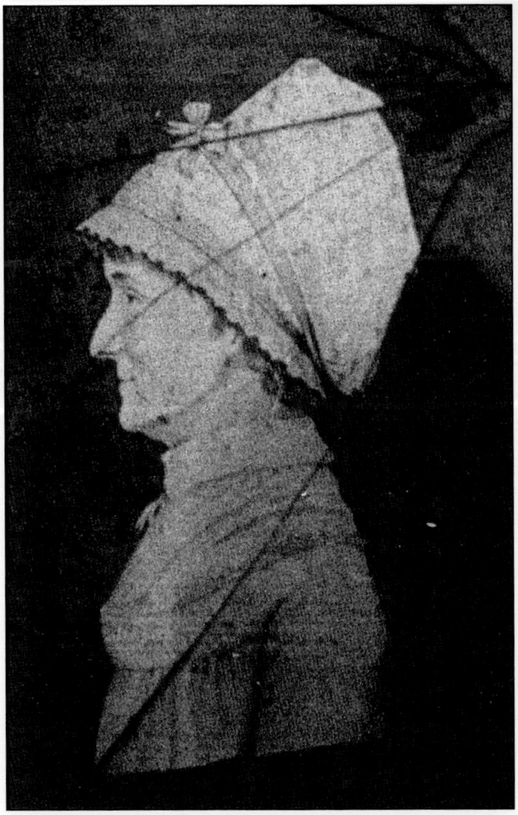

In 1770, Mary Ann Christian Abigail Ferguson from Frederick Town married Joseph Chapline Jr., who was practicing law in that city. The couple lived in their country estate called Mount Pleasant, northwest of Sharpsburg. The history of St. Paul's Episcopal Church tells of a minister being invited by Captain Chapline and "his lady" to be their guest at their Mount Pleasant home. Chapline Jr. was appointed captain in the Revolutionary War. (Courtesy Bonnard J. Morgan Sr.)

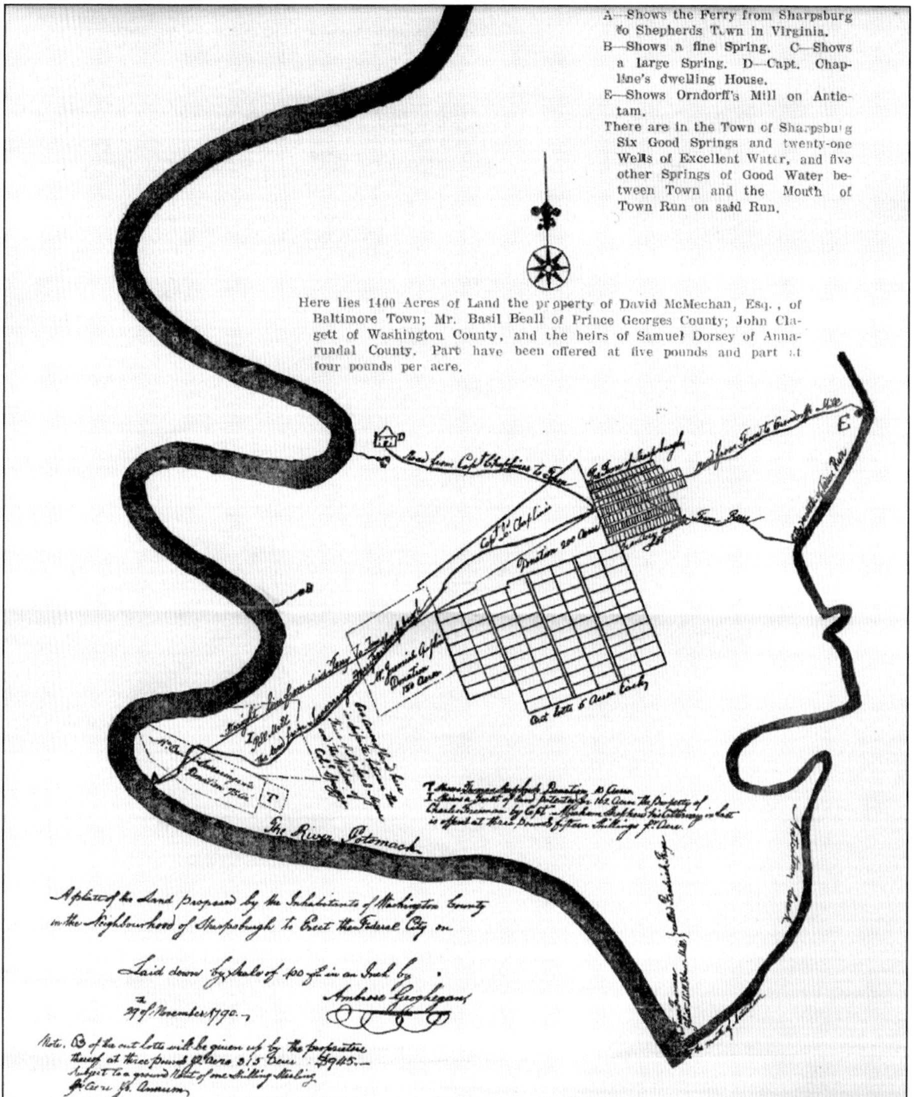

FAC-SIMILE COPY OF MAP OF PROPOSED CAPITOL CITY

(Reduced to One-fifth Original Size)

The author has taken the liberty to eliminate the hand written description as shown on the original in the Library of Congress and substituted in lieu thereof type printed at the top hereof. It is hoped the substitution will make it more easily read. See letters printed on pages 175, 176, 177.

In 1790, Capt. Joseph Chapline Jr. proposed that the nation's capital be near Sharpsburg. This drawing is "a platt of the Land proposed by the Inhabitants of Washington County in the Neighborhood of Sharpsburgh to Erect the Federal City on." Between "The River Potomack" and the Antietam Creek is noted land to be donated by Chapline and others as well as land available for sale at 3 or more pounds per acre. The sellers of the out lots were to be paid also "a ground rent of one shilling sterling per acre per annum." East of town is Orndorff's Mill. At the mouth of the Antietam Creek is "Frederick Forge." Along the Potomac are marked two springs. One is near Chapline's "Dwelling House," Mount Pleasant. The other spring is probably the location of Joseph Chapline Sr.'s home place. Town Run flows from the Great Spring in town to its entrance into Antietam Creek. Washington did not choose Sharpsburg, and as it had lost its bid for the county seat, so, too, did it lose its bid to be the country's capital. (Courtesy WCFL/WMR.)

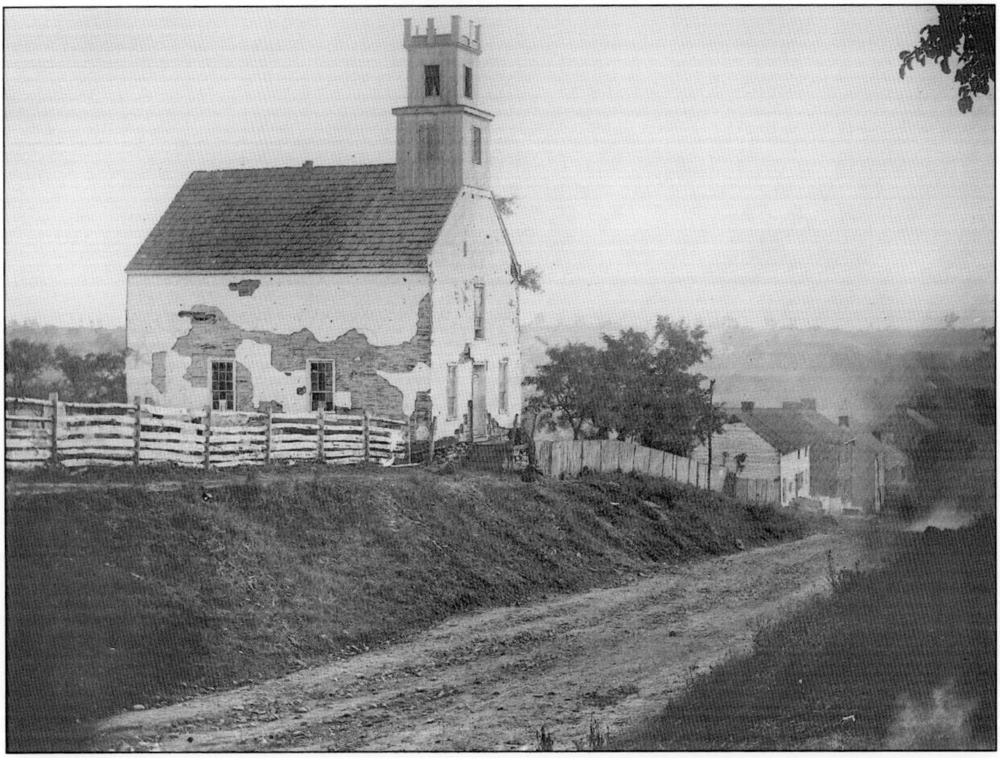

The first Lutheran church in Sharpsburg was built in 1768 on land deeded by Joseph Chapline Sr. for the price of one peppercorn to be paid annually. The log church was 33 feet by 38 feet. Until 1832, services were in German. This 1862 photograph by Alexander Gardner shows the damaged church following the Battle of Antietam. Confederate forces used the church as a signal tower, and the Union troops shelled the building at the east end of town. Two men sit near the front door. On a wood panel, an unidentified itinerant artist painted the damaged church and added six houses west into town. Most of the houses are not identified, but one twin double-chimney house still stands at 120 East Main Street. (Above, courtesy Library of Congress; below, courtesy Rosita Ray.)

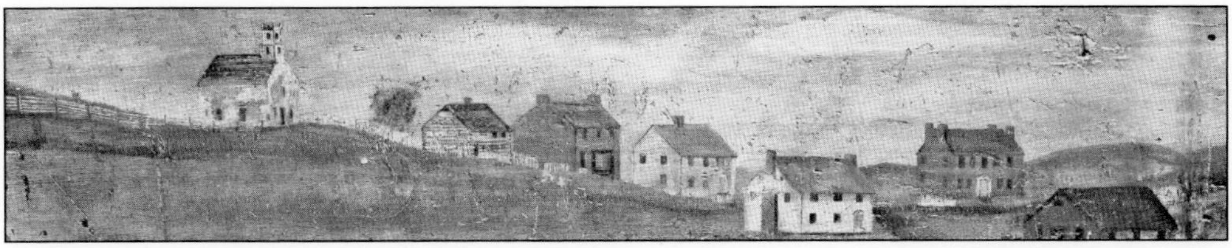

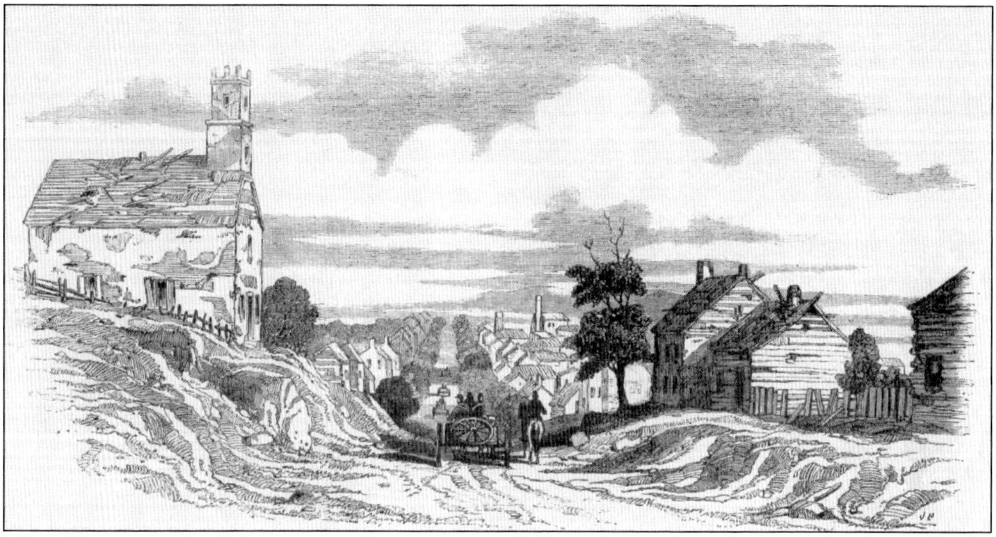

This illustration by J. B. appeared in the October 18, 1862, issue of *Frank Leslie's Illustrated Newspaper.* The scene, which shows great damage to the roof and fence, gives an expanded view of Main Street looking west from the church. The street scene includes soldiers in a wagon and on a horse as well as buildings on the north side of Main Street. The tallest tower identifies St. Paul's Episcopal Church. (Courtesy WCFL/WMR.)

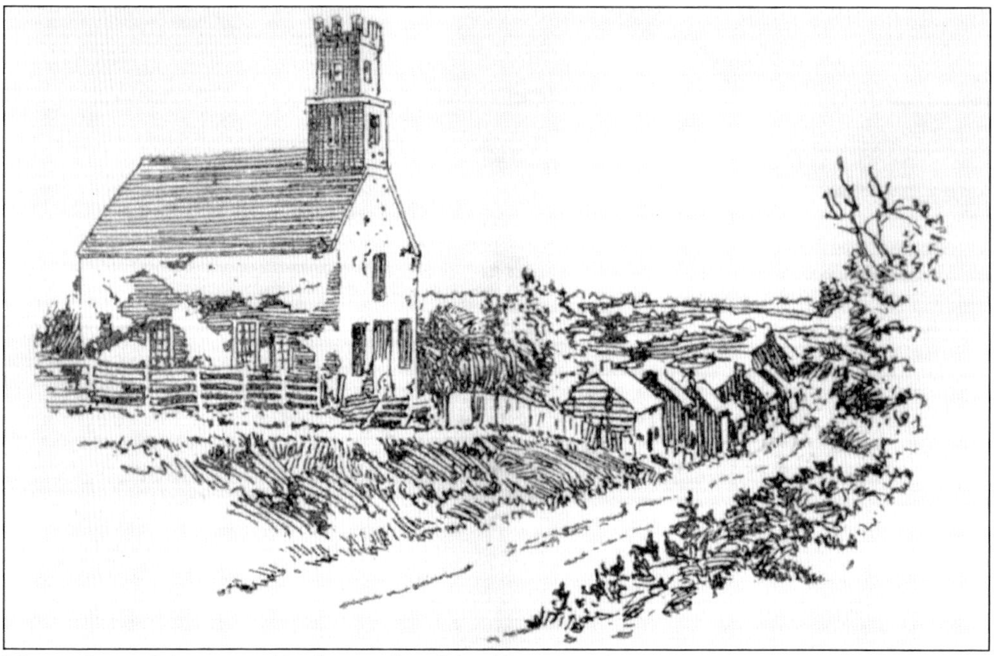

This etching of the original Lutheran church building, based on Alexander Gardner's photograph, emphasizes the damaged stucco. The church was used as a Federal hospital until February 1863. Pews were used to make coffins, and some soldiers were buried in the adjoining cemetery, where headstones date from 1774. After its service as a hospital, the church was deemed unfit for worship and was torn down in April 1863. (Courtesy Holy Trinity Memorial Evangelical Lutheran Church.)

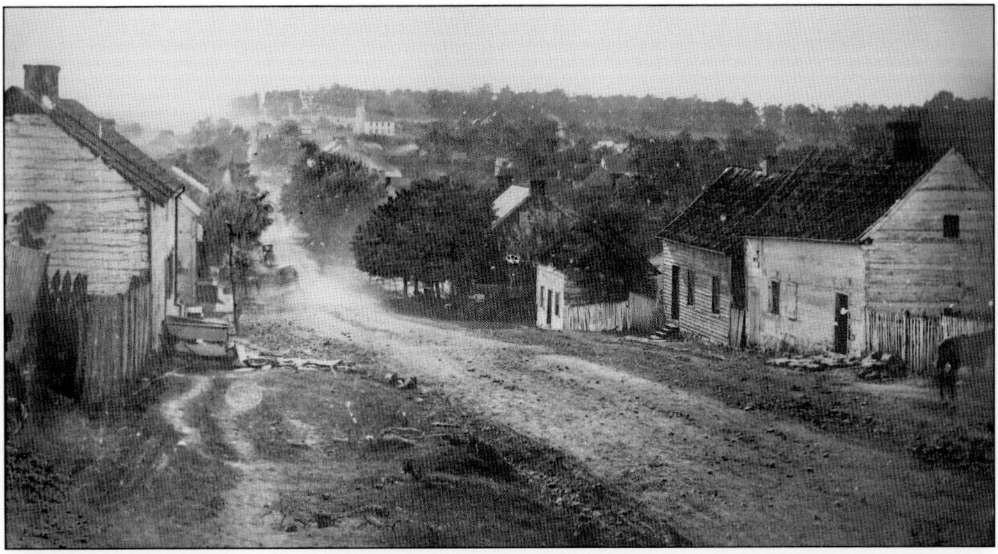

This Alexander Gardner photograph shows Main Street looking west from a point near the old Lutheran church site. It shows typical log houses without porches and with different exterior treatments. The house at the left, perhaps that of Maggie Hoffmaster in 1862, is whitewashed; the house at the right appears to be covered with clapboards. The Episcopal church is visible in the distance. (Courtesy Library of Congress.)

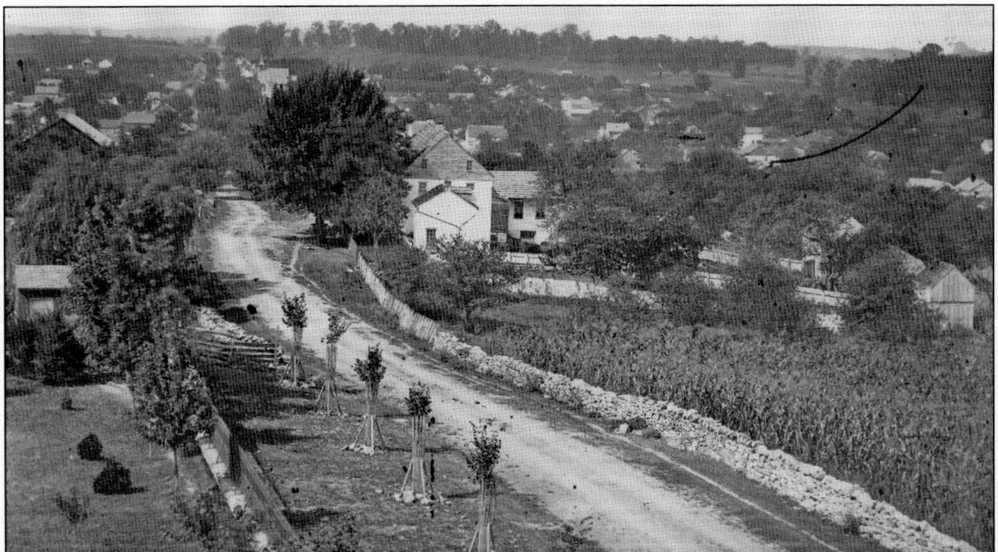

This 1877 photograph by William H. Tipton looking west from the National Cemetery shows the town of Sharpsburg recovering from the Battle of Antietam. Note the different kinds of fencing. Unmortared stones border the cornfield. Wooded paling fences enclose the yard next to the home on the right. Newly planted and braced trees line the north side of the street. (Courtesy NPS/ANB.)

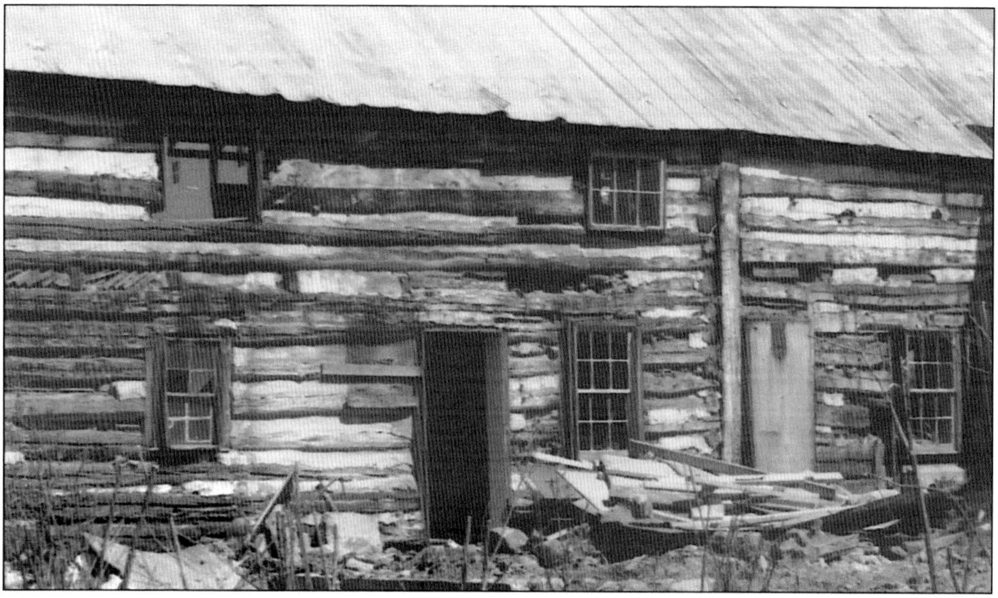

This 1985 photograph shows Raymond Howard's house at 204 East Main Street before it was demolished. The log house appears to have had two sections. The picture shows the kind of fill and rubble, boards and stones, put between logs before they were mortared. This may be the structure shown on the 1877 map on Lot 146 owned by J. Grice. (Courtesy Rosita Ray.)

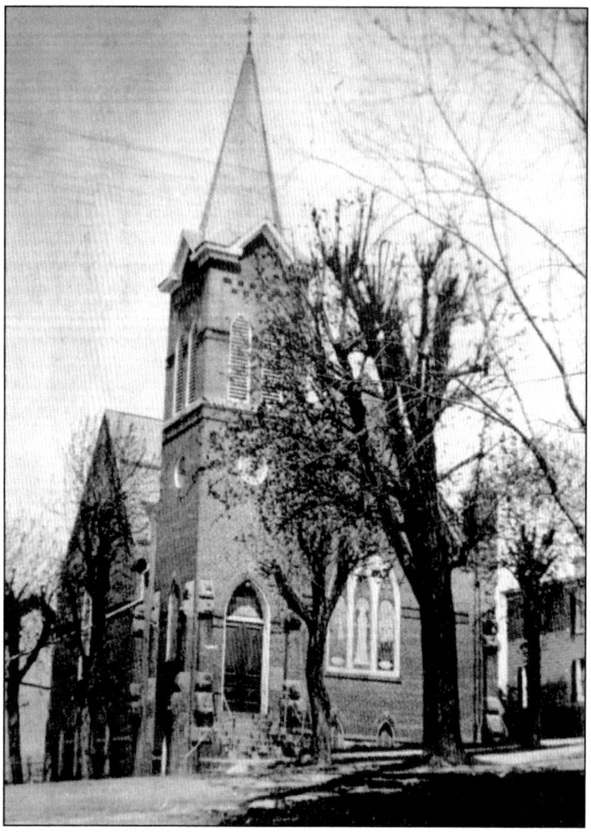

The cornerstone of the Holy Trinity Memorial Evangelical Lutheran Church was laid on September 17, 1892, the 30th anniversary of the Battle of Antietam. A church history says the building was dedicated on May 25, 1898, as a memorial to "the Federal Soldiers who fought and those who fell at the Battle of Antietam." Everything in the church, including the bricks, was a memorial. A fire on December 23, 1942, left only the brick walls. (Courtesy Holy Trinity Memorial Evangelical Lutheran Church.)

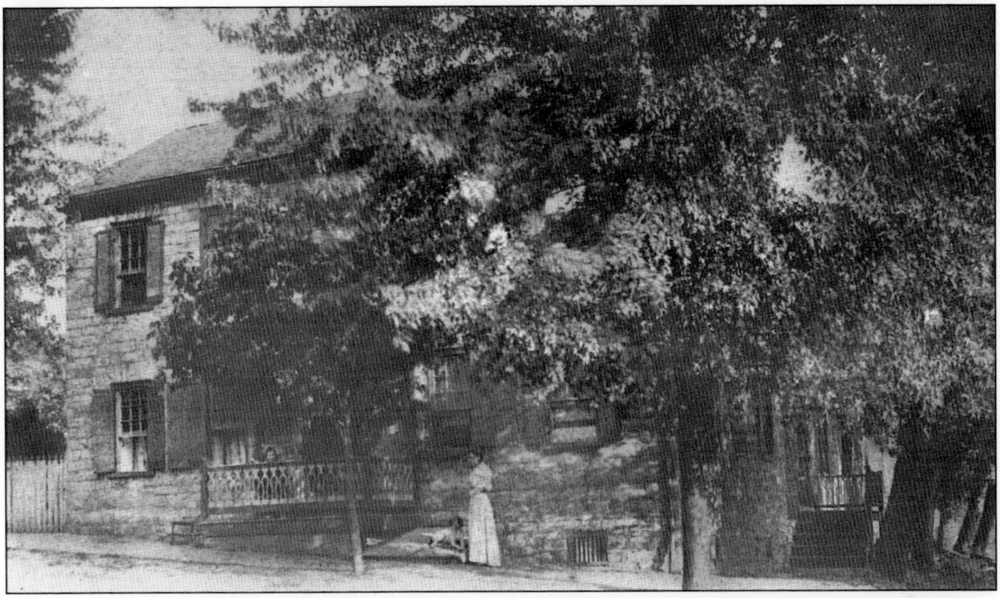

This "Grey-Stone House" on Lot 145 at the southeast corner of Church and Main Streets became the Piper House when Daniel Piper bought it in 1839 from Samuel Detrick for $1,705. The date of construction is thought to be about 1790. The house remained in the Piper family until 1968. It is one of the four cut-stone houses in Sharpsburg. The upstairs has a large ballroom that has a spring-supported floor. At the rear on the second floor is a small room that was reportedly once the room of Emory Summers, a slave owned by the Pipers. Aimee Smith is eating watermelon at the entrance of the springhouse in the garden, which still has the original stone retaining walls. The house was placed on the National Register of Historic Places in 1999. (Both, courtesy Rosita Ray.)

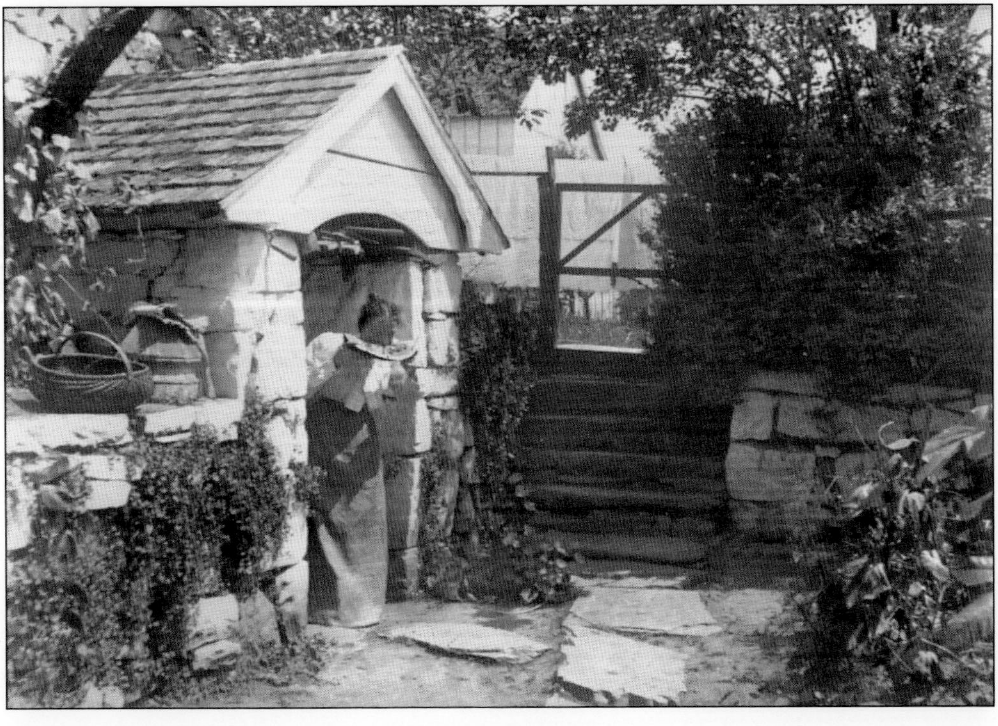

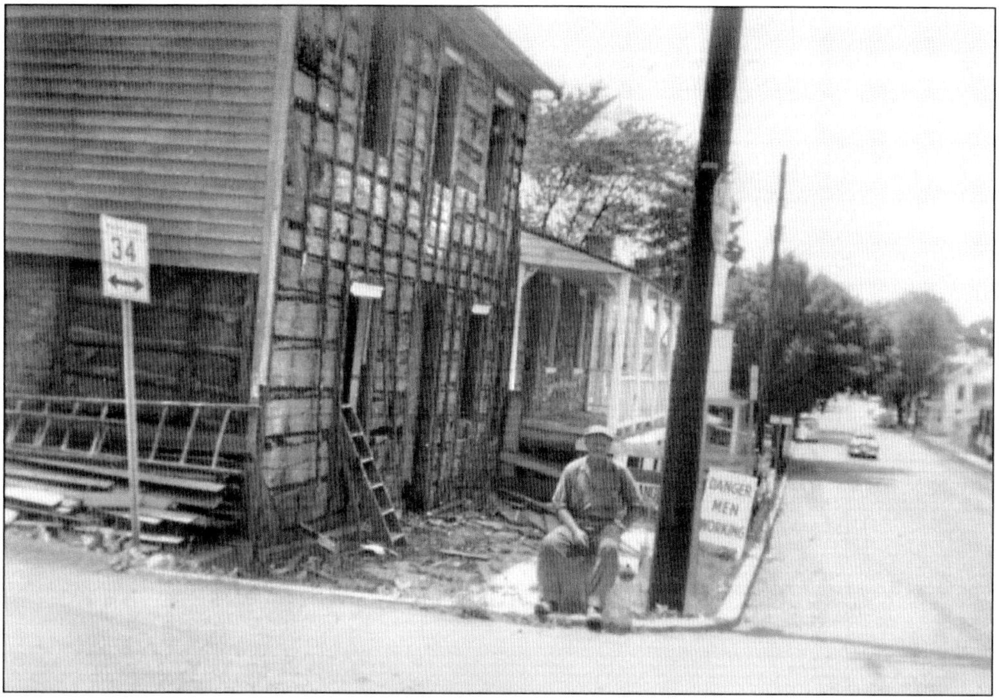

This house, being razed in 1957 to make way for a service station, stood on the southwest corner of Church and Main Streets. The 1877 map indicates a Miller Estate on Lot 7. Items found in the demolition date from the 1820s. The building had been used as a school and, perhaps, as a stop on the Underground Railroad. Phil Lum sits on the large stone that is called the "slave block." (Courtesy WCFL/WMR.)

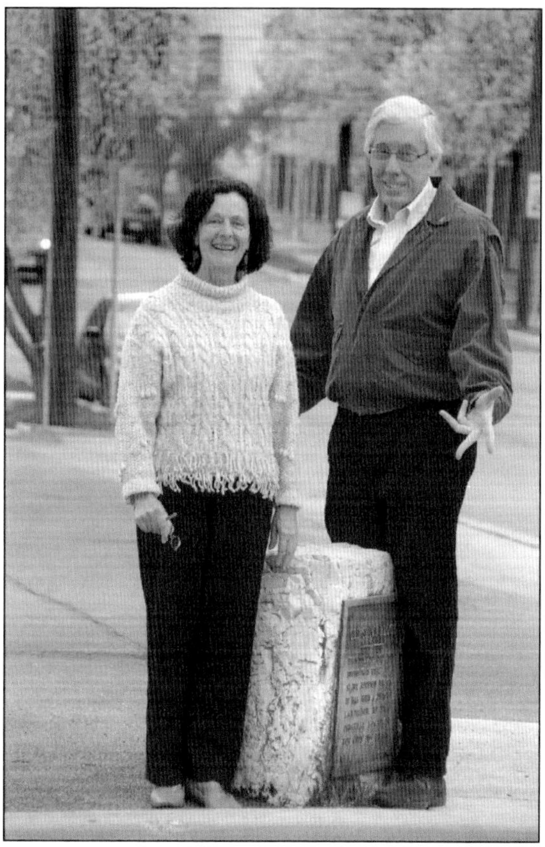

The plaque on the stone says the stone was used as a slave auction block for 65 years and that it has been at this location for 150 years. Most residents discount the "slave block" story and believe the stone was simply a carriage stepping stone. The authors are standing at this famous landmark on the corner in Sharpsburg, Maryland. (Photograph by Tim Doyle.)

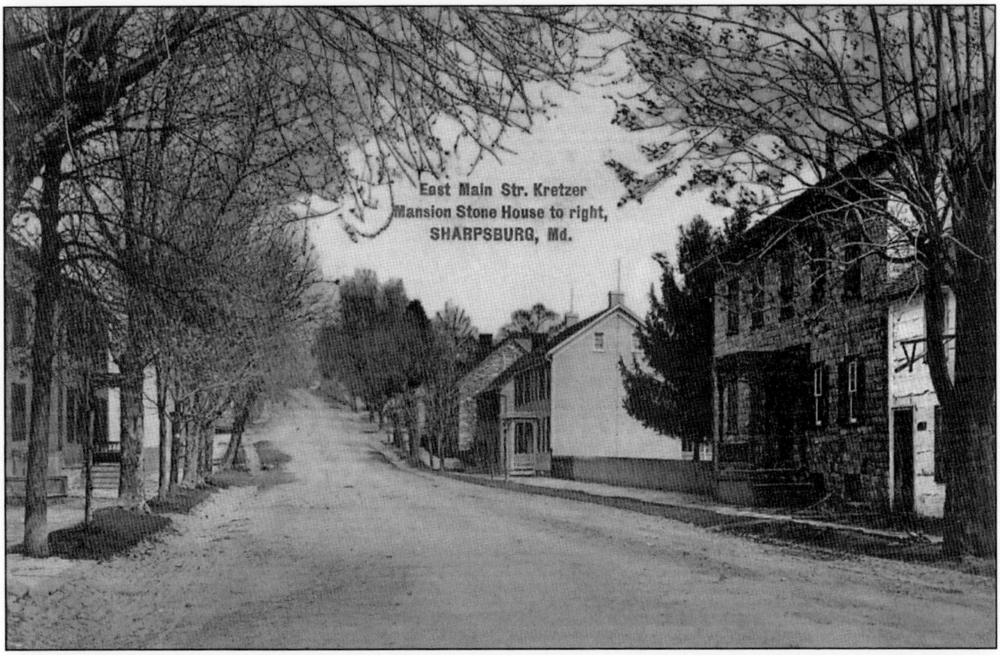

The stone house on the right of this postcard is the home owned by John Kretzer in 1862. It was built on Lot 5 by 1831. The Kretzer family opened the four-room cellar to town residents during the battle. Different sources say 60 to 200 people hid there. Kretzer's daughter Theresa saved their U.S. flag by making the Confederate soldiers think she had burned it when she had only hidden it in "ashes." (Courtesy Stephen Recker.)

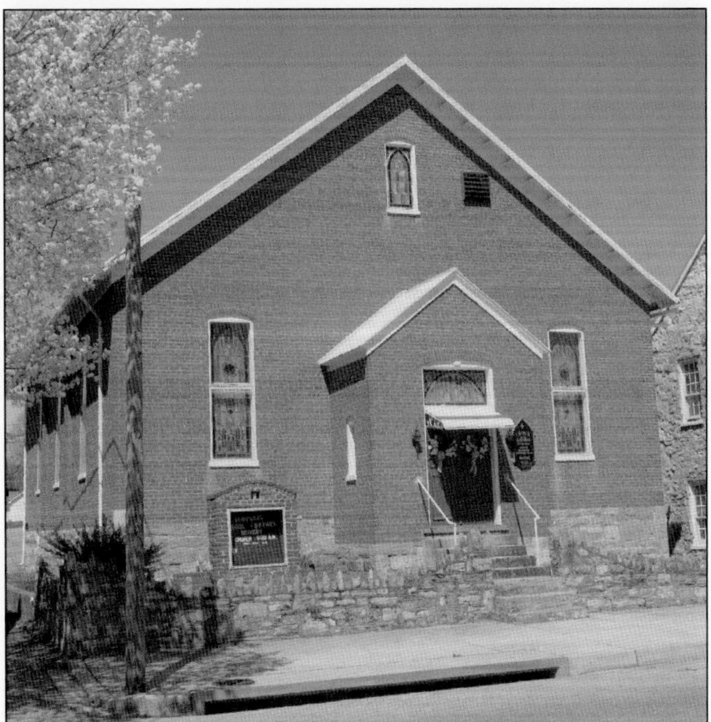

When the congregation of the Dunker church on the battlefield outgrew that building, it constructed a church on half of Lot 52, 123 East Main Street. The building was dedicated on January 1, 1899. The congregation left the Manor Church of the Brethren in 1950 and is now called the Sharpsburg Church of the Brethren. The church was rededicated on December 26, 1999. (Photograph by Tim Doyle.)

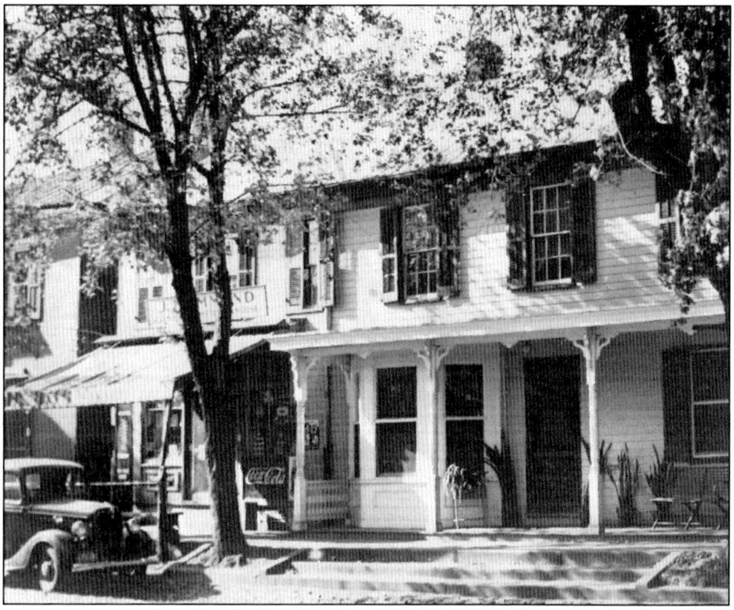

Situated at 117 East Main Street, the Josiah Hammond family residence was conveniently located next door to the family's J. Hammond General Merchandise store at 115 East Main Street. The store's sign can be seen above the awning and behind the tree in this 1930s photograph. (Courtesy Frank Hammond.)

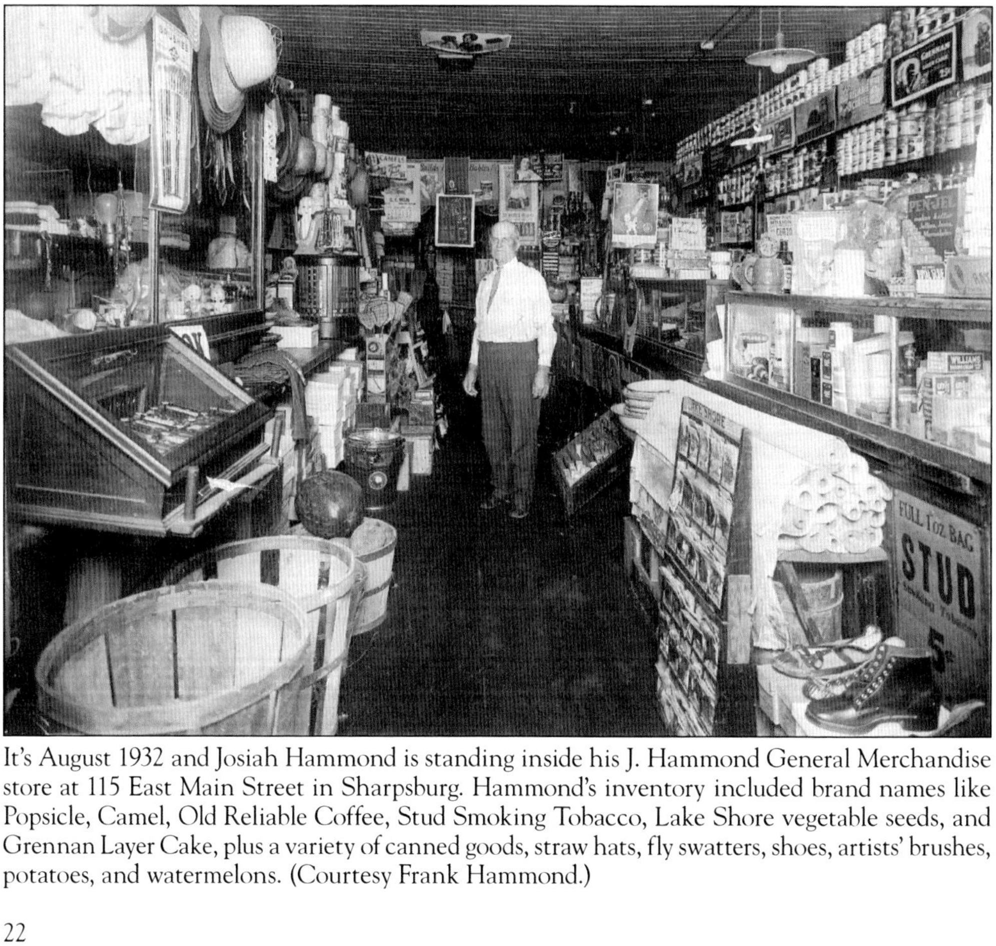

It's August 1932 and Josiah Hammond is standing inside his J. Hammond General Merchandise store at 115 East Main Street in Sharpsburg. Hammond's inventory included brand names like Popsicle, Camel, Old Reliable Coffee, Stud Smoking Tobacco, Lake Shore vegetable seeds, and Grennan Layer Cake, plus a variety of canned goods, straw hats, fly swatters, shoes, artists' brushes, potatoes, and watermelons. (Courtesy Frank Hammond.)

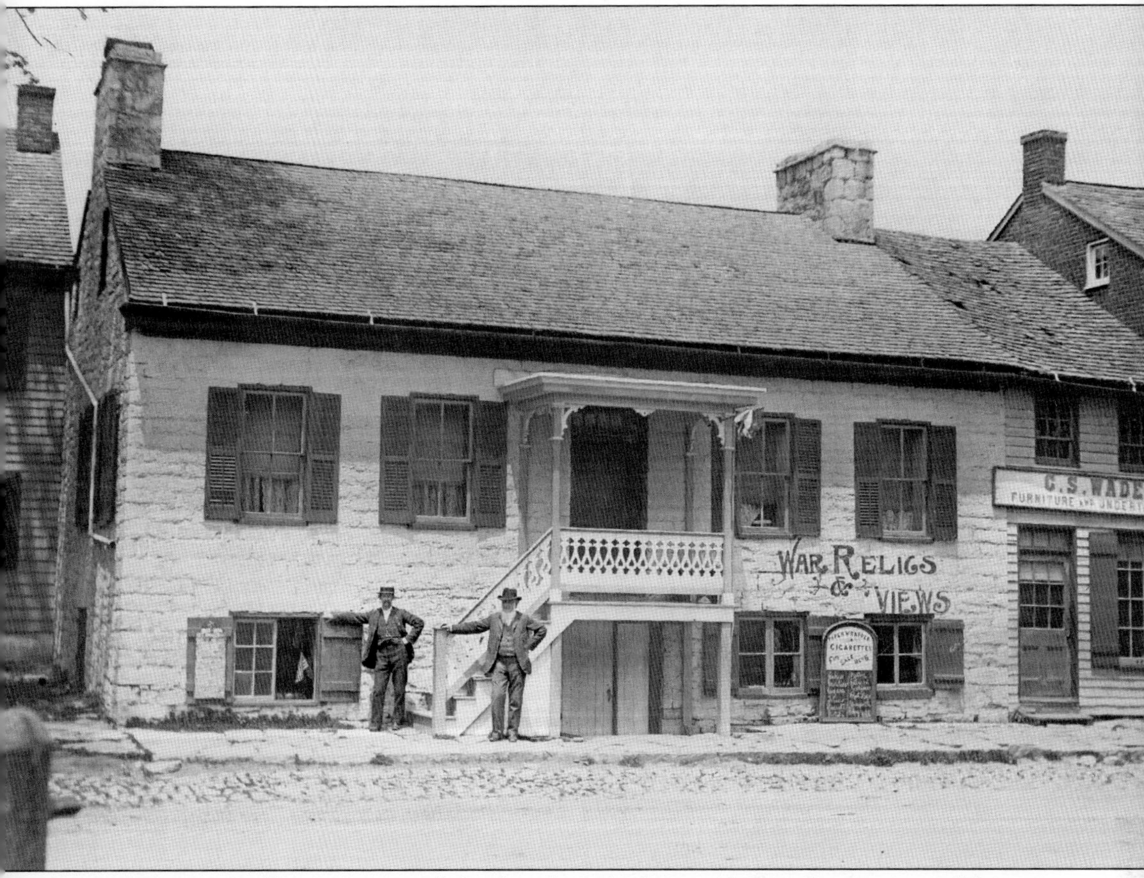

Oliver Thomas Reilly, the man with his hand on the batten shutter, became so well known that his name is part of this historic stone house, the Good-Reilly House. From this residence he published and sold postcards, candy, and cigarettes and offered battlefield history, relics, and tours. He was five years old at the time of the battle, and he became a guide at 15. His 1906 *Battlefield of Antietam* includes stories that longtime residents told him. Starting in 1906, he wrote the Sharpsburg news column for the *Shepherdstown Register*. He erected a monument on the battlefield in 1927 "to the memory of the Old Dunkard Church. The oak tree that stood in front and the Union Civil War Veterans of Sharpsburg, MD." C. S. Wade's shop was built about 1895 between the stone house and the brick building visible at the right, which is now Bender's Tavern. Martin L. Burgan for a few years offered competing tours and postcards from a shop in the brick building. (Courtesy WCHS.)

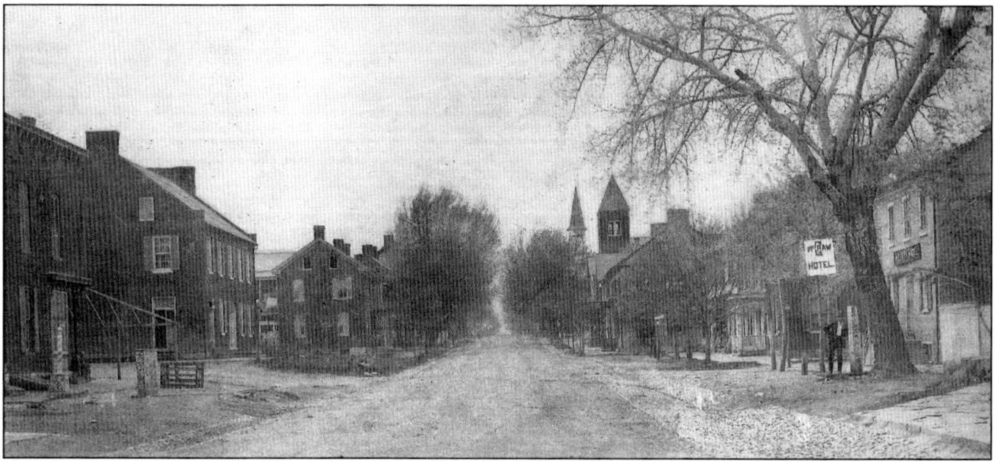

These two images show Main Street from the Public Square looking west in the early 1900s. The scene today has barely changed except for street improvements. The earlier photograph has a man leaning against an advertisement for some kind of cake soap. The McGraw Hotel and the City Hotel were next to each other. The large brick building on the left side of the square is the Jacob Grove building, made famous by Robert E. Lee and his generals as their meeting place. In the Martin L. Burgan postcard, published about 1912, the Grove house has acquired a porch and an Antietam Hotel sign above the side door. Bob DeLauney owned the hotel at that time. The skinny steeple is no longer on the Methodist church. (Above, courtesy Stephen Recker; below, courtesy Earl Roulette.)

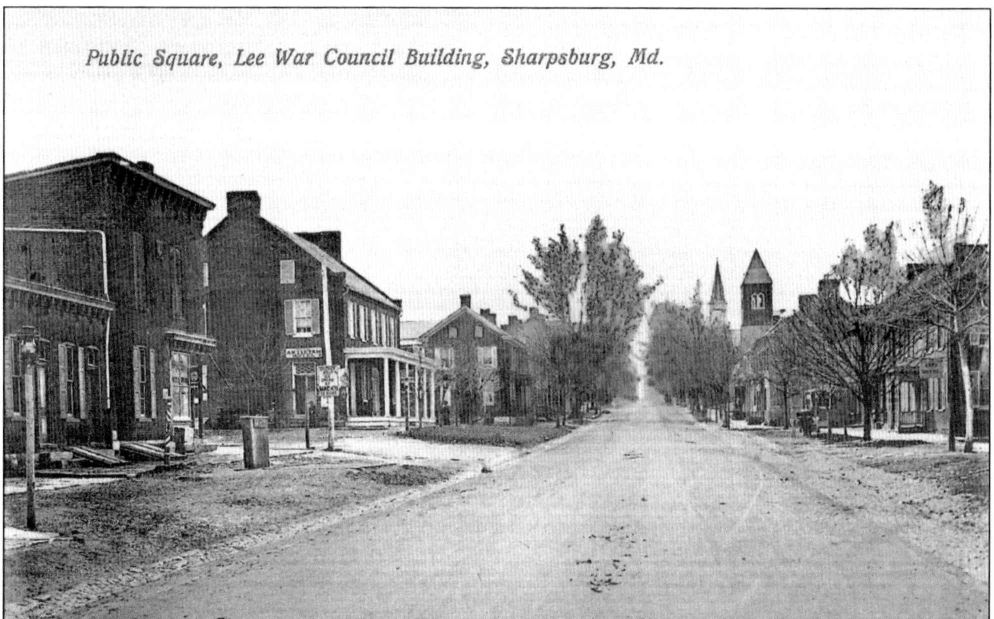

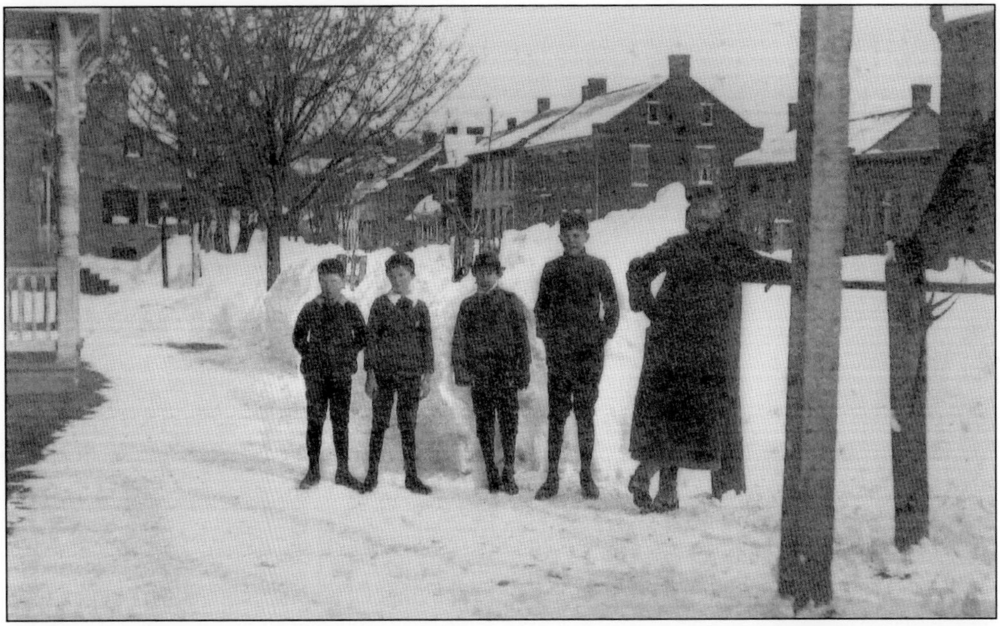

The man and four boys stand before a huge pile of snow in this 1899 photograph. The location is given as "in front of Dr. Biggs' house." They are in the area just east of the house at the town square close to the bank building. Across the street, behind the horse's head, the Masonic Hall can be seen. (Courtesy SHS.)

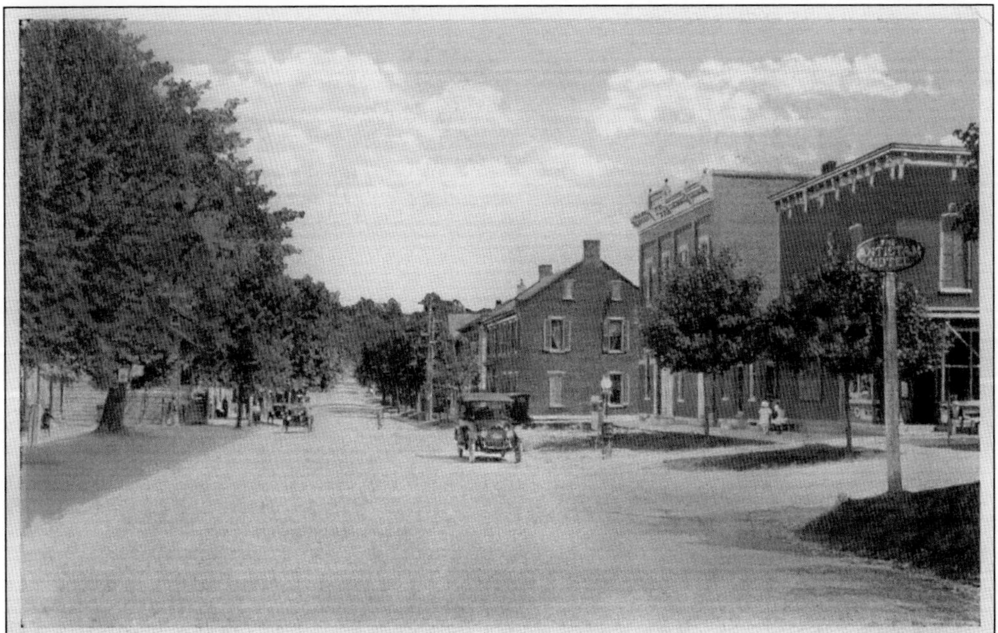

This postcard's photograph was taken from a spot just west of the town square. The Antietam Hotel has a new sign, the trees are bigger, and Main Street looks like a one-way street for the few automobiles. The view looking east today has more cars, but the buildings are the same. On the left, just past the steps, is O. T. Reilly's souvenir shop, with apparent business. (Courtesy authors' collection.)

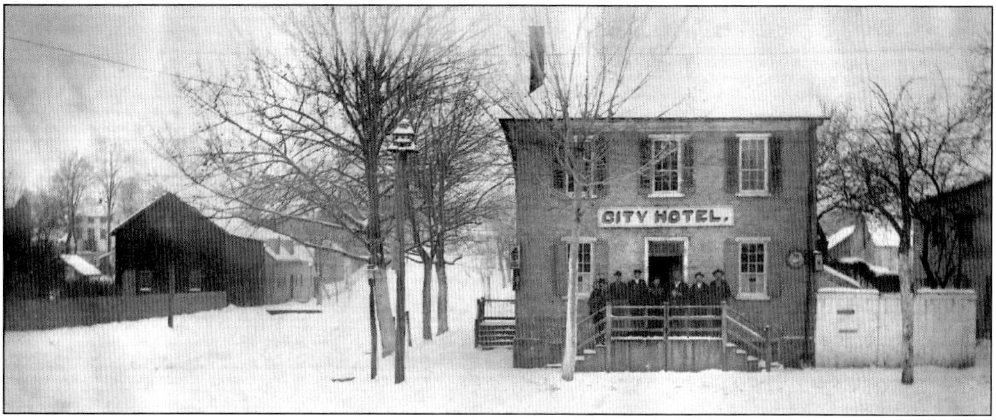

These two pictures could have been taken from the same spot on the southeast corner of the square years and seasons apart. The stepping-stones in the street kept shoes clean and dry from this often-flooded corner. On the left is a porchless Grove house. Above the second-floor window on Dr. Bigg's house is a hole caused by artillery fire during the Battle of Antietam. The City Hotel is on Lot 49 of the 1877 map and is labeled the Shay House, John Shay proprietor. The owner from 1900 to 1920 according to Barron's *History of Sharpsburg* was W. H. Highbarger. Seven men and a child pose on the front steps of this stone building, which has been modified with brick additions, gables, and porches. (Above, courtesy Marian and Syd Gale; below, courtesy WCFL/WMR.)

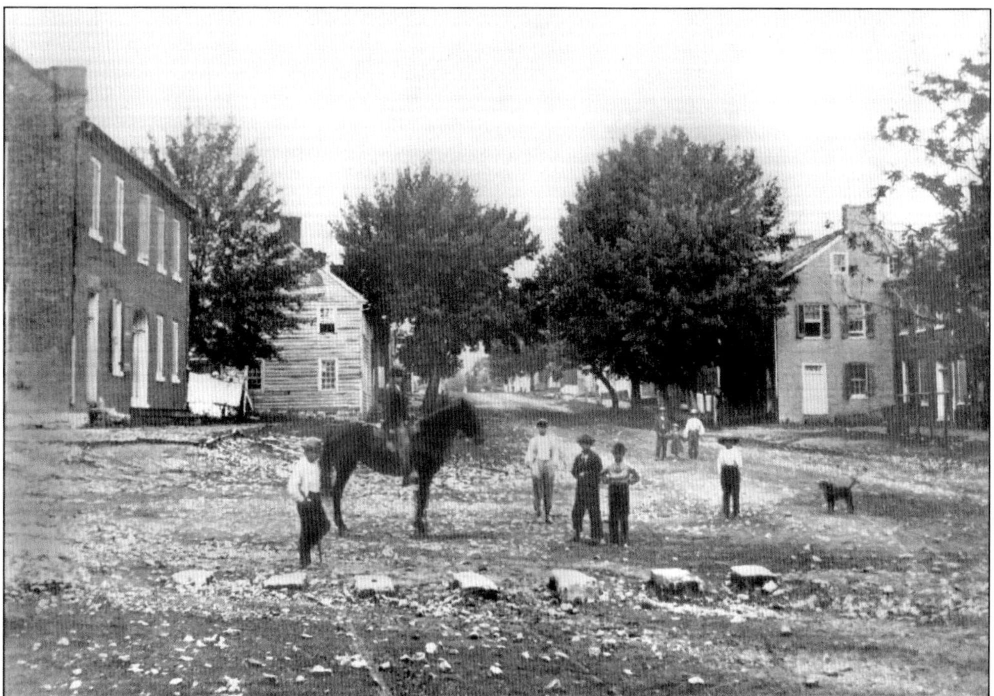

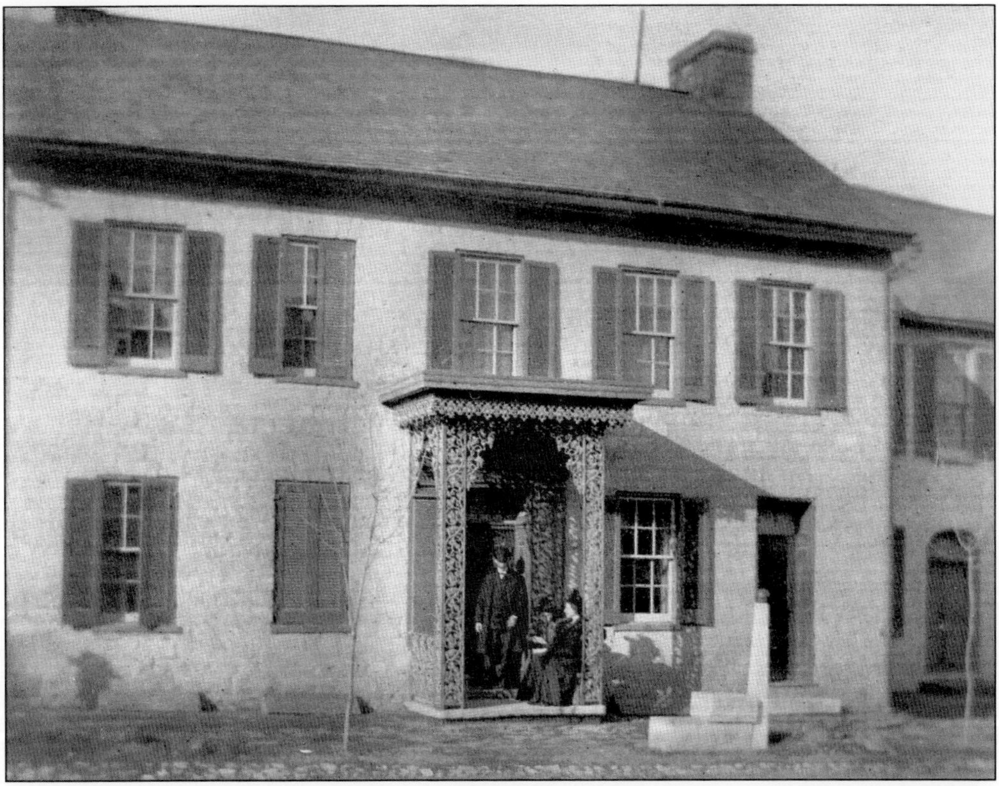

Three well-dressed persons sit in the sunshine at the front entrance of the Biggs House. The hitching post and carriage steps are still in front of the house. According to an article in the *Maryland Cracker Barrel* by Colleen Stone, they were used by Pres. Abraham Lincoln and Pres. William McKinley. She wrote that slaves once lived in the attic and that the ghost of Stella Biggs opens the cellar door. (Courtesy Marian and Syd Gale.)

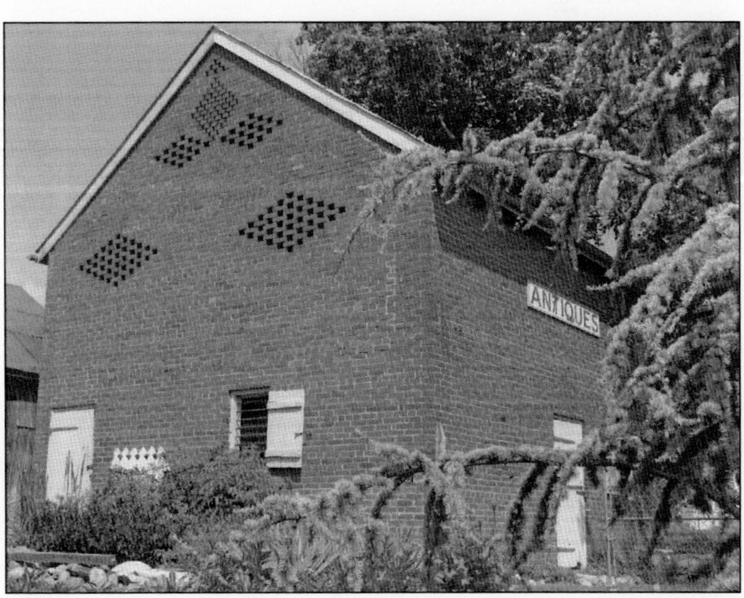

Confederate troops burned the brick stable, the horse barn that sits at the alley behind the Biggs House. Charred joists are visible in the structure that the present owners use as an antiques shop. The decorative ventilators, unusual for a small building, are common in larger brick end barns throughout this area in Washington County. (Photograph by Tim Doyle.)

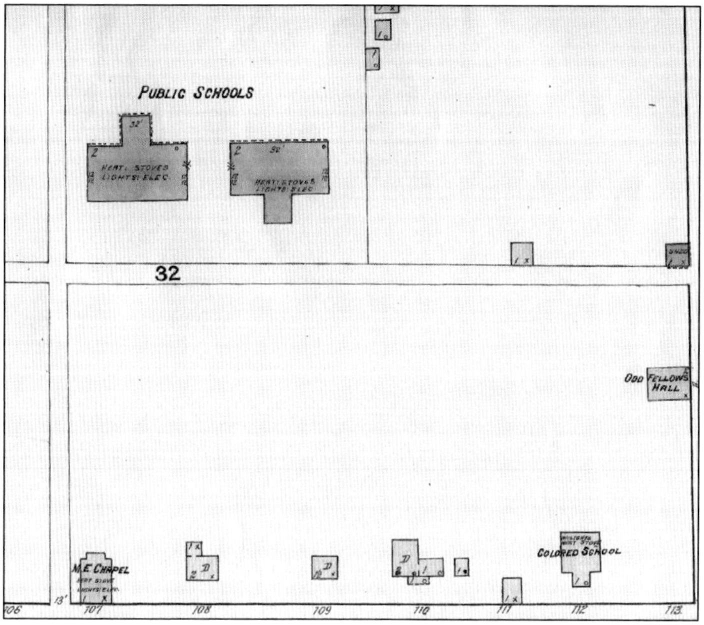

This 1922 Sanborn Insurance Map shows the locations of Sharpsburg's schools and the Methodist Episcopal chapel (Tolson's). The public schools for white children and Tolson's Chapel have heat stoves, lights, and electricity. The colored school is labeled as having a heat stove and no lights. This 1922 map also shows the location of the black Odd Fellows Hall, labeled the "Negro Hall" in Barron's *History of Sharpsburg*, on Church Street. (Courtesy WCFL/WMR.)

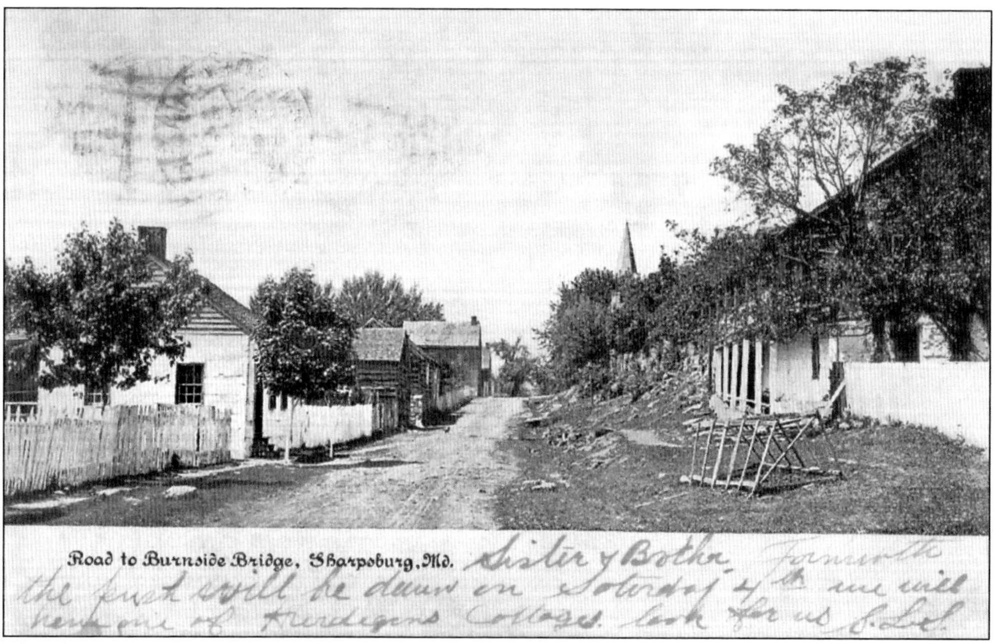

The date on this postcard is illegible; the 1877 map shows only two structures on the left side of this street, now Church Street. The large wooden structure near the house on the right might be some kind of hay rack. The log houses and fences are like those seen on other streets in town. The steeple marks the location of the Lutheran church on the corner of Church and Main Streets. (Courtesy Stephen Recker.)

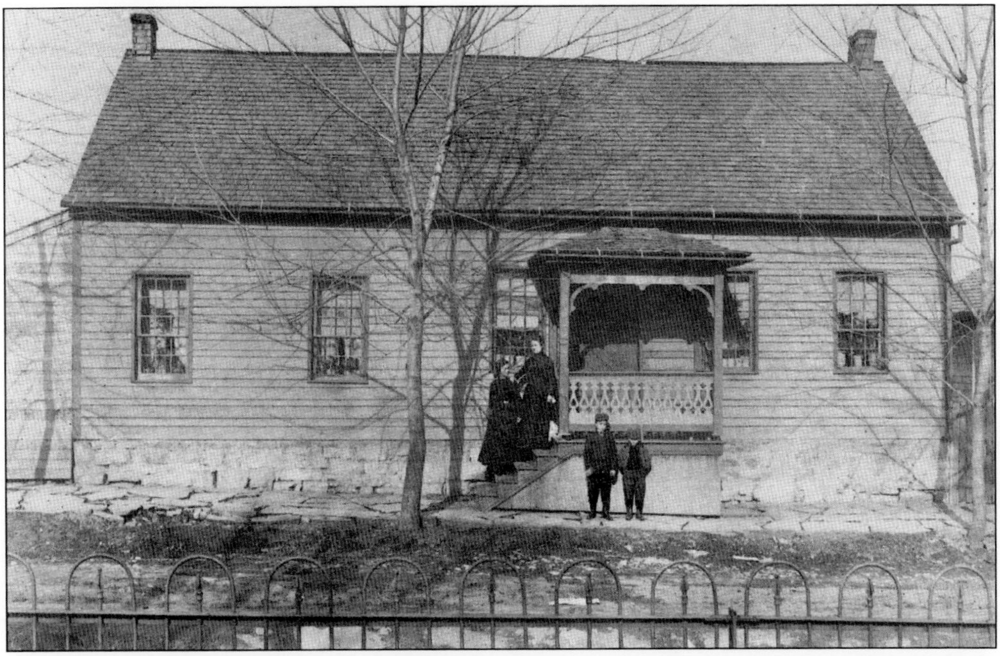

These two photographs show what can happen to a house over 150 years. The wrought-iron fence surrounded the Sharpsburg school grounds across the street from 113 East Antietam Street. The house began as two log cabins sitting next to each other in 1829. Jacob Kretzer bought the two cabins from George Cronise and used one cabin as a blacksmith shop. The family lived in the other, which had a summer kitchen behind it. At some point, the two cabins were joined. Jacob died in 1833, a victim of the cholera epidemic that swept the area. His son Benjamin Franklin Kretzer was the owner of this property in 1877. The survey map designates him as F. Kretzer. John Eavey, the schoolteacher, added the second story. Descendants of the Kretzer family owned the property until 2007. (Both, courtesy SHS and Linda Irvin-Craig.)

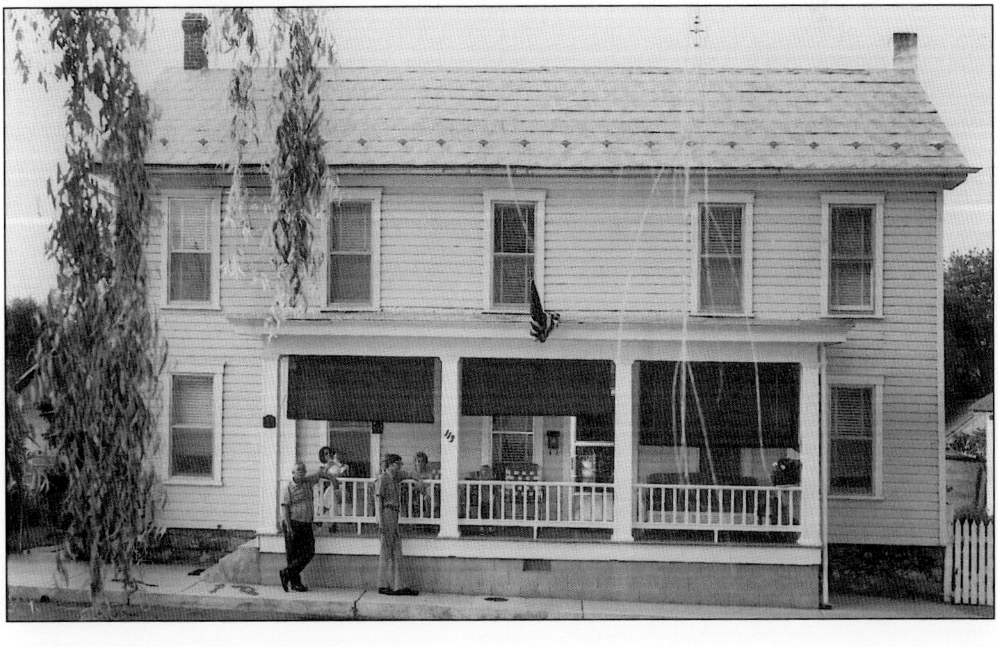

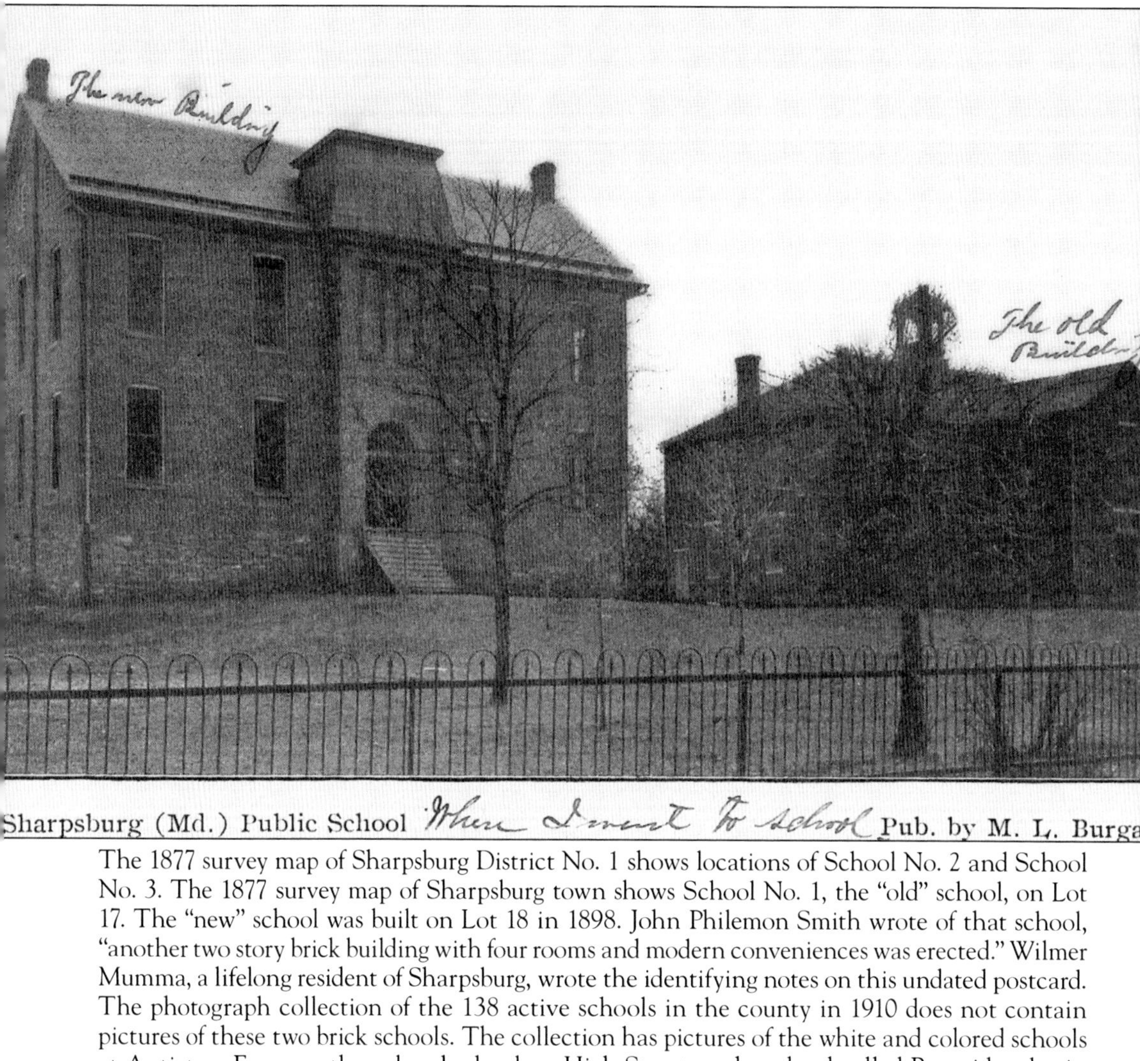

The 1877 survey map of Sharpsburg District No. 1 shows locations of School No. 2 and School No. 3. The 1877 survey map of Sharpsburg town shows School No. 1, the "old" school, on Lot 17. The "new" school was built on Lot 18 in 1898. John Philemon Smith wrote of that school, "another two story brick building with four rooms and modern conveniences was erected." Wilmer Mumma, a lifelong resident of Sharpsburg, wrote the identifying notes on this undated postcard. The photograph collection of the 138 active schools in the county in 1910 does not contain pictures of these two brick schools. The collection has pictures of the white and colored schools at Antietam Furnace, the colored school on High Street, and a school called Burnside, also in District 1. (Courtesy Stephen Recker.)

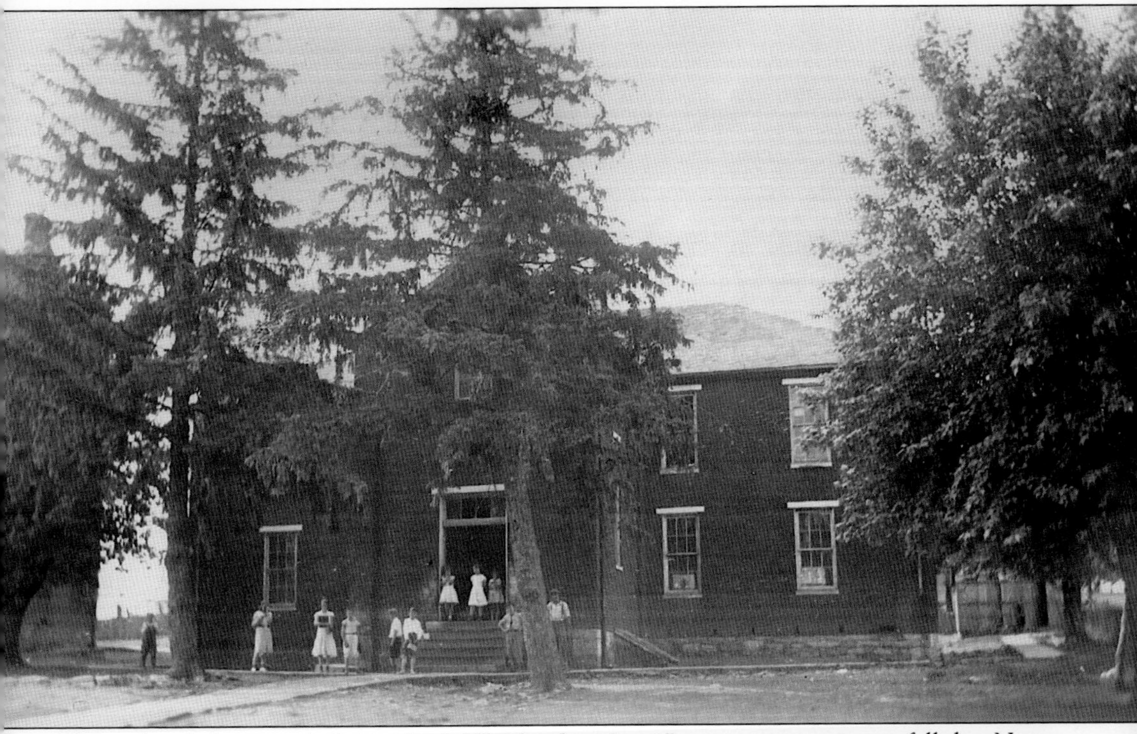

The undated photograph shows the "old" school on Lot 17 on a warm spring or fall day. Note the boxes or boards propping open the windows on the first floor. This brick building with "four commodious rooms" was built in 1870. It replaced a brick building about a half block south of Chapline Street, on what is now Mondel Road. The Town of Sharpsburg turned that building into the town jail. Barron's *History of Sharpsburg* reports that in 1882, five teachers were responsible for 325 children. The "new" school, visible on the left, was built to relieve the crowded condition. Sharpsburg Elementary School moved to its current location on West Main Street in 1936. After these schools closed, the Federal Silk Mill operated in the buildings for about five years and then used them for storage. This building burned in 1954. Current owners bought the property in 1973 and razed the remaining building, which was in bad repair. (Courtesy Stephen Recker.)

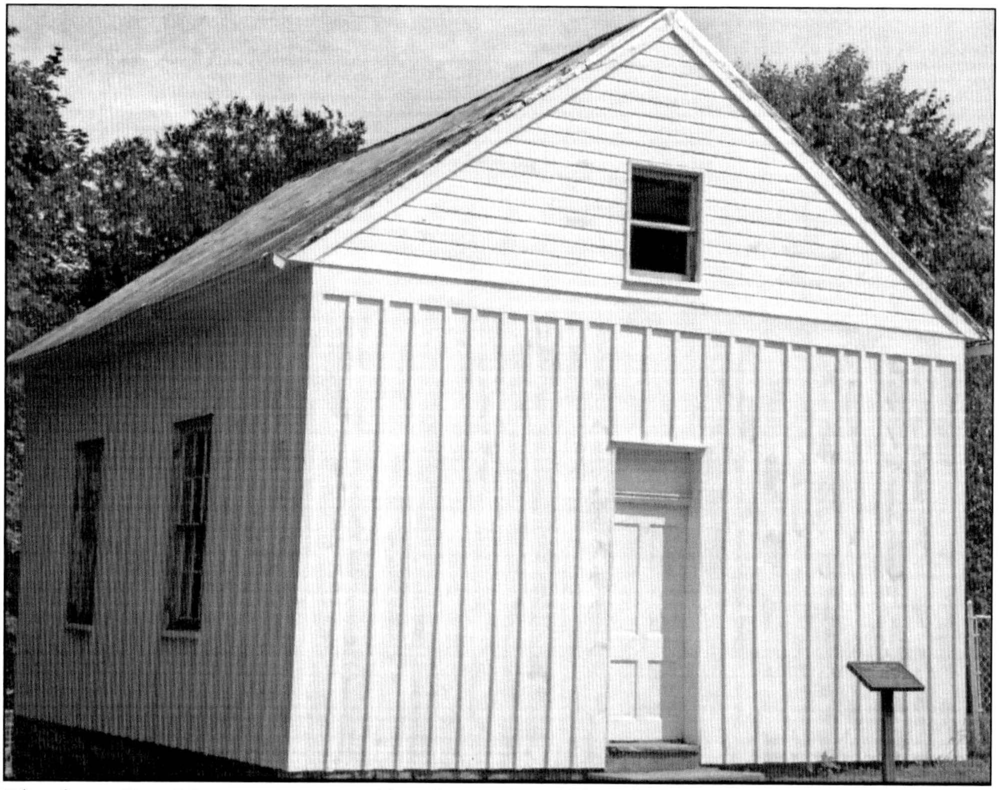

Thanks to Save Historic Antietam Foundation (SHAF) and the nonprofit Friends of Tolson's Chapel, the small church at 111 East High Street is beginning to resemble the original log building that was covered with board-and-batten siding. The African American community, made up of free and newly freed persons, built their church and named it for John R. Tolson, pastor for the Colored Methodist Episcopal circuit of Hagerstown. The cornerstone was laid on October 20, 1866. Virginia Cook, a member of the congregation, told that the church was built by "anyone who could drive a nail." Stones in the Fairmont Cemetery, visible through the chain-link fence, date from 1893. The last person buried here was Virginia Cook in 1996. (Above, restoration photograph by Tim Doyle; below, courtesy Historic American Building Survey, Library of Congress.)

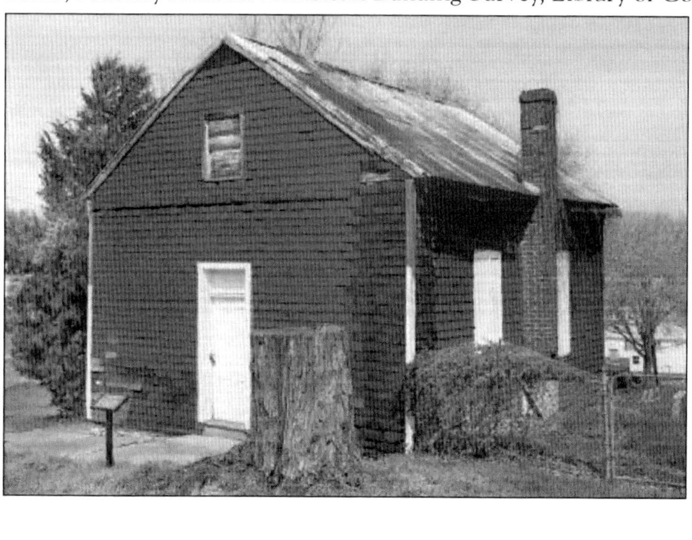

This building covered with red asbestos shingles served the black community as its church and as its school. In April 1868, the Freedman's Bureau sent Ezra Johnson, a white man, to be the teacher. In what he called the "American Union school," he taught children during the day, adults at night, and on Sundays had a Sabbath school. The black families of Sharpsburg paid his monthly salary, $6.50. (Courtesy Historic American Buildings Survey, Library of Congress.)

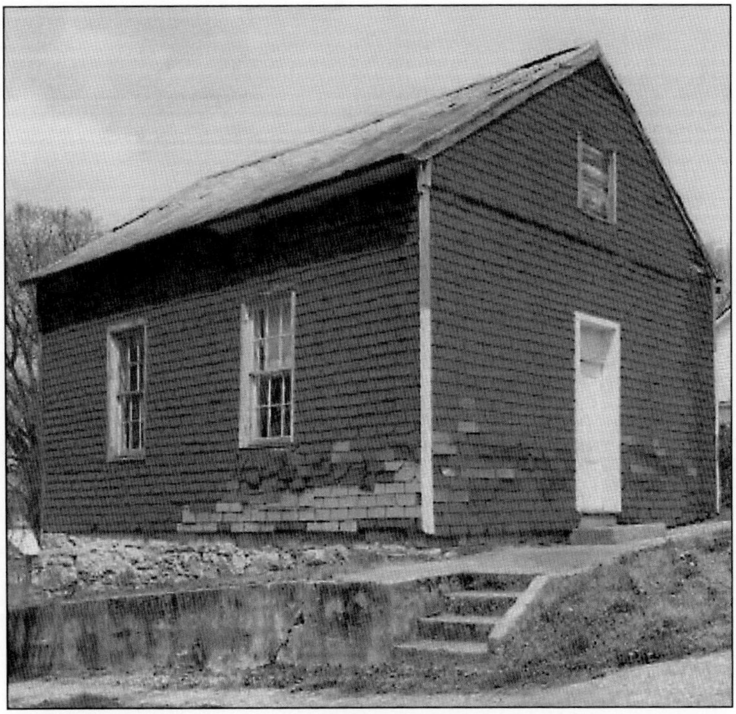

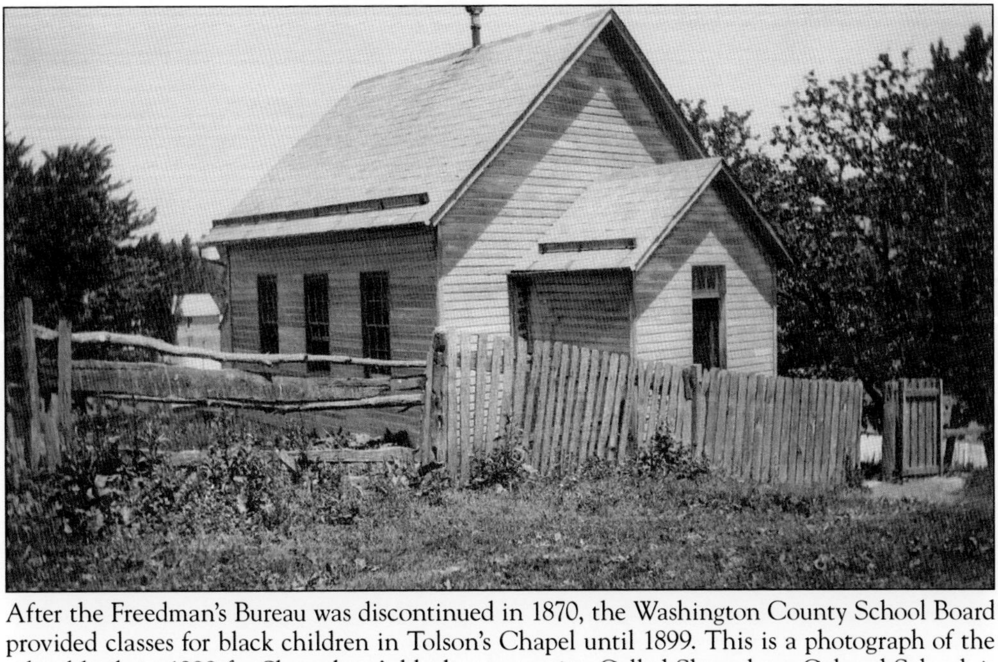

After the Freedman's Bureau was discontinued in 1870, the Washington County School Board provided classes for black children in Tolson's Chapel until 1899. This is a photograph of the school built in 1899 for Sharpsburg's black community. Called Sharpsburg Colored School, it was on the corner of High and Church Streets, about a block from Tolson's Chapel and a block from the schools for white children. (Courtesy WCFL/WMR.)

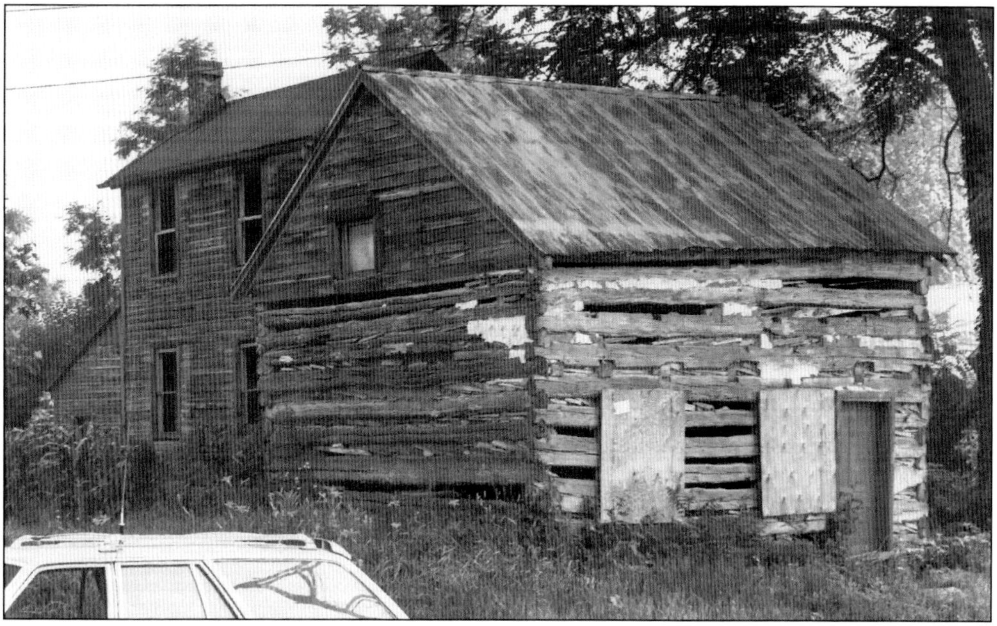

The 1973 watercolor of the Glass House that hangs in the Sharpsburg Public Library shows a log cabin much different from the structure in the photograph. Both, however, show the large walnut tree that was on the property. The date of construction is unidentified but has been thought to be as early as 1723. The 1799 deed transferring the property from Jacob and Elizabeth Smith to Peter Glass specified houses and outbuildings on the 103-foot-by-206-foot lot. The house remained in the Glass family until 1972, when Mrs. James Ardinger gave the badly deteriorating cabin to the Town of Sharpsburg. Unfortunately, the project to restore the house where it stood was not completed. Roger Fairbourn acquired the house in the early 1980s. He had it carefully dismantled and stored for a future reconstruction. The Washington County Rural Heritage Museum began reconstruction of the house in its village at the Washington County Agricultural Education Center on Maryland Route 65 in 2009. The house now sits about 3 miles from its original location on Lot 82. (Above, courtesy Jim Ardinger; below, courtesy Sharpsburg Public Library.)

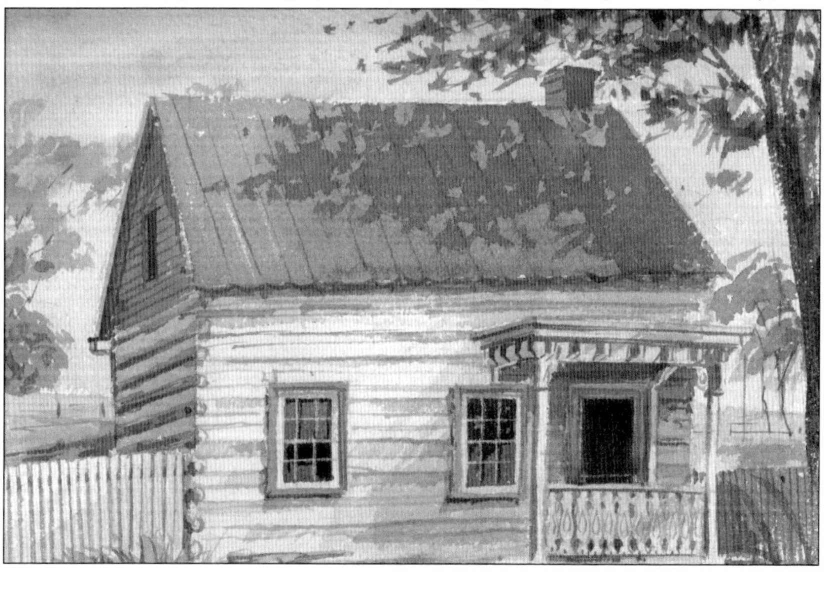

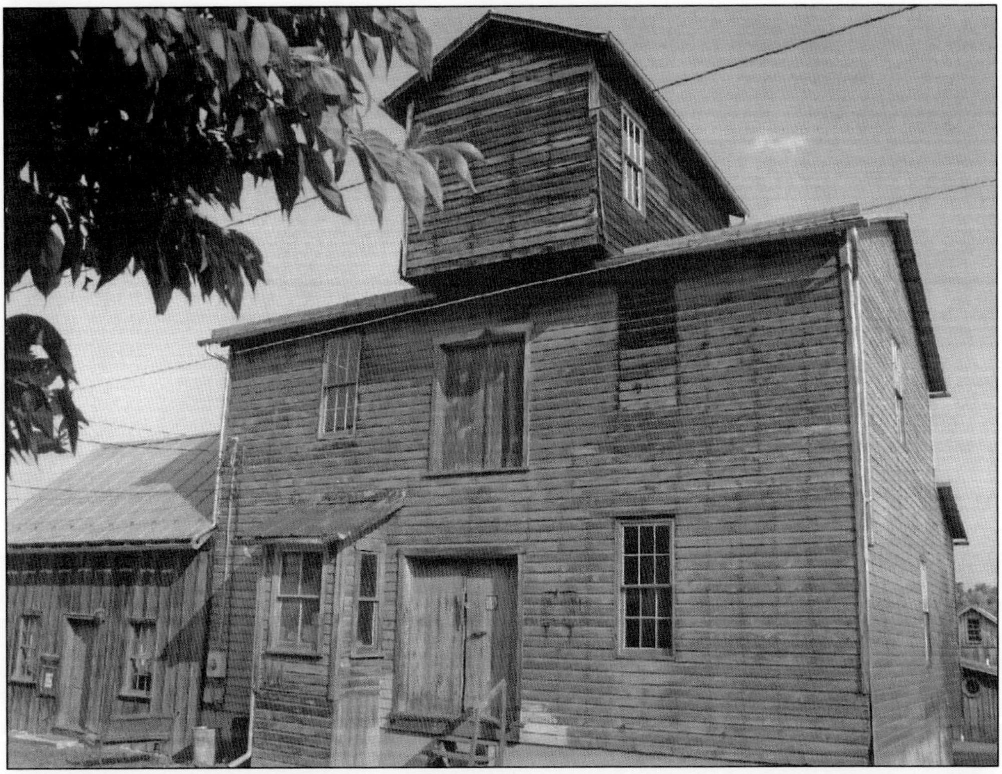

This odd-looking wooden structure on East Chapline Street is next to the old cemetery of the Reformed Calvinist Church. It is the Clipp Feed and Grain Mill, built in 1924. It operated as a mill until the late 1960s. The current owner purchased the property in 1996 and hopes to restore the mill and make it a working museum. A small log cabin is visible behind the mill. (Photograph by Tim Doyle.)

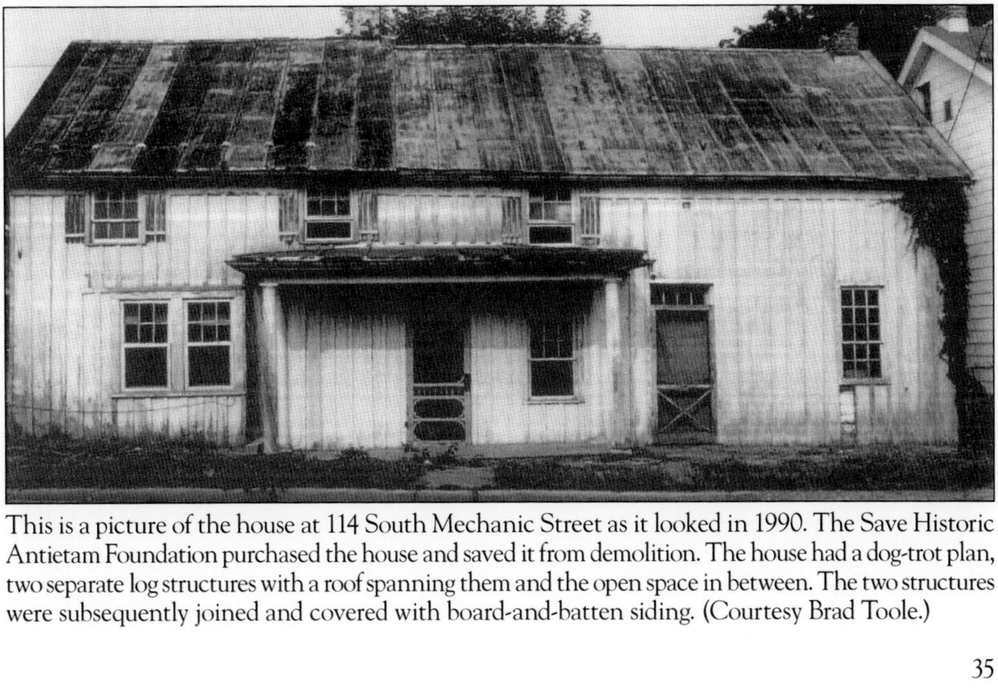

This is a picture of the house at 114 South Mechanic Street as it looked in 1990. The Save Historic Antietam Foundation purchased the house and saved it from demolition. The house had a dog-trot plan, two separate log structures with a roof spanning them and the open space in between. The two structures were subsequently joined and covered with board-and-batten siding. (Courtesy Brad Toole.)

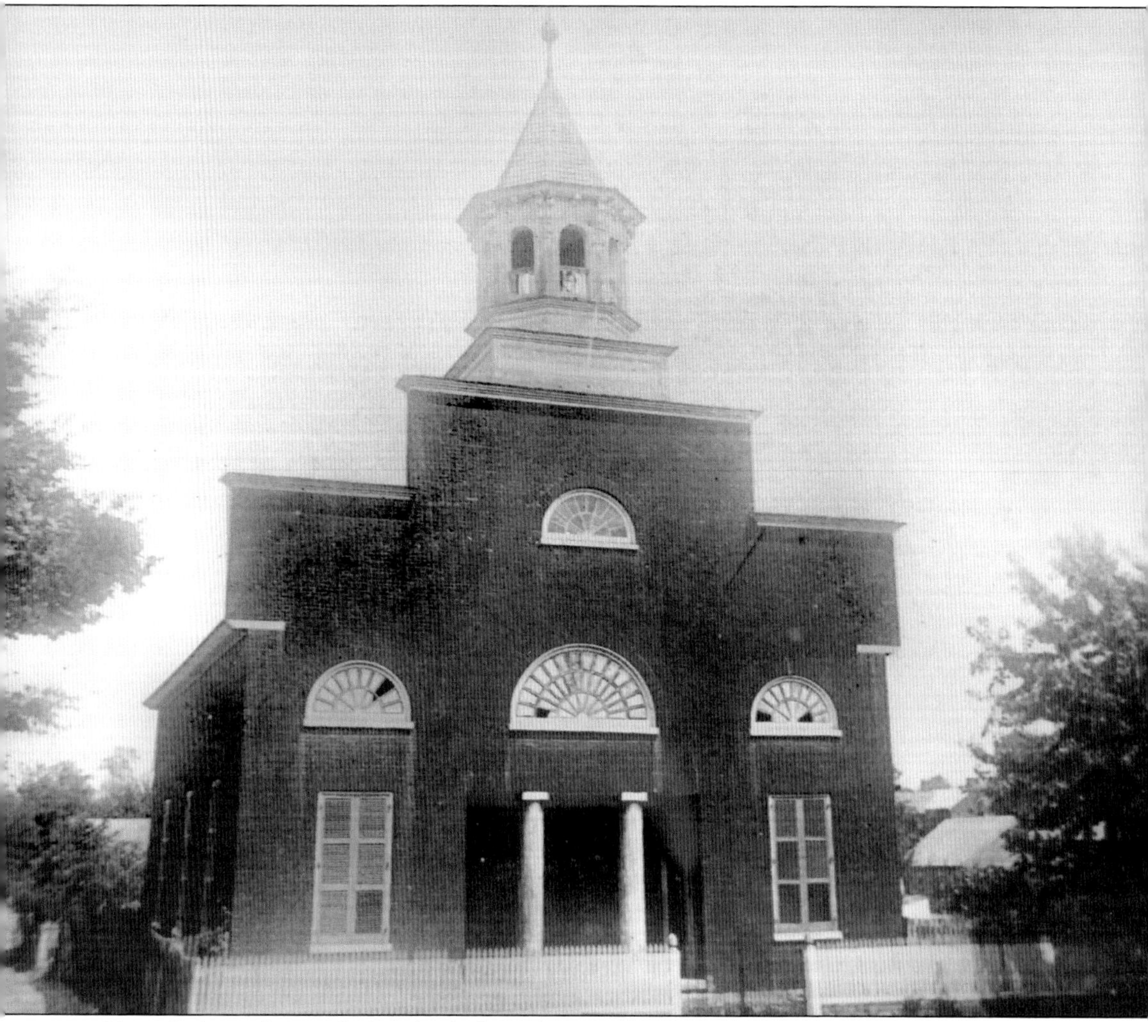

Christ Reformed United Church of Christ (UCC) had its first incarnation in 1769 on Lot 61, East Chapline Street. It was known as the German Reformed Church of the first Reformed Calvinist Church. Its cemetery contains graves dating from 1775. In 1832, the first church building was torn down, and the congregation moved to this building on Lot 46, purchased from Mary Ground in 1830. Grafton Smith presented this image to the church in 1954. In 1890, the pillars were incorporated into the front wall of the remodeled church and lunette windows were bricked in. This building served as a hospital for wounded Union soldiers following the Battles of Antietam and Gettysburg. The distinctive belfry is easily located on drawings of Sharpsburg at the time of the Battle of Antietam. (Courtesy Christ Reformed UCC.)

The 1890 renovation of the church followed its use as a hospital, when it was greatly injured. Lizzie K. Miller of the Ladies Aid Society wrote letters inviting member of Grand Army posts to donate memorial windows to the repaired church. The 16th Regiment of Connecticut Volunteers is memorialized in the large hand-leaded window in the center of the church. Another stained-glass window anonymously donated memorializes the 11th Connecticut Volunteers. (Courtesy Christ Reformed UCC.)

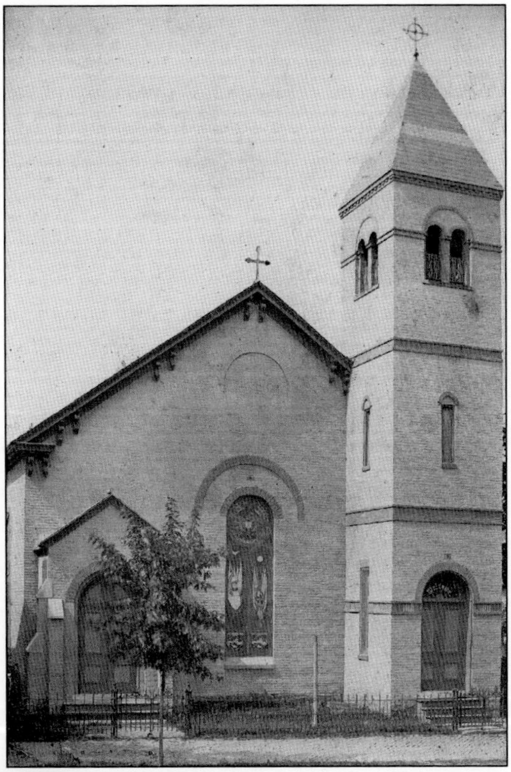

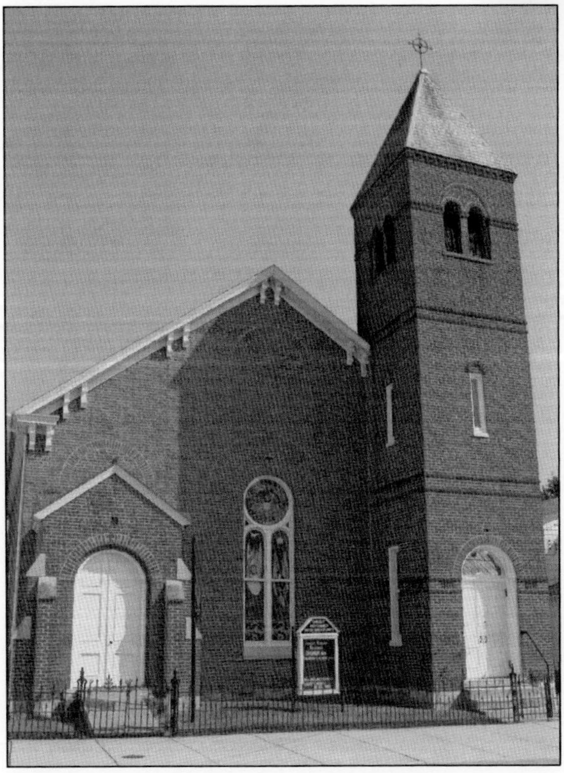

The church standing today was rededicated in 1891. A Moller organ was installed in 1946. In 1965, Sunday school rooms were added at the back of the church on land donated by Mr. and Mrs. J. Fred Roulette. The building is registered as a Maryland Historic Site. The current pastor is Rev. Delancy L. Catlett. (Courtesy Christ Reformed UCC.)

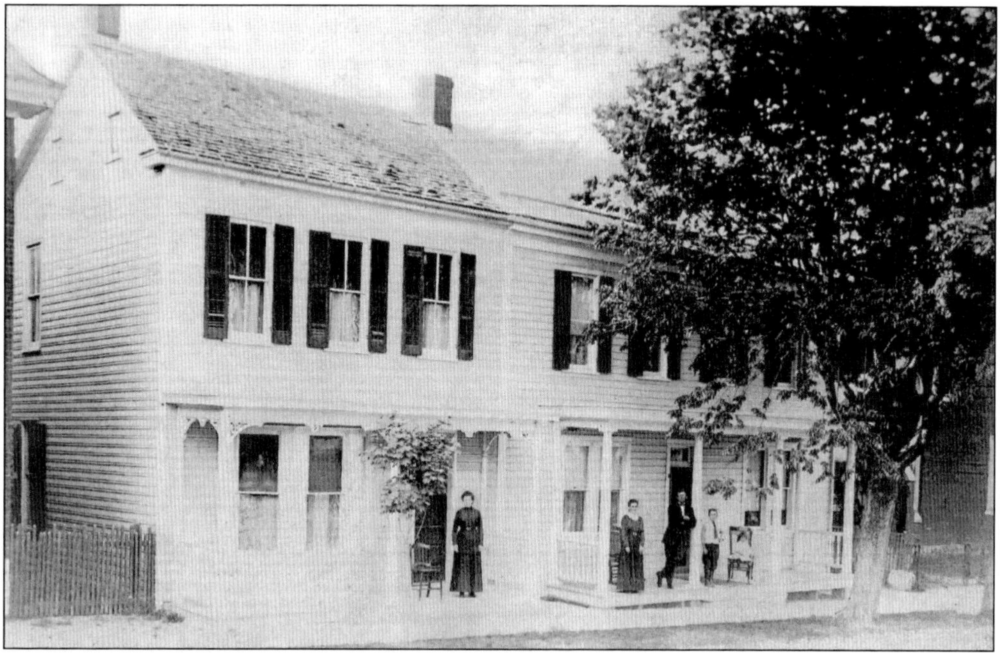

These photographs show the front and back of the houses at 121 and 123 West Main Street, the east half of Lot 45. Three adults and two children in their Sunday best posed for this pair of pictures, although the little girl is not in the backyard view. A man in the alley next to the Reformed church seems to be an unexpected passerby. Note the electric pole on Main Street. The Methodist church next door no longer has its tower. Family tradition tells that Mary Houser and her children hid in their cellar and could hear sounds of the battle. In 1871, Mary Jane and Barney Houser sold their home and part of their half-lot to Henry Schamel for $950. Ten days later, they sold the other 20 feet of the lot to Elias Spong for $482. (Both, courtesy authors' collection.)

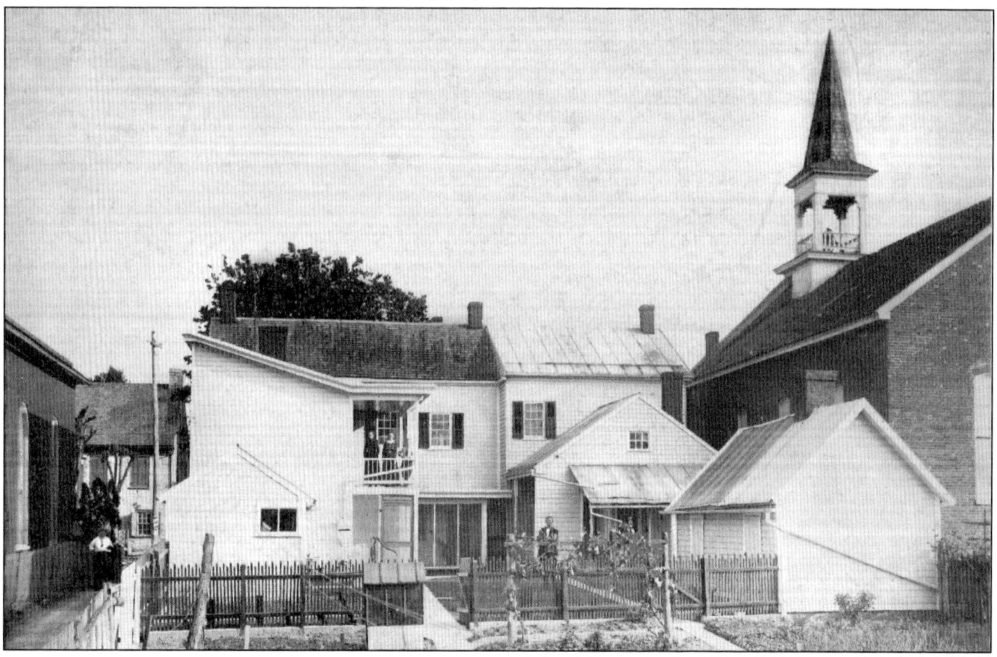

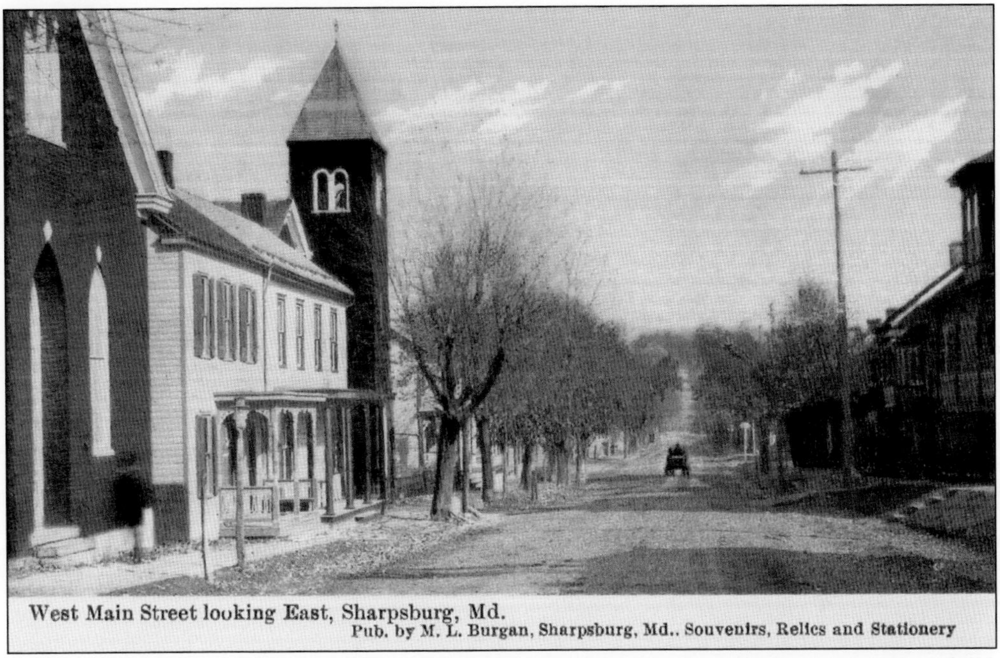

Between the Methodist church, left, and the Reformed church are the two houses at 121 and 123 West Main Street. On the right near the horse-drawn wagon is the oval sign for the Antietam Hotel. All elements help date this postcard to be about 1914. It was published by Martin L. Burgan, purveyor of souvenirs, relics, and stationery at his shop on East Main Street. (Courtesy Stephen Recker.)

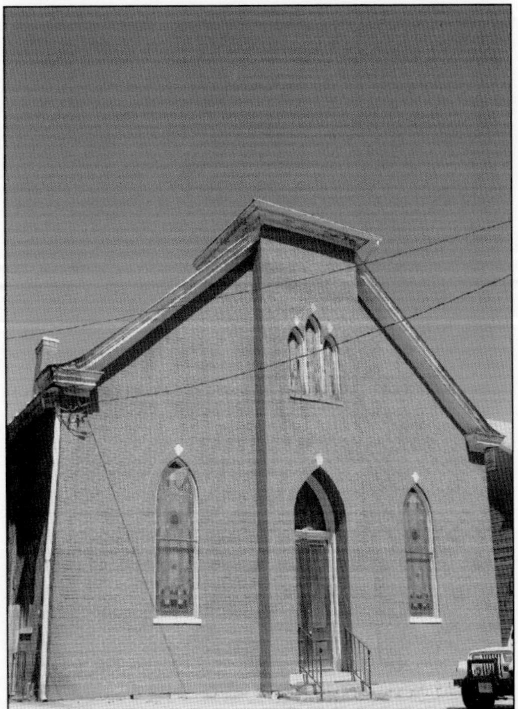

This building on Lot 45 was built after the first Methodist church on Hall Street was torn down. The cornerstone on this building at 125 West Main Street reads, "Wesley Chapel, Oct. 24, 1857." A cupola and bell were added when the church was rededicated in 1864. Old photographs of Main Street show a tall steeple on this building. The church was discontinued in 1938. The building is privately owned. (Photograph by Tim Doyle.)

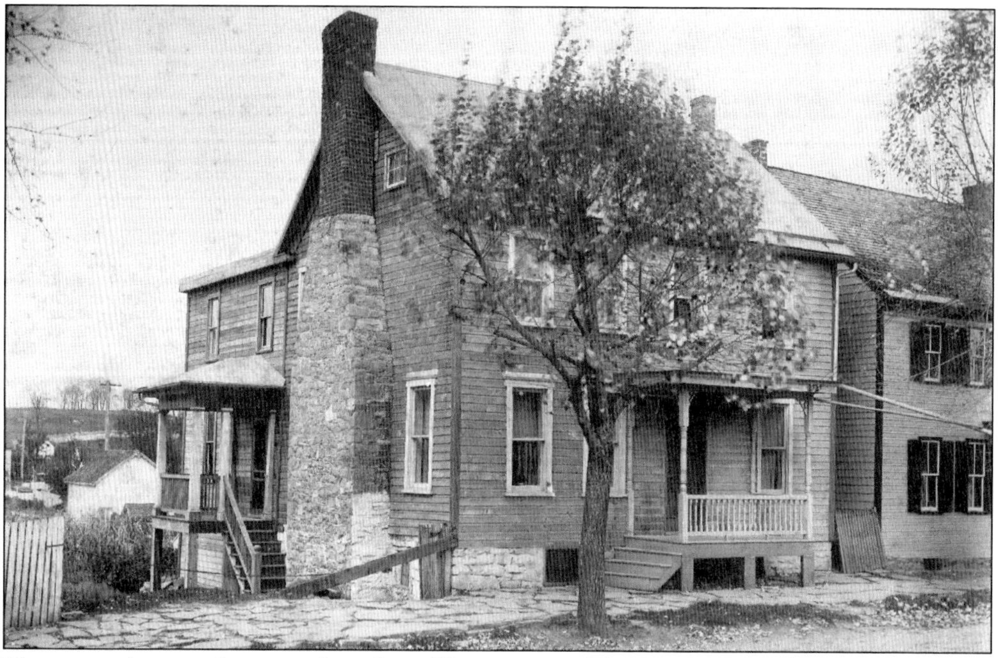

These two photographs were taken about 50 years apart. The first picture, taken by C. D. Young, shows the Mumma home at 135 West Main Street being repaired about 1955. This structure appears on the 1877 map on Lot 43, owned by Soloman Renner. Between the time of the first photograph and the second, the house operated as the Antietam Museum and later fell into a neglected state. The Town of Sharpsburg purchased the house and coordinated its preservation, ensuring that it would keep its historic features and contribute to Sharpsburg's character. The front porch was rebuilt to match the side porch, and a second-floor window was added. The 2008 photograph shows that downspouts no longer pass above a fieldstone sidewalk. The stone foundation and chimney are remortared, and the wooden siding is painted. (Above, courtesy WCFL/WMR; below, photograph by Tim Doyle.)

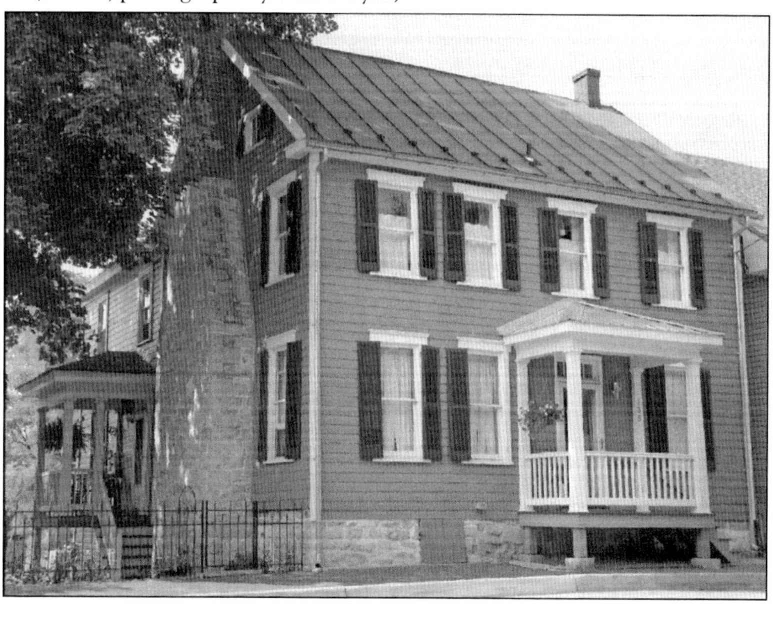

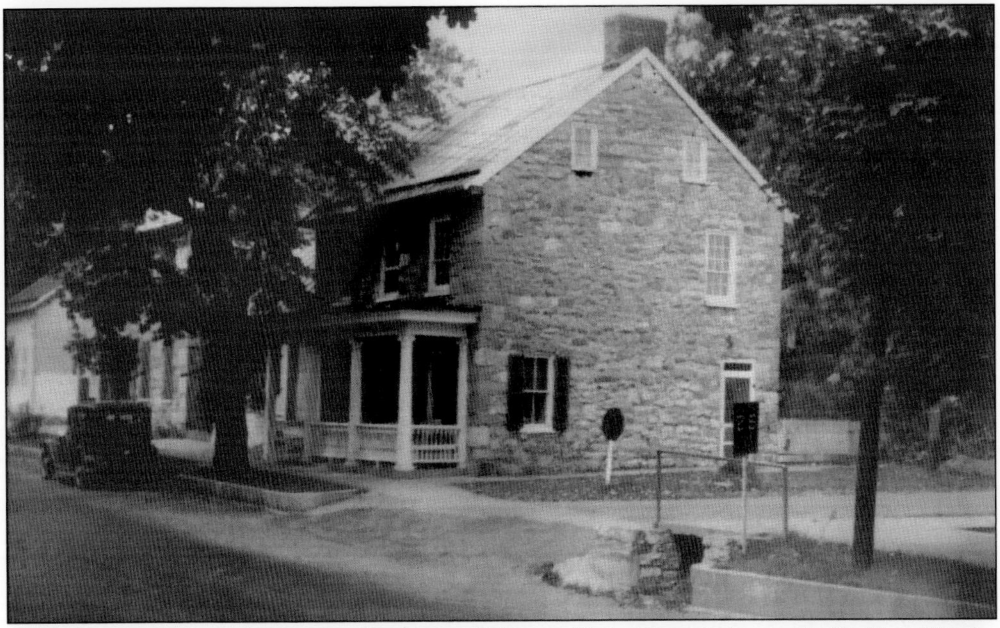

This stone house is on the National Register of Historic Places. It is on the east half of Lot 130, the lot Joseph Chaplin Sr. willed to his daughter Sarah in 1769. In 1832, Jacob Highbarger, a "house carpenter," bought the half-lot for $45 and had the house built. The 1877 map has Highbarger as owner, but he sold the house to Elias Spong that year. Oliver T. Reilly bought it at public sale in 1896 and owned it until 1910. The stone of the house is different from the blue-gray stone of the other stone houses in town. The log portion, an example of corner post log construction rare in Sharpsburg, was used as a workshop and for various stores. After a connecting doorway to the stone house was cut, the log structure served as a kitchen. (Above, courtesy Barry Rowekamp, M.D.; below, photograph by Tim Doyle.)

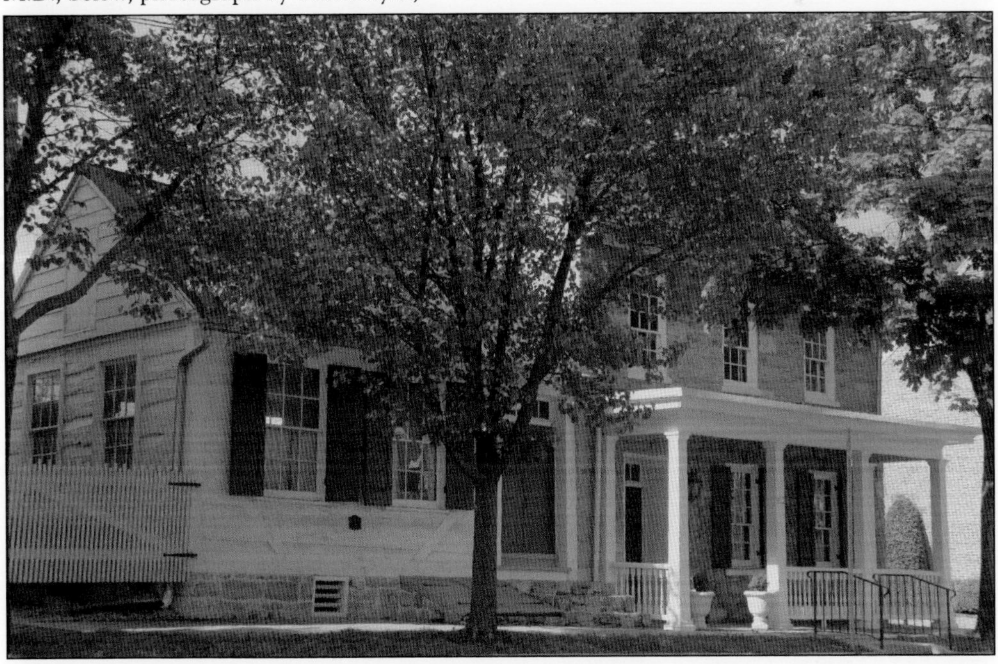

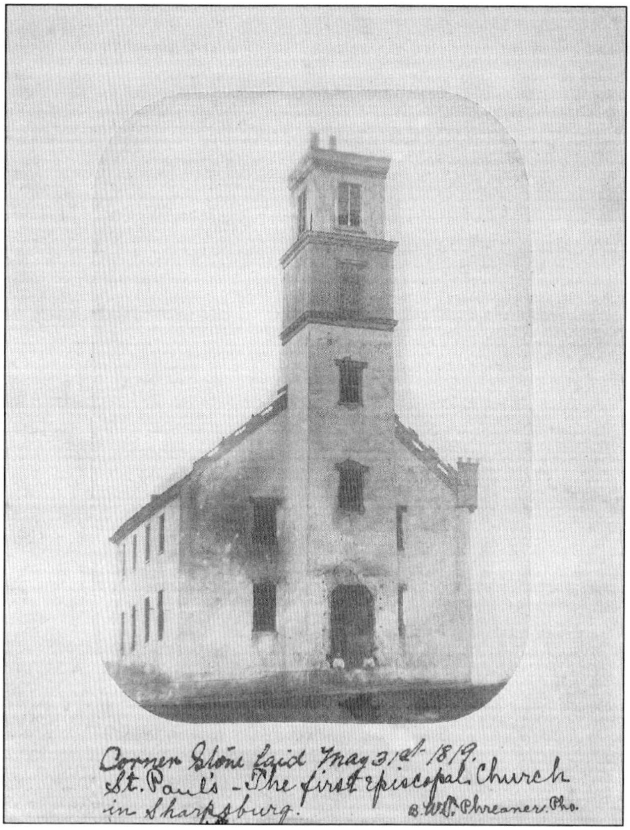

St. Paul's Episcopal Church was organized in 1818. Before this rough-cut stone building with its massive tower was erected, the congregation met in the old Lutheran church. The cornerstone for this building on Lot 132 was laid on May 31, 1819. Joseph Chapline Jr. deeded the lot to the church's trustees and wardens. His daughters, Jane and Sarah, taught in the Sunday school; his wife donated the bell that hung in the tall tower. The church was consecrated on July 29, 1831. This undated photograph by B. W. T. Phreaner shows the church after the Battle of Antietam, when it was used as a Confederate and then a Union hospital. The building was so severely damaged by cannon fire and use as a hospital that, like the original Lutheran church, it was declared unfit for worship and torn down. (Courtesy St. Paul's Episcopal Church.)

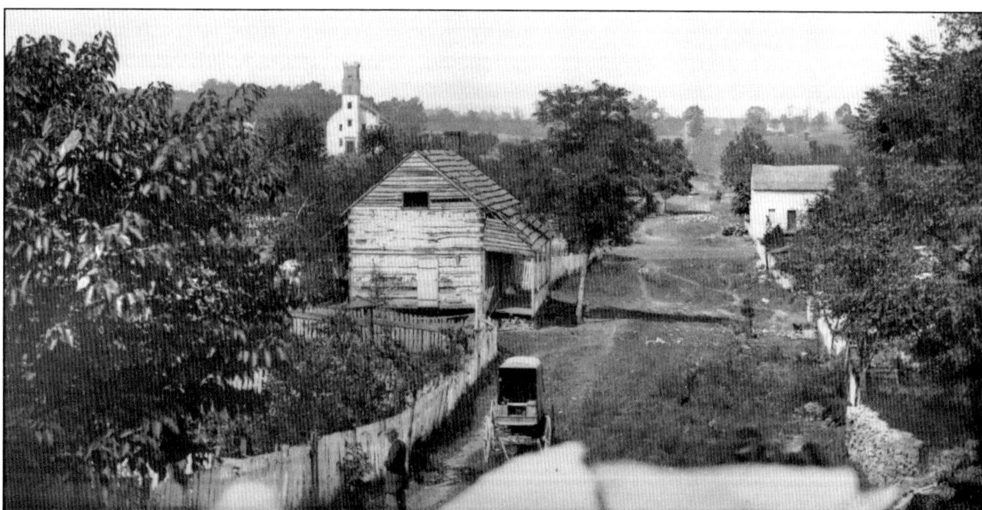

This September 1862 Alexander Gardner photograph shows the road that is now South Hall Street, looking north. The Episcopal church is in the background. The porch on the whitewashed log house, perhaps on Lot 114, is unusual; most log houses had plain fronts. Wood-paling fences were common around the backyard garden and livestock area. The carriage might be the photographer's wagon. (Courtesy Library of Congress.)

The cornerstone for the new St. Paul's building was laid on October 30, 1871. The congregation held services in the Lutheran and German Reformed churches during its construction. The belfry was finished in 1877. The original bell, which had been removed before the battle and hidden, was rehung. The new building, when debt free, was consecrated in September 1885. The date on the photograph is "circa 1906." (Courtesy St. Paul's Episcopal Church.)

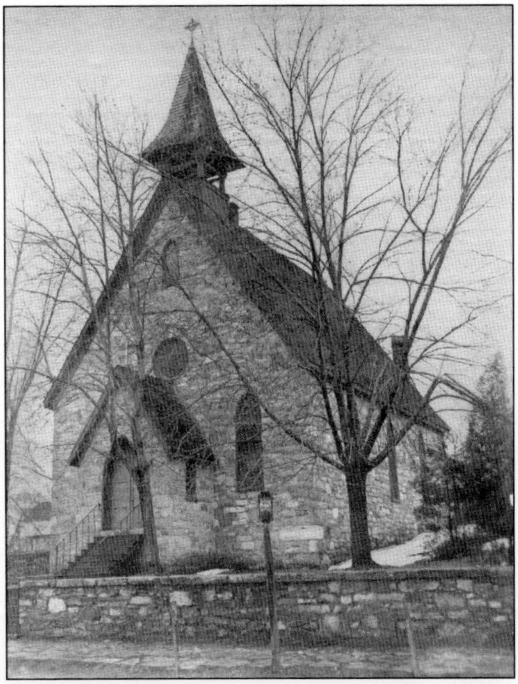

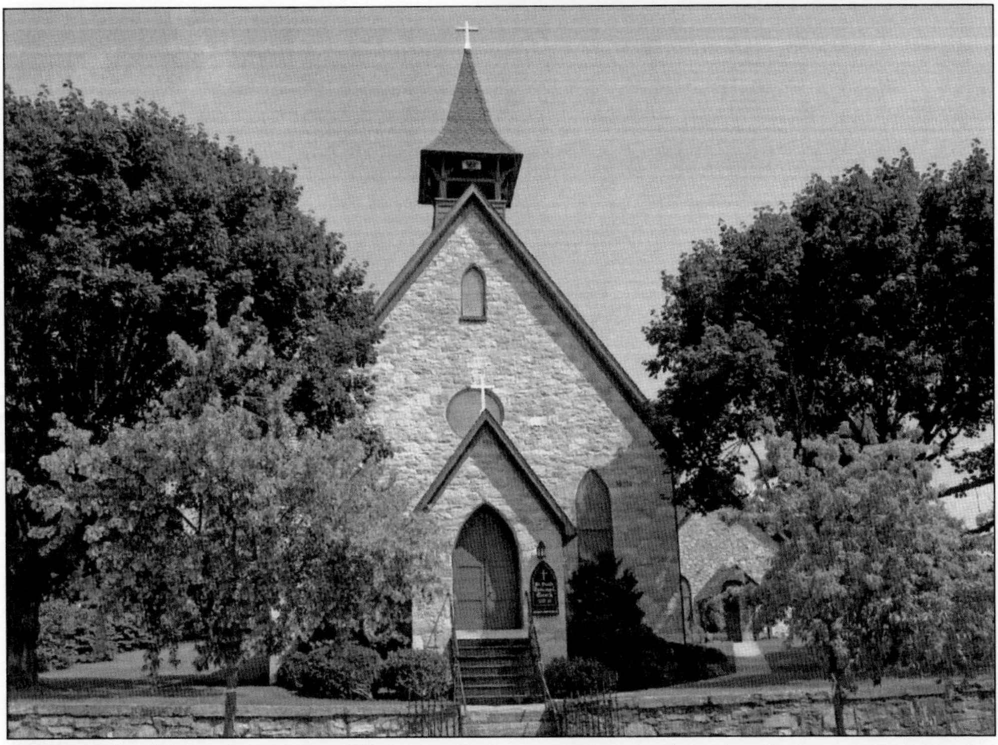

The church rebuilt after the Civil War contains stones from the first church. It is on the same lot but closer to the street. The church's social hall, built in 1965, is close to the site of the original building. The circular window above the entrance door is a memorial to Capt. Fanning C. Tucker, who died of wounds received during the battle. (Photograph by Tim Doyle.)

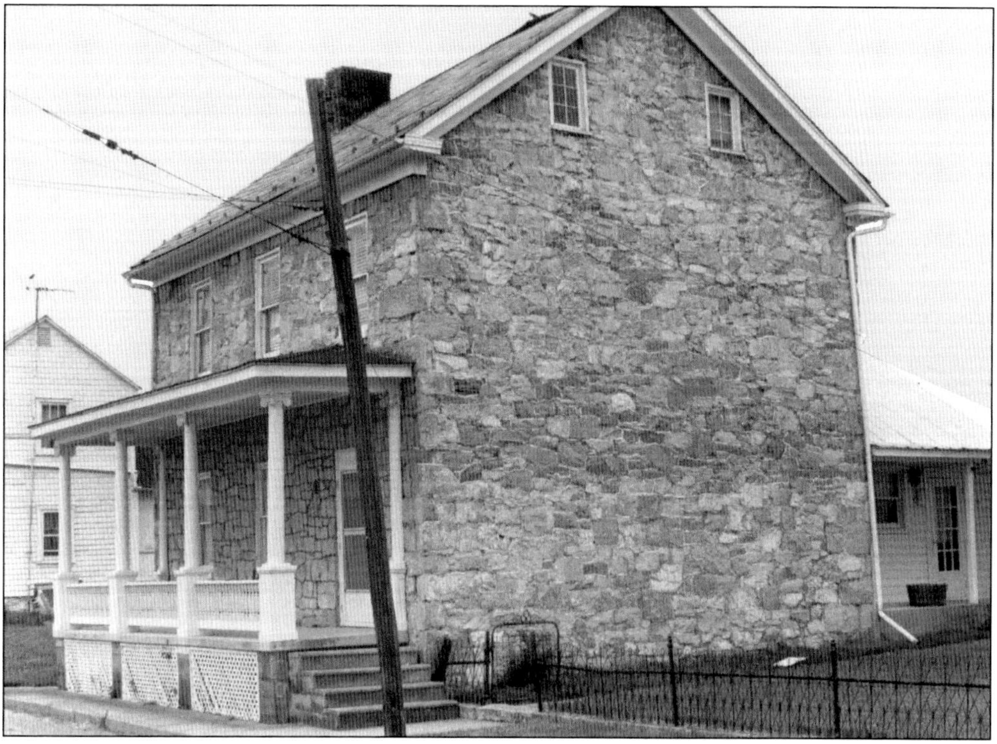

This house on West Chapline Street has been called the Founder's House, but the historic resource study for Sharpsburg could not verify the construction date or original owner. Researcher Paula Reed, Ph.D., concludes that the house was built between 1810 and 1820, possibly by John Jones Hays, nephew of Joseph Chapline Jr. (Courtesy WCFL/WMR.)

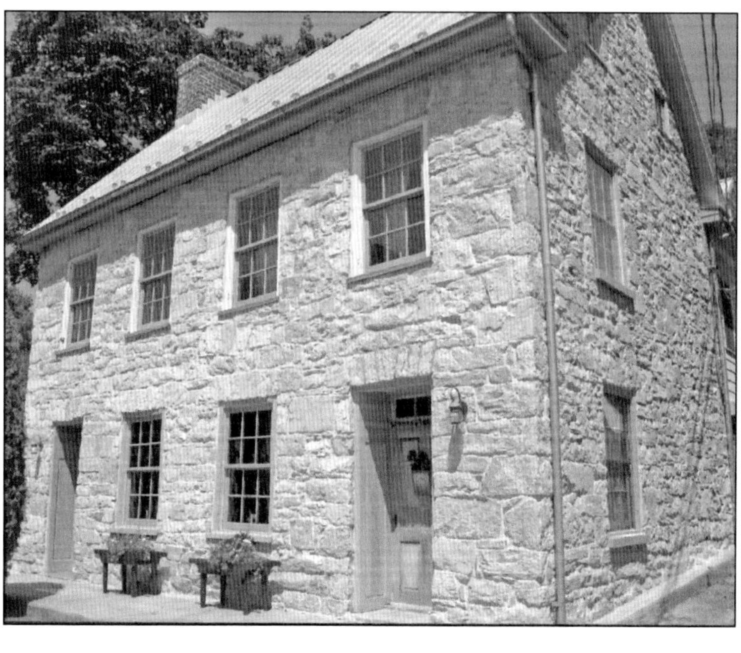

At the other end of Chapline Street, across from Clipp's Mill, is this roughly hewn stone house that may date from 1853, the date recently found written on a board in the house. This house on Lot 79 has unusual "book-end" entrances. The current owner has raised the roof of the original four-room stone structure and added a two-story wing at the rear. (Photograph by Tim Doyle.)

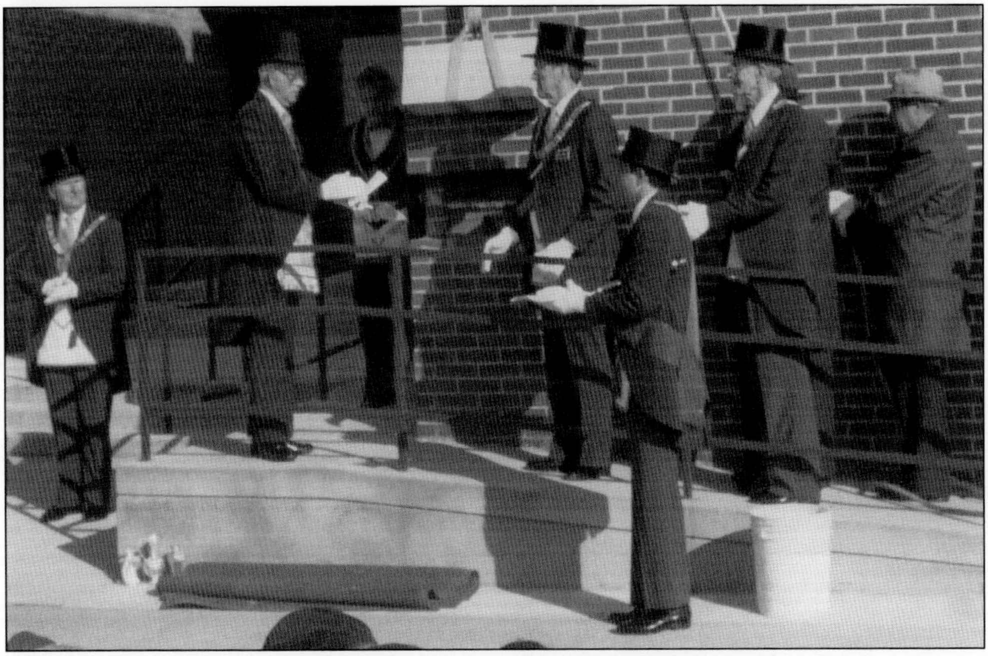

The original cornerstone from the 1936 Sharpsburg Elementary School is suspended above its new location in the remodeled and enlarged school on West Main Street. This rededication took place on November 29, 1983, at 1:15 p.m. All staff and students attended. The ceremony was performed by members of the Sharpsburg Eureka Lodge 105 and representatives of the state Masonic lodge. The program for the first cornerstone laying in 1936 shows that the same lodge presided then. During the ceremony, the master recited, "We are assembled in the open day, under the broad Canopy of Heaven, to lay the Corner-Stone of this building . . . may this building continue for centuries a credit to this community and a blessing to the citizens thereof." Dr. William Hess gave the address; the benediction was given by Rev. H. D. Chapman. (Both, courtesy Sharpsburg Elementary School.)

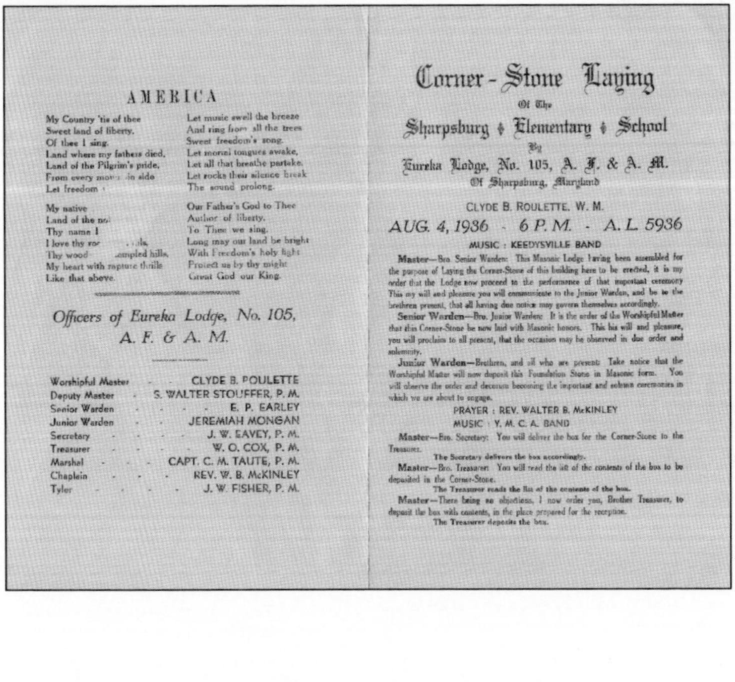

AMERICA

My Country 'tis of thee
Sweet land of liberty,
Of thee I sing.
Land where my fathers died,
Land of the Pilgrim's pride,
From every mo... ...in side
Let freedom ...

My native
Land of the no...
Thy name I
I love thy ro... ...ils,
Thy wood... ...empled hills,
My heart with rapture thrills
Like that above.

Let music swell the breeze
And ring from all the trees
Sweet freedom's song.
Let mortal tongues awake,
Let all that breathe partake,
Let rocks their silence break
The sound prolong.

Our Father's God to Thee
Author of liberty,
To Thee we sing.
Long may our land be bright
With Freedom's holy light
Protect us by thy might
Great God our King.

Officers of Eureka Lodge, No. 105,
A. F. & A. M.

Worshipful Master	CLYDE B. POULETTE
Deputy Master	S. WALTER STOUFFER, P. M.
Senior Warden	E. P. EARLEY
Junior Warden	JEREMIAH MONGAN
Secretary	J. W. EAVEY, P. M.
Treasurer	W. O. COX, P. M.
Marshal	CAPT. C. M. TAUTE, P. M.
Chaplain	REV. W. B. McKINLEY
Tyler	J. W. FISHER, P. M.

Corner-Stone Laying
Of The
Sharpsburg Elementary School
By
Eureka Lodge, No. 105, A. F. & A. M.
Of Sharpsburg, Maryland

CLYDE B. ROULETTE, W. M.

AUG. 4, 1936 - 6 P. M. - A. L. 5936

MUSIC : KEEDYSVILLE BAND

Master—Bro Senior Warden: This Masonic Lodge having been assembled for the purpose of Laying the Corner-Stone of this building here to be erected, it is my order that the Lodge now proceed to the performance of that important ceremony This my will and pleasure you will communicate to the Junior Warden, and he to the brethren present, that all having due notice may govern themselves accordingly.

Senior Warden—Bro. Junior Warden: It is the order of the Worshipful Master that this Corner-Stone be now laid with Masonic honors. This his will and pleasure, you will proclaim to all present, that the occasion may be observed in due order and solemnity.

Junior Warden—Brethren, and all who are present: Take notice that the Worshipful Master will now deposit this Foundation Stone in Masonic form. You will observe the order and decorum becoming the important and solemn ceremonies in which we are about to engage.

PRAYER : REV. WALTER B. McKINLEY

MUSIC : Y. M. C. A. BAND

Master—Bro. Secretary: You will deliver the box for the Corner-Stone to the Treasurer.

The Secretary delivers the box accordingly.

Master—Bro. Treasurer: You will read the list of the contents of the box to be deposited in the Corner-Stone.

The Treasurer reads the list of the contents of the box.

Master—There being no objections, I now order you, Brother Treasurer, to deposit the box with contents, in the place prepared for the reception.

The Treasurer deposits the box.

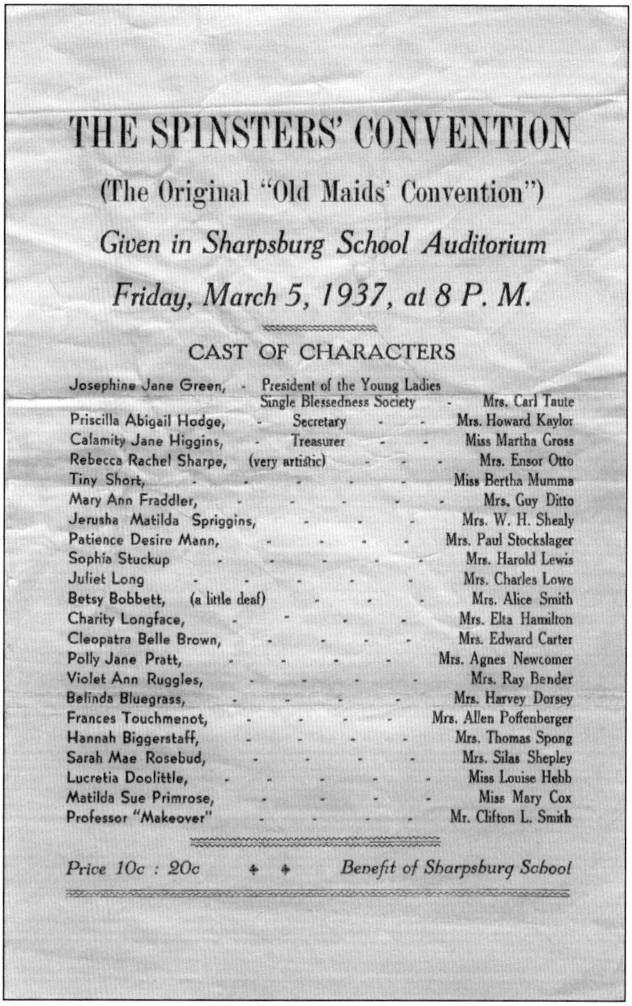

THE SPINSTERS' CONVENTION

(The Original "Old Maids' Convention")

Given in Sharpsburg School Auditorium

Friday, March 5, 1937, at 8 P. M.

CAST OF CHARACTERS

Character	Role	Cast
Josephine Jane Green,	President of the Young Ladies Single Blessedness Society	Mrs. Carl Taute
Priscilla Abigail Hodge,	Secretary	Mrs. Howard Kaylor
Calamity Jane Higgins,	Treasurer	Miss Martha Gross
Rebecca Rachel Sharpe,	(very artistic)	Mrs. Ensor Otto
Tiny Short,		Miss Bertha Mumma
Mary Ann Fraddler,		Mrs. Guy Ditto
Jerusha Matilda Spriggins,		Mrs. W. H. Shealy
Patience Desire Mann,		Mrs. Paul Stockslager
Sophia Stuckup		Mrs. Harold Lewis
Juliet Long		Mrs. Charles Lowe
Betsy Bobbett,	(a little deaf)	Mrs. Alice Smith
Charity Longface,		Mrs. Elta Hamilton
Cleopatra Belle Brown,		Mrs. Edward Carter
Polly Jane Pratt,		Mrs. Agnes Newcomer
Violet Ann Ruggles,		Mrs. Ray Bender
Belinda Bluegrass,		Mrs. Harvey Dorsey
Frances Touchmenot,		Mrs. Allen Poffenberger
Hannah Biggerstaff,		Mrs. Thomas Spong
Sarah Mae Rosebud,		Mrs. Silas Shepley
Lucretia Doolittle,		Miss Louise Hebb
Matilda Sue Primrose,		Miss Mary Cox
Professor "Makeover"		Mr. Clifton L. Smith

Price 10c : 20c ✦ ✦ *Benefit of Sharpsburg School*

The Spinsters' Convention was presented in the auditorium of the new Sharpsburg School as a school benefit. The cast included town residents with family names that appear on the 1877 survey map. Apparently there was a sense of political correctness; the title of the original play *Old Maids' Convention* had been changed, but it is still printed on the program. (Courtesy Sharpsburg Elementary School.)

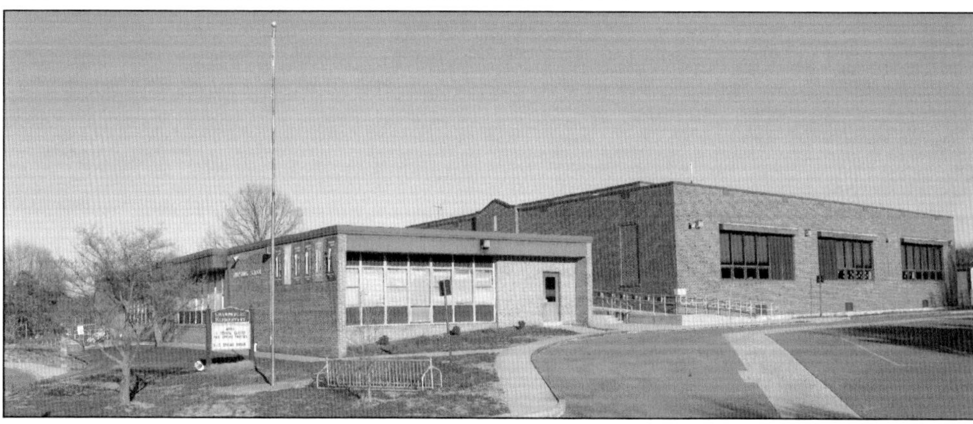

Sharpsburg Elementary School on West Main Street incorporates and surrounds the 1936 building. The old limestone wall is visible at the left edge of this 2009 photograph. A pointed gable of the old entrance is visible as part of the larger 1983 addition. The relaid cornerstone is just to the right of the ramp. (Photograph by Tim Doyle.)

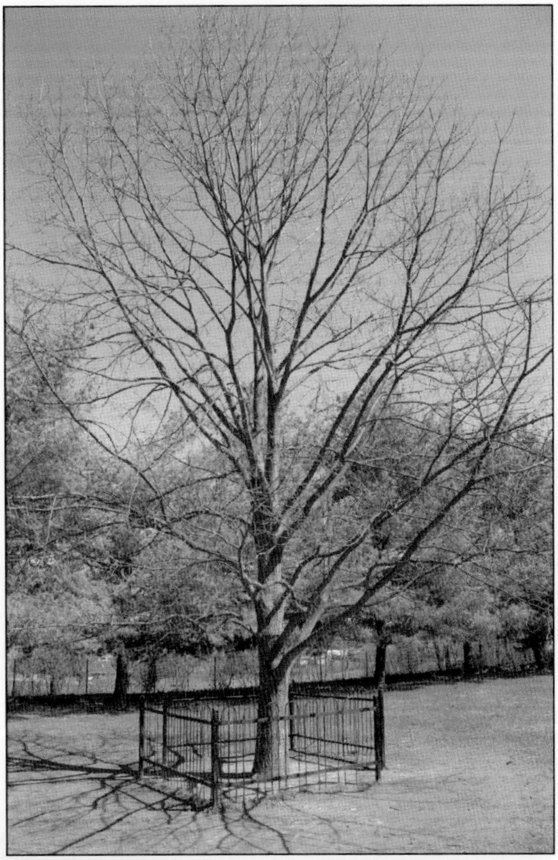

This oak tree, planted as a memorial on the playground of the school, is enclosed by parts of the iron fence that surrounded the old schools on East Antietam Street. The close-up view of the fence shows that some of the interior stakes, and even one of the arches, have disappeared. Mrs. Ronald Milburn (Patsy) of Sharpsburg remembered that some of the fence from the old schoolyard had been saved, but, she said, none was on the Antietam Street property when she and her husband bought it in 1973. This fence appears in this book on the pictures of the old schools and on the photograph of the house at 113 East Antietam Street. School officials have been unable to identify the person who was to be memorialized. (Both photographs by Tim Doyle.)

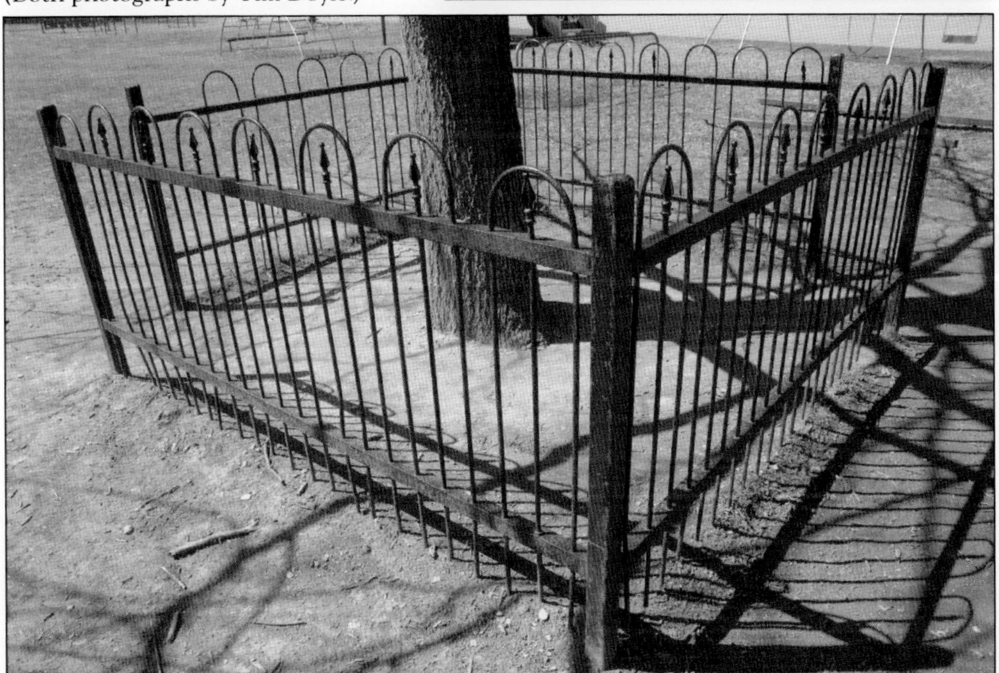

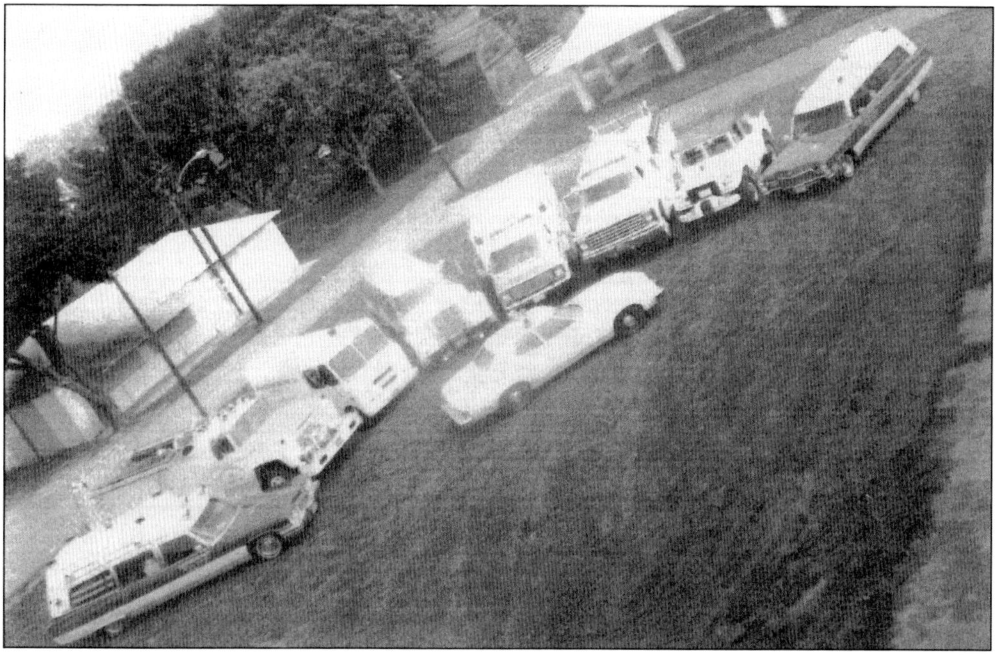

In 1943, eight men with $16 and a donated pumping unit took a training course and formed the Sharpsburg Volunteer Fire Company. This photograph shows that first pumper, second from the right. The building at the left was their first fire hall. It was financed by selling concrete blocks for $1 each. The company had fund-raisers and borrowed money to build another fire hall on West Chapline Street. (Courtesy Sharpsburg Volunteer Fire Company.)

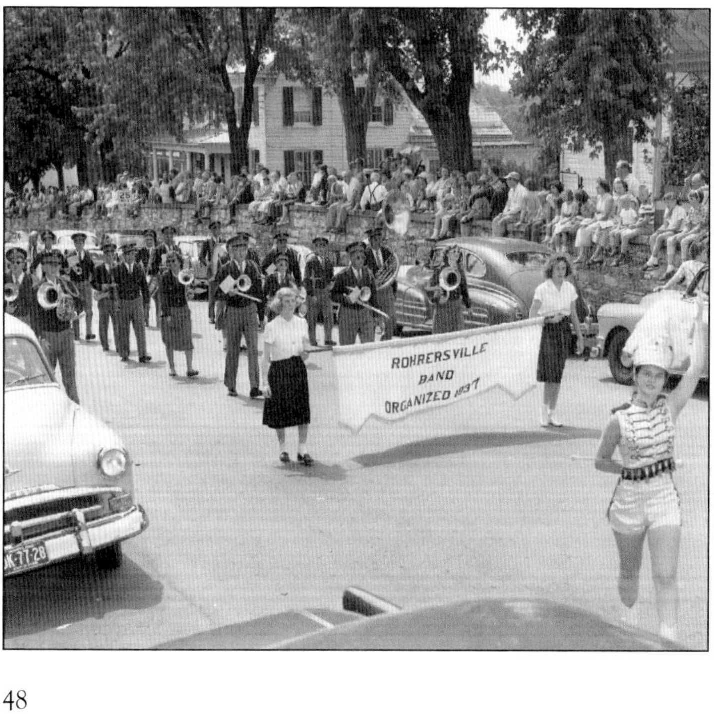

Sharpsburg has observed Memorial (Decoration) Day since 1867. The Rohrersville Band has marched in every Sharpsburg Memorial Day Parade, except for two, since 1895. In this 1957 photograph, the band approaches the end of the parade at the top of the hill while observers sit on the stone walls that line East Main Street. Before the May parade, the band presents a concert at the square after the wreath-laying ceremony. (Courtesy WCFL/WMR.)

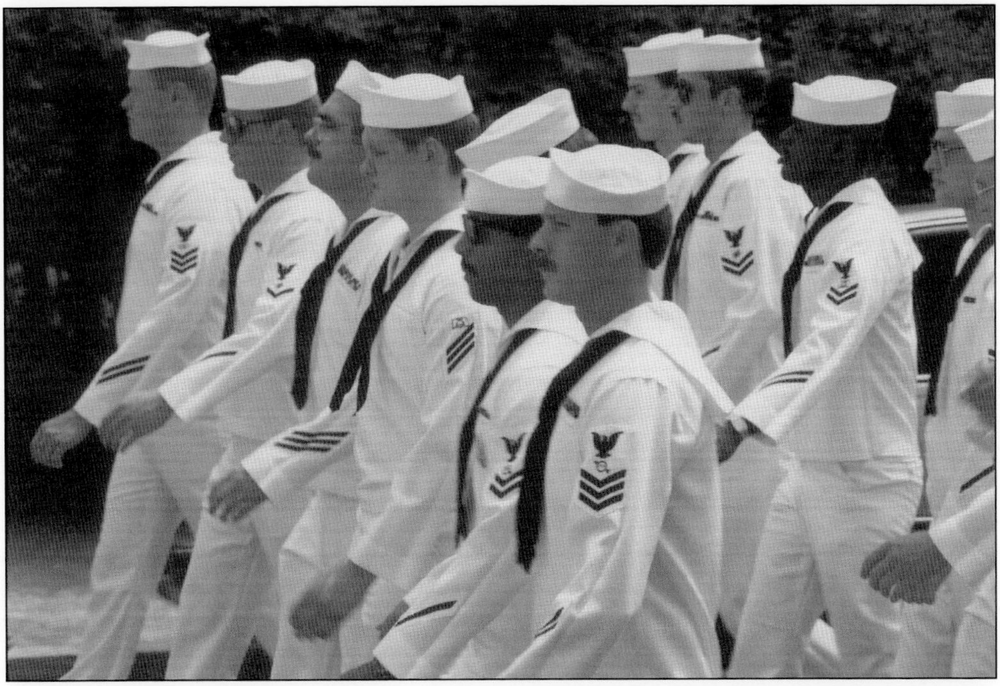

These sailors are crew members from the USS *Antietam* (CG-54). They had visited the elementary school and presented this picture of the ship to the school. They are shown marching in the Memorial Day parade on May 30, 1987, the 120th observation of the service of American citizens in armed conflicts. On that Memorial Day, Page T. Otto, commander of Antietam Post 236 American Legion, said, "This addition of a new ship to the fleet of the U.S. Navy to carry the name USS *Antietam* is of great distinction and recognition." Beverly Byron, 6th District Maryland congresswoman, was asked to name the guided missile cruiser. The ship was christened on April 19, 1987, and was commissioned on June 6, 1987. It is 567 feet long, weighs 9,500 tons, and is capable of speeds over 30 knots. (Above, courtesy St. Paul's Episcopal Church; below, courtesy Jeffrey Saylor.)

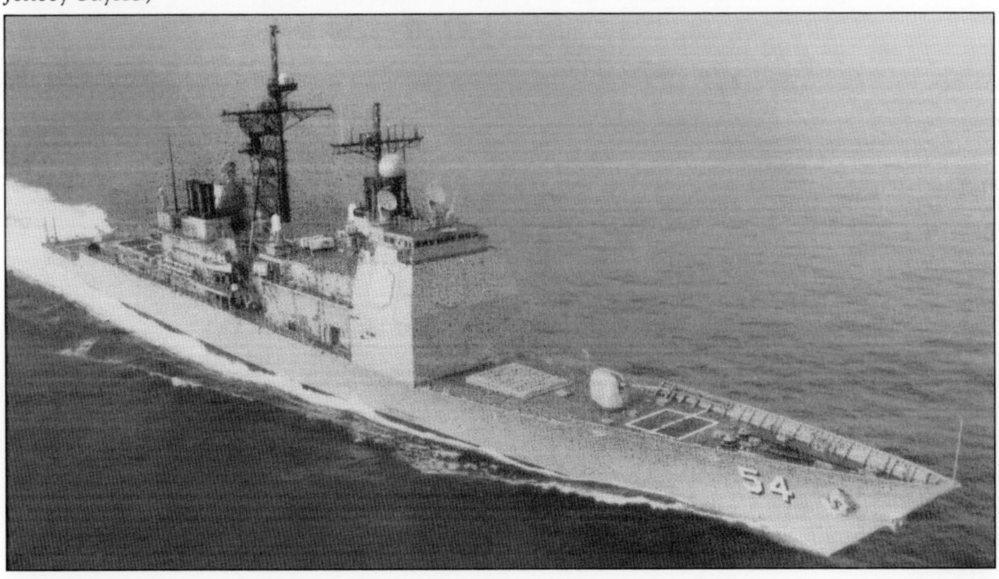

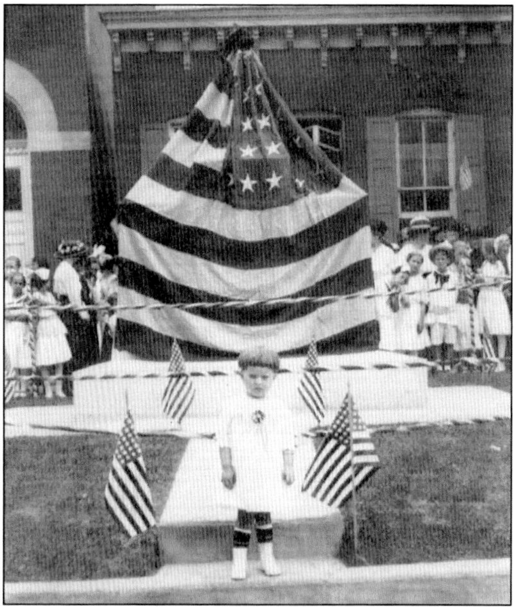

Albina Renner Roulette stands in front of the still-veiled World Wars monument that lists 66 names. The inscription reads, "Erected by citizens of Sharpsburg Dist. In recognition of the patriotism shown by all who answered our country's call in the World War. 1917–1919." The back, inscribed after 1945, reads, "Dedicated to the men and women of District 1 who devotedly served their country in World War II." (Courtesy authors' collection.)

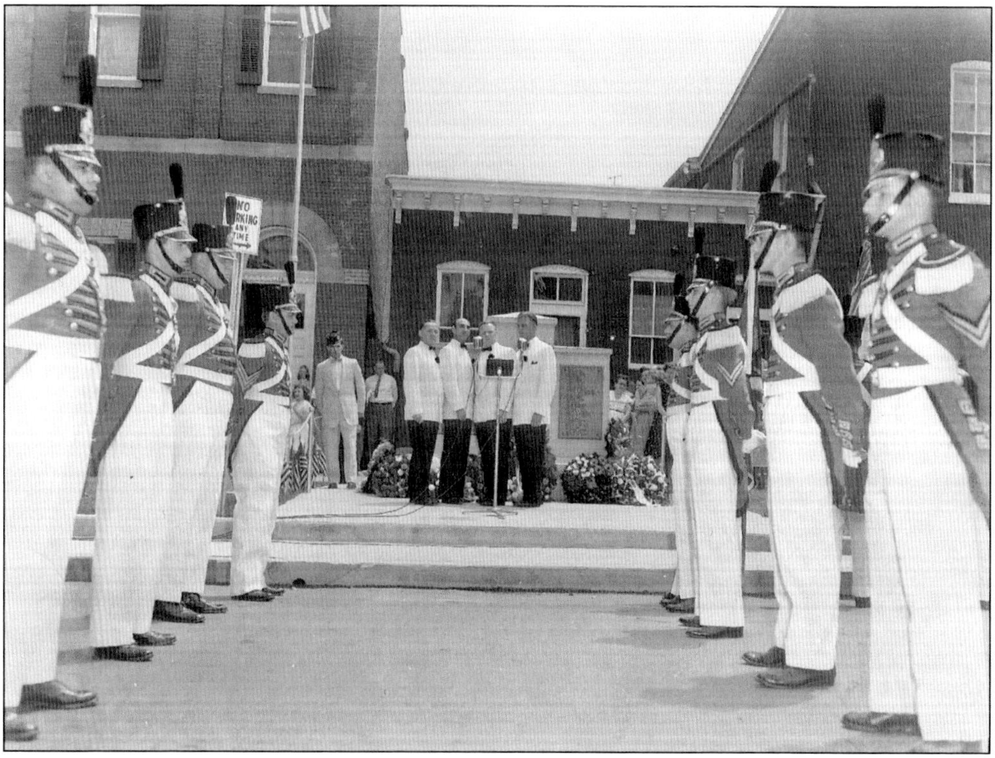

Before the Memorial Day parade each year, wreaths are laid at the monuments in front of town hall. The World Wars monument is visible behind the quartet. About 100 area citizens served in World War II. Korean and Vietnam veterans' monuments were unveiled in November 1987. The Sharpsburg area raised two full companies for the Union army during the Civil War. Singing are, from left to right, Kenneth Sinn, Joe Schindler, Paul Berger, and Clark Jennings. (Courtesy Stephen Recker.)

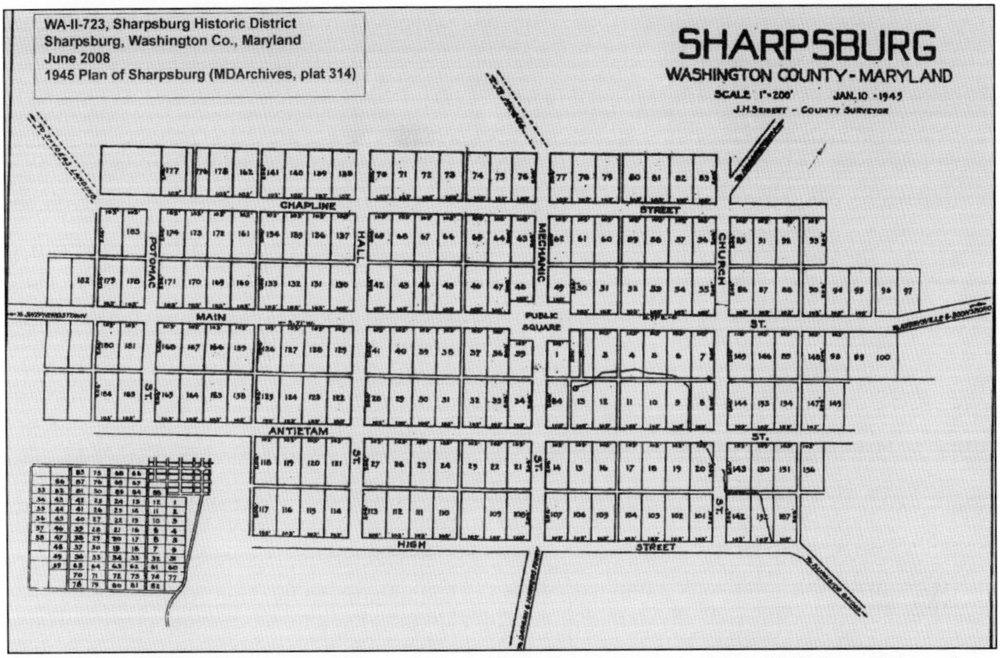

The 1887 survey map has been referenced throughout this chapter, but this 1945 plan of Sharpsburg that hangs in town hall could have served to locate houses, churches, and schools. The out lots southwest of town were 5-acre plots used as family or commercial gardens at the time of the Civil War. The 1950s photograph taken by Gene Virts for Fairchild Aircraft shows the out lots at the bottom right as empty fields. At the top right (east of town) is Antietam National Cemetery with the large white Soldiers' Monument. Across the street is Mountain View Cemetery. The old brick schools are still standing on East Antietam Street. The 1936 elementary school is at the end of West Main Street in the lower left-hand corner of the photograph. The three churches on West Main Street all have steeples. (Above, courtesy Paula S. Reed and Associates; below, courtesy WCFL/WMR.)

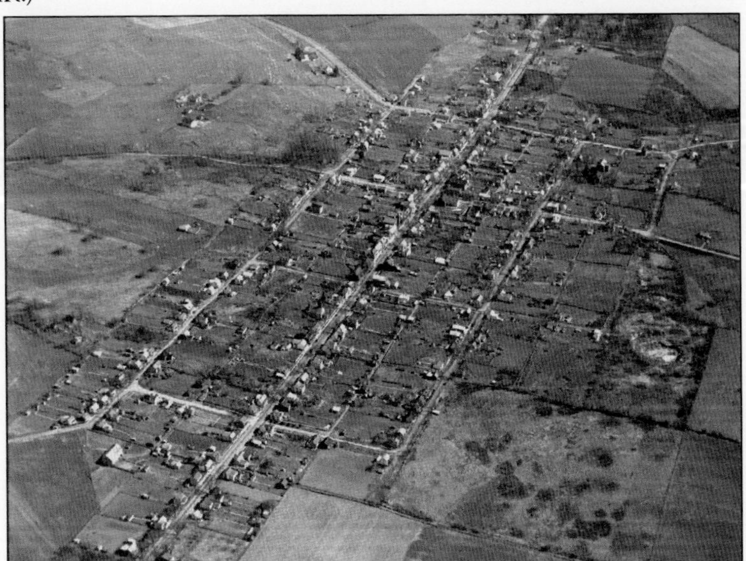

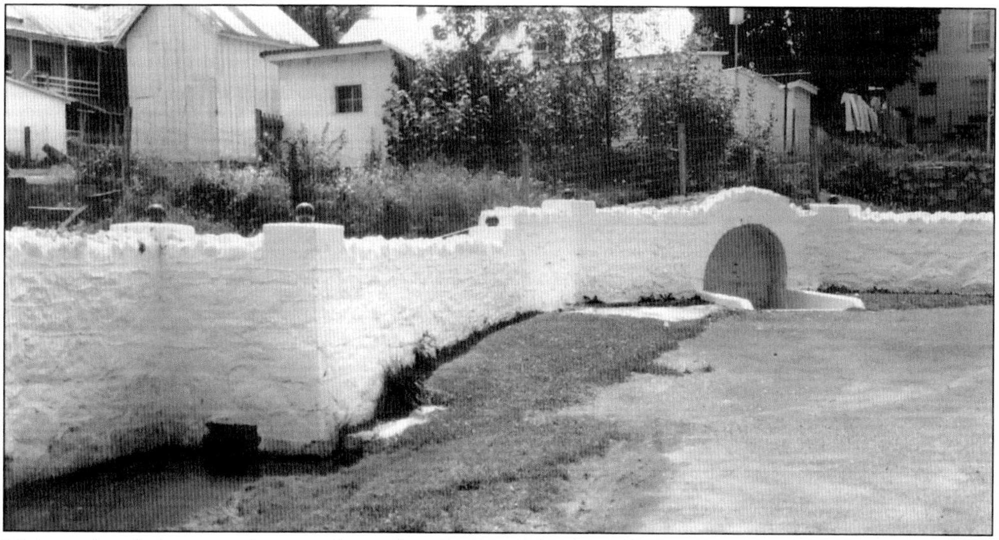

This undated photograph was taken after the WPA built and mortared these stone walls around the Big Spring in the 1930s. Seven cannonballs top the corner pillars. The area in front of the spring has been paved. The stream emerges from an opening in the wall and flows, as the Town Run, into the Antietam Creek. The 1877 survey map shows that William Brashear owned Lot 13, the site of the Great Spring. (Courtesy WCHS.)

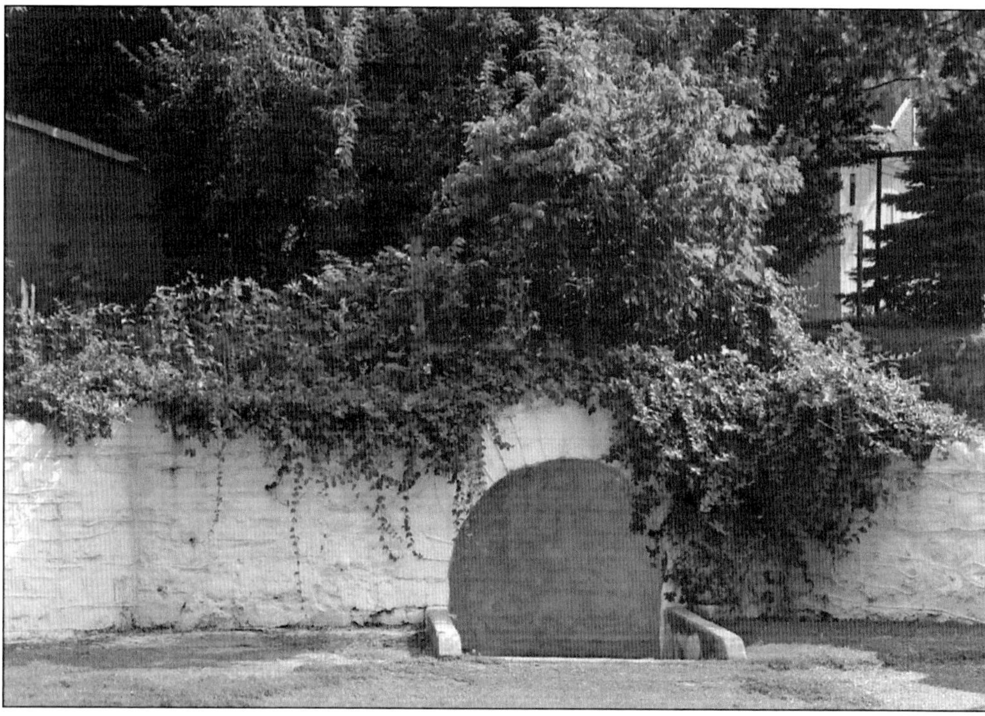

The wire fence behind the spring still stands but is almost covered with summer vines and ivy. In 1969, the Town of Sharpsburg installed water lines for town residents. Sharpsburg's water source is now the Potomac River and the Great Spring—kept tidy by the Sharpsburg Historical Society, other volunteers, and the town—which serves as a reminder of the town's origin and history. (Photograph by Tim Doyle.)

Two

The People

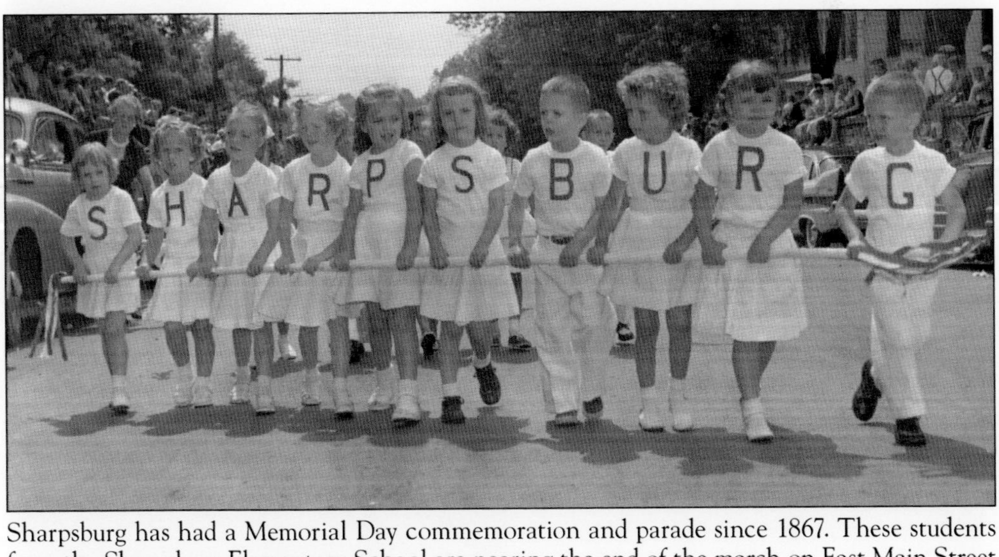

Sharpsburg has had a Memorial Day commemoration and parade since 1867. These students from the Sharpsburg Elementary School are nearing the end of the march on East Main Street on May 30, 1957. They are kept in order and in line by the pole, but they are not in step as they work hard to get to the top of the hill. (Courtesy *Maryland Cracker Barrel*.)

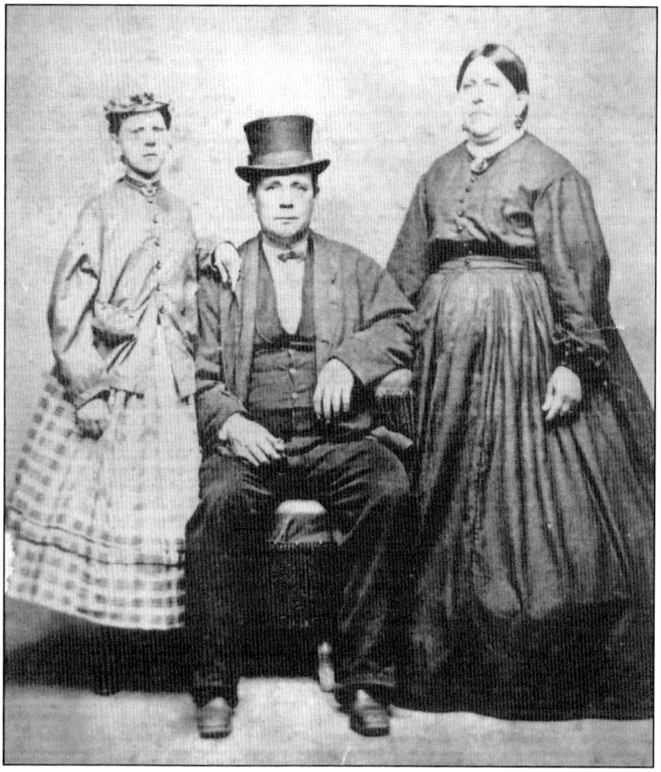

Pictured here about 1866 are, from left to right, Lillie Virginia (Smith) Rohr (1856–1936); Judge David Smith, nicknamed "Shoemaker" (1819–1892); and Mary Ann (Keedy) Smith (1814–1872). The family lived in the stone house at the corner of North Mechanic and West Chapline Streets at the time of the battle. Mary Ann Smith and her four children hid in the cellar while shell and shrapnel flew around and into the house. (Courtesy NPS/ANB.)

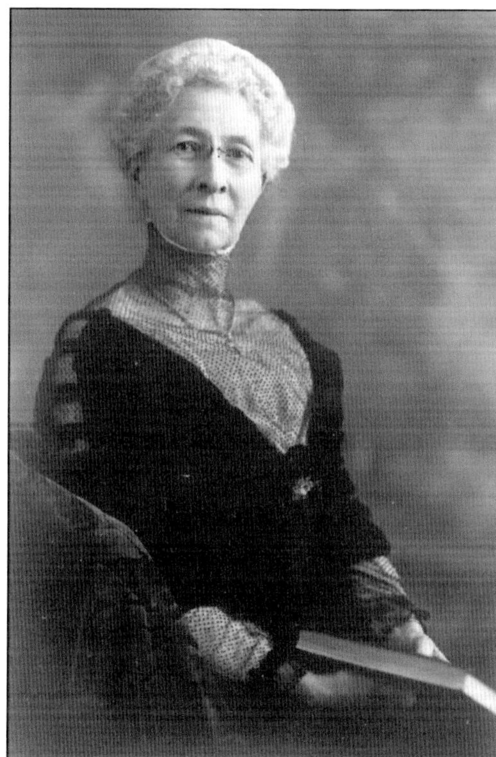

This is a formal portrait of Elizabeth Riley (Piper) Showman Dye (1840–1925). Her parents were Henry and Elizabeth (Keedy) Piper. Her first husband, Raleigh Showman, died on the same date, April 8, 1863, that their first son, David William, died. She remarried Maj. P. Edwin Dye in 1878. She is buried in Mountain View Cemetery in Sharpsburg. (Courtesy Rosita Ray.)

This backyard portrait includes descendents of the Daniel Piper family. From left to right are (first row) Susan (Piper) Miller (born 1845) and Elizabeth, mother of Raleigh Sherman (born 1863), who changed his name from Showman; (second row) Raleigh; Raleigh's nephew Marcellus Stow (born 1902); Raleigh's niece Elizabeth Stow (born 1905); and Mary Ellen (Piper) Smith, sister of Elizabeth and Susan. (Courtesy Rosita Ray.)

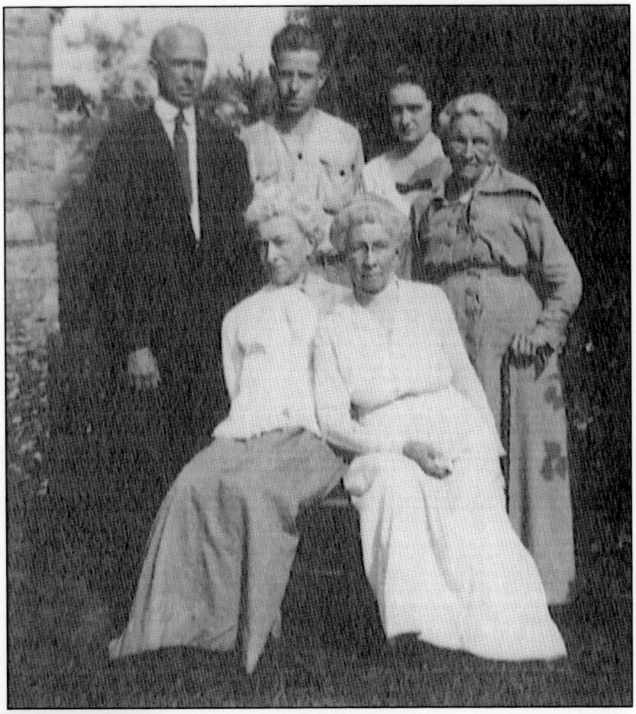

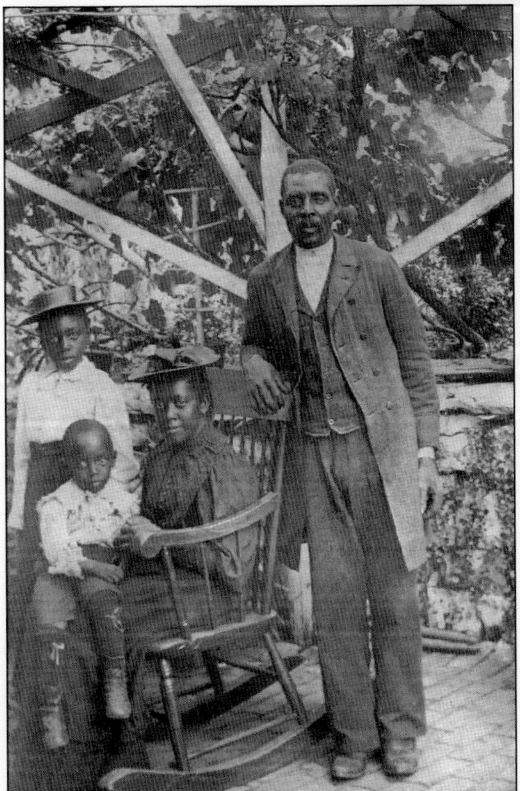

This is the family of Emory Summers, who once lived in this house as a slave of the owner Henry Piper. They are under the grape arbor in late summer in the garden of the Piper House. After the Civil War, the Pipers gave Summers a home on their farm, north of Sharpsburg. A note in the book *Too Afraid to Cry* says Summers lived in Sharpsburg off East Chapline Street in 1920. (Courtesy Rosita Ray.)

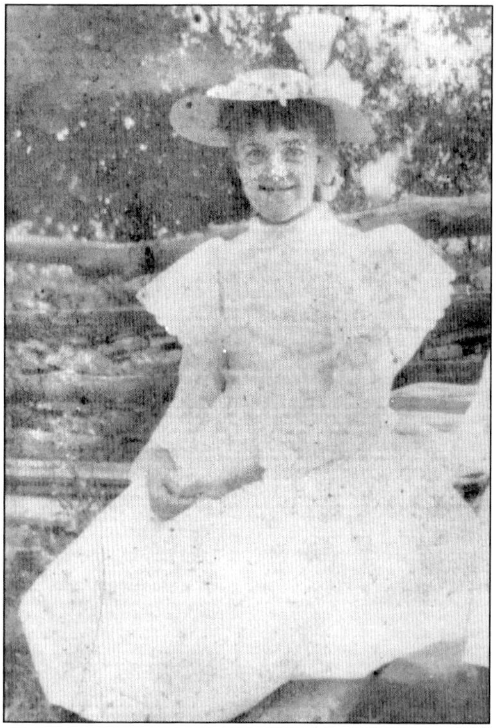

Myrta Irene Snavely appears to be about 10 years old in this photograph. She married John Walter Roulette in 1885. They lived in town for about 10 years before they moved to a farm just west of town. Five of their eight children lived into adulthood. One son, Robert Earl, lived on the farm with his wife, Annabelle, until he died in October 2008. (Courtesy Earl and Annabelle Roulette.)

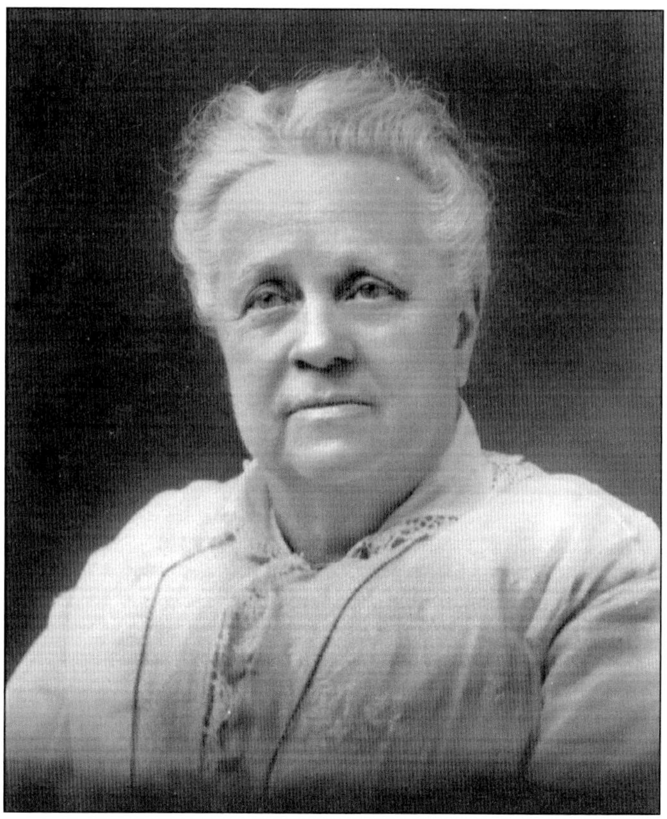

The note on the back of this photograph says simply, "Grandmother Snavely." She is the wife of Joseph Snavely, Myrta Irene (Snavely) Roulette's mother, and the grandmother of Earl Roulette. She spent part of her childhood at Belinda Springs. (Courtesy Earl and Annabelle Roulette.)

William Roulette, his wife, Margaret, and their six children hid in the cellar of their home as the Battle of Antietam raged above them. They survived the battle, but their 20-month-old daughter Carrie May died in October 1862. John Roulette, a son, later moved to town to the stone house at 201 West Main Street. It is sometimes called the Hays Highbarger Roulette House. (Courtesy Earl and Annabelle Roulette.)

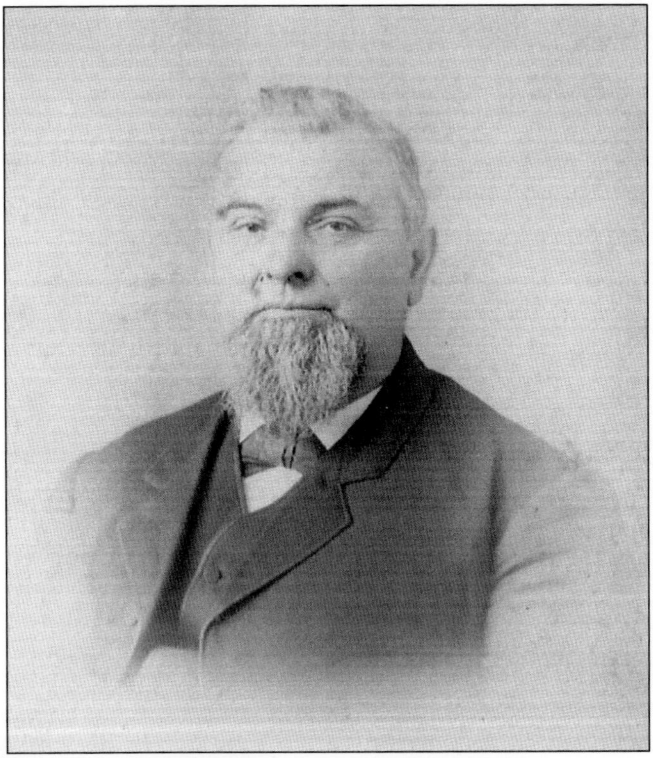

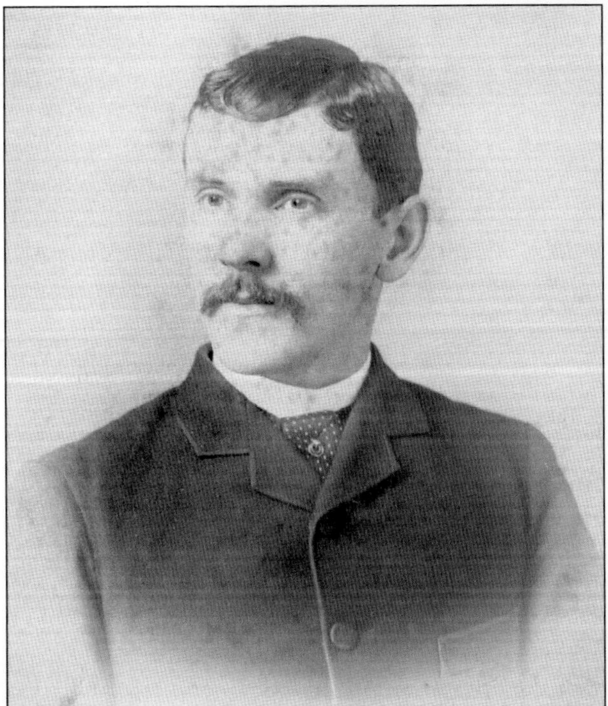

Franklin Roulette was a grandson of William Roulette of the Roulette farm near Bloody Lane on the Antietam National Battlefield. He was one of eight children of John W. and Myrta Irene (Snavely) Roulette. Franklin served as a bombardier in the South Pacific in World War II. He was a teacher at South Hagerstown High School. (Courtesy Earl and Annabelle Roulette.)

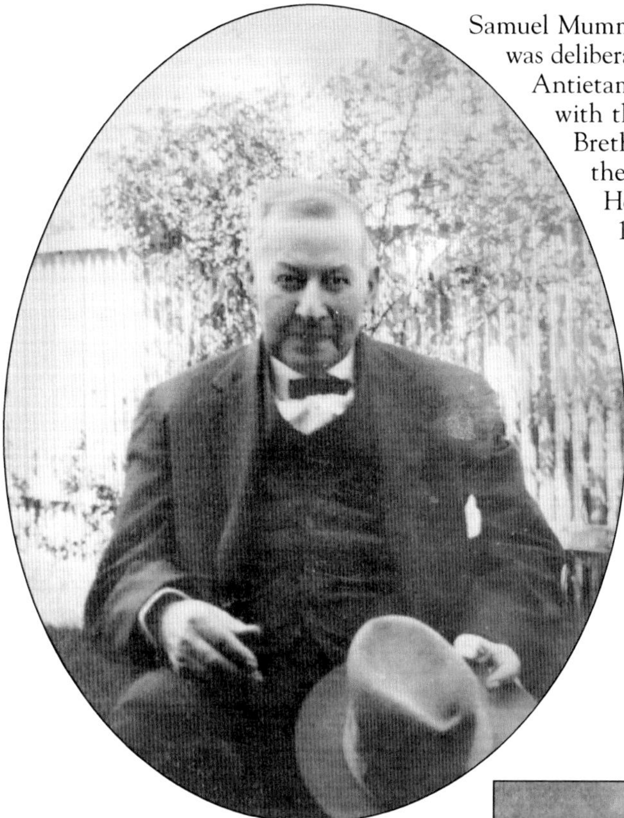

Samuel Mumma Jr. lived in the only home that was deliberately destroyed during the Battle of Antietam. The family fled, taking nothing with them, to the Manor Church of the Brethren to escape the fighting. After the battle, they lived in the Sherrick House. Mumma, pictured here about 1920, became the postmaster in Sharpsburg, as did his son Victor Reichard Mumma. (Courtesy Bonnard J. Morgan Sr.)

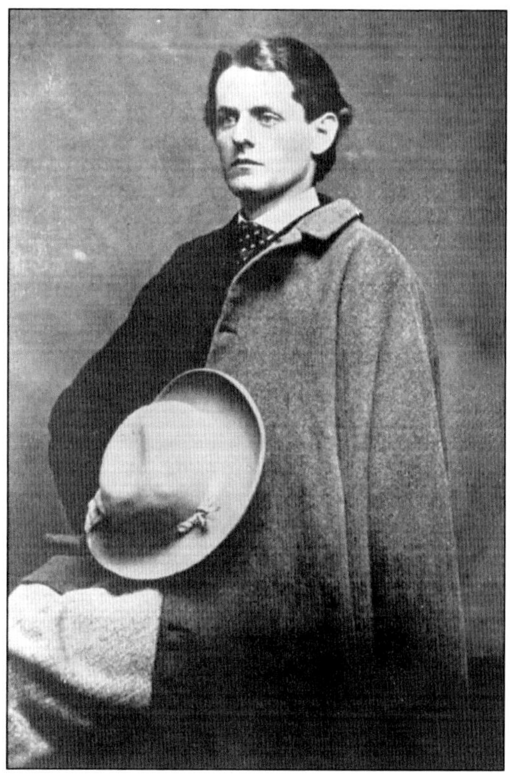

Henry Kyd Douglas grew up near Sharpsburg at Ferry Hill Place on the Potomac River. He enlisted in the Confederate army and became a member of Stonewall Jackson's staff. He was the youngest brigade officer in the Civil War. During the battle, he managed to visit his parents, unionists, at Ferry Hill. He practiced law in Hagerstown and never married. (Courtesy WCHS.)

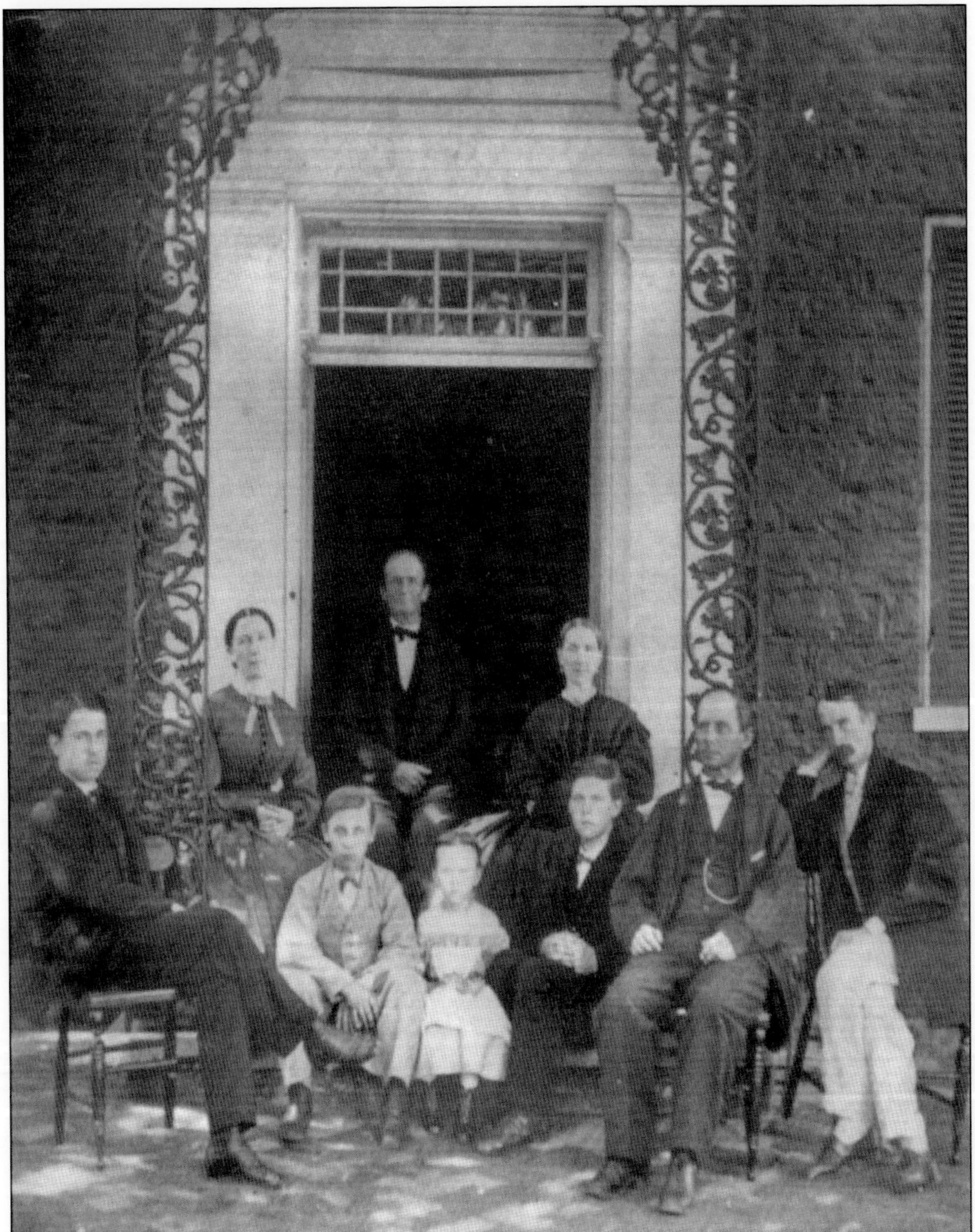

The Dr. Augustine Biggs family sits before their stone home on West Main Street with its fancy Victorian iron grill work. The physician married twice and had four children. The local limestone house was built in 1789 on Lot 47. The brick addition was constructed sometime before 1850, when Biggs bought the house. Biggs began practice in Sharpsburg in 1836 and instituted a health care plan for workers at the Antietam Furnace. The house was hit by artillery fire during the Battle of Antietam, and a hole caused by cannon is visible on the second floor of the gable end of the house. Biggs, a Union supporter, filed a claim for damage to the house and the brick stable at the rear of the property. After the Civil War, he designed the National Cemetery. He retired from the practice of medicine in 1887. He died in 1889. (Courtesy Marian and Syd Gale.)

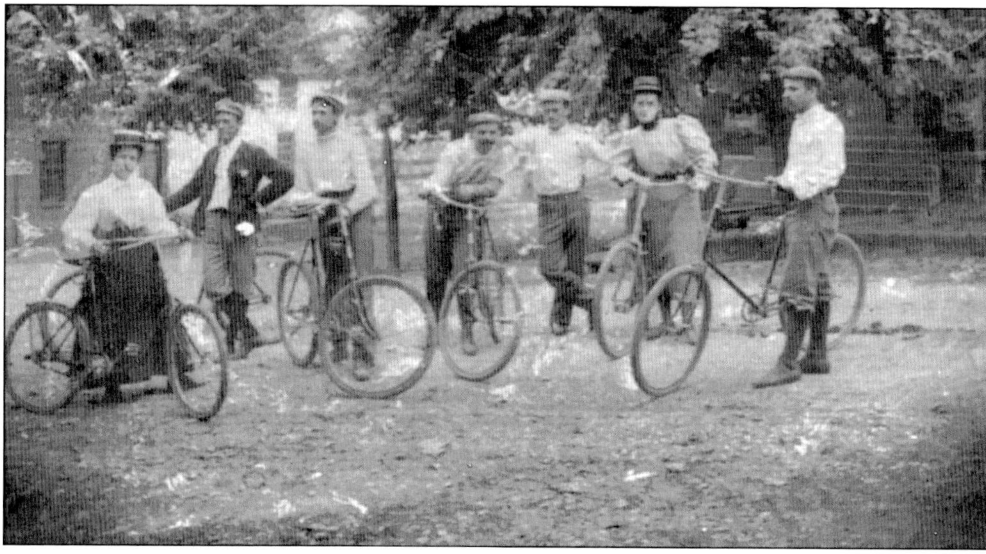

The photograph identifies place and date, "Sharpsburg, Washington Co., Aug. 13, 1890," but the participants' names are not given. The cyclists appear to be in town; a street lamp is in the middle background, and some kind of sign is at the left. The group of seven has only six bikes, but all are dressed for the outing with hats for all and long skirts for the women. (Courtesy Rosita Ray.)

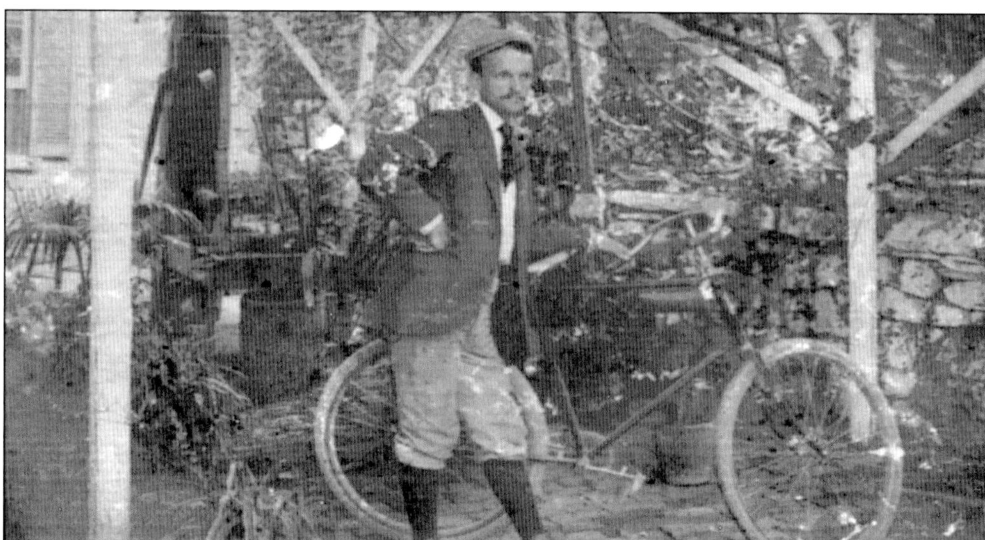

Raleigh Showman and his bike on August 13, 1890, are in the backyard of the Piper House. The fashionable Washington, D.C., lawyer was 27 years old. He is standing in front of the stone retaining wall and the grape arbor, which is no longer there. To the left in the background can be seen the handle of a cucumber pump, also no longer there. (Courtesy Rosita Ray.)

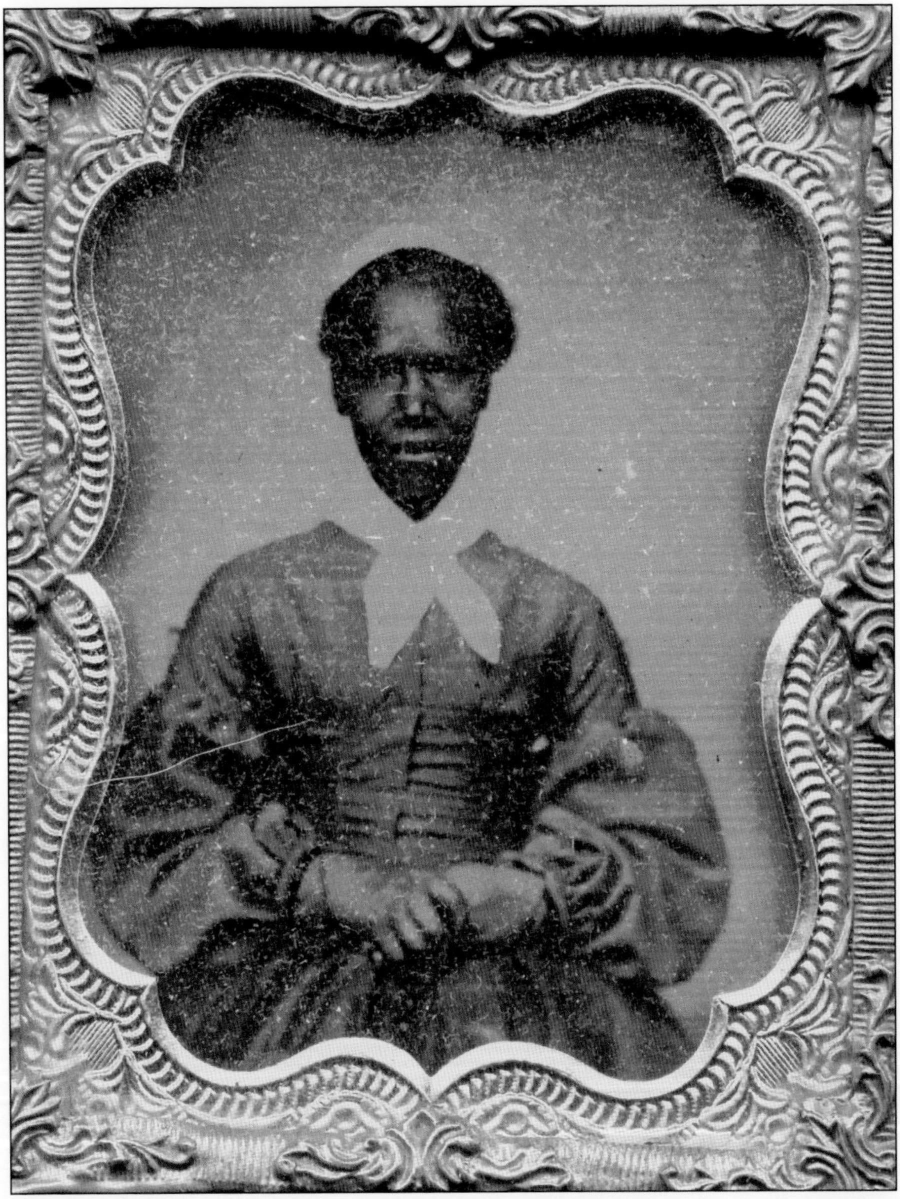

This 3-inch-by-3-inch daguerreotype is of Nancy Campbell (1814–1892). Andrew Miller freed her by deed of manumission in June 1859. The Washington County Orphans Court granted the free 46-year-old woman of "extraordinary good conduct and good character as proven to us by the testimony of William Rulett" permission to remain in Maryland for one year from November 25, 1859. The 1860 census records Nancy Campbell, free black, living with the William Roulette family. She stayed on the Roulette farm when it was turned over to Benjamin Franklin Roulette. She had joined the Manor Dunker Church near Tilghmanton while still a slave and probably went there with the William Roulette family when they, like others, traveled there for safety before the battle. She is buried in the Manor Church cemetery, where her tombstone reads "Nancy Camel." In her last will and testament of June 20, 1885, she gave $50 "to the Manor Church of the Tunker denomination" and $20 to Tolson's Chapel, although she was not a known member of the black church in Sharpsburg. (Courtesy Earl and Annabelle Roulette.)

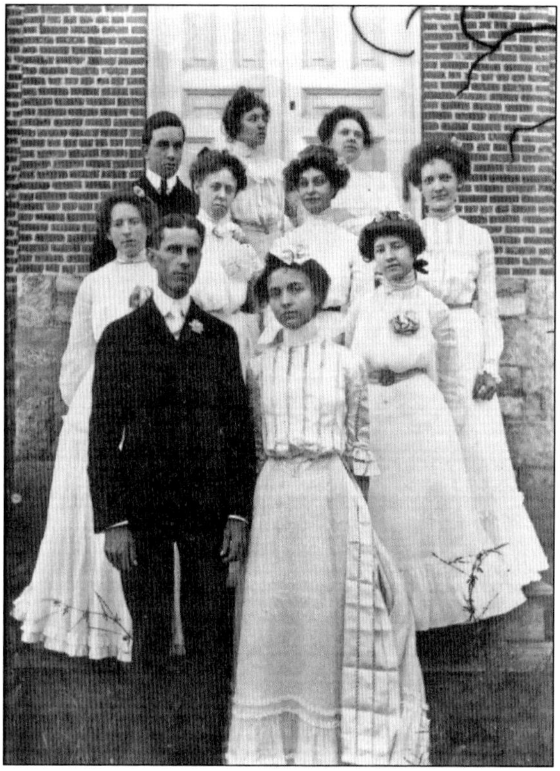

On the steps of the "new" Sharpsburg school on July 16, 1902, is the wedding party of John Wesley Eavey and Idella Cordelia Smith. John Eavey later became the principal of the school. From left to right are (second row) Iva Eavey and Ethel Rohrer; (third row) Gertrude Smith, Elta Schamel, and Mary Eavey; (fourth row) the bride's brother Claude Smith, Mabel Rohrer, and an unidentified woman. (Courtesy *Maryland Cracker Barrel*.)

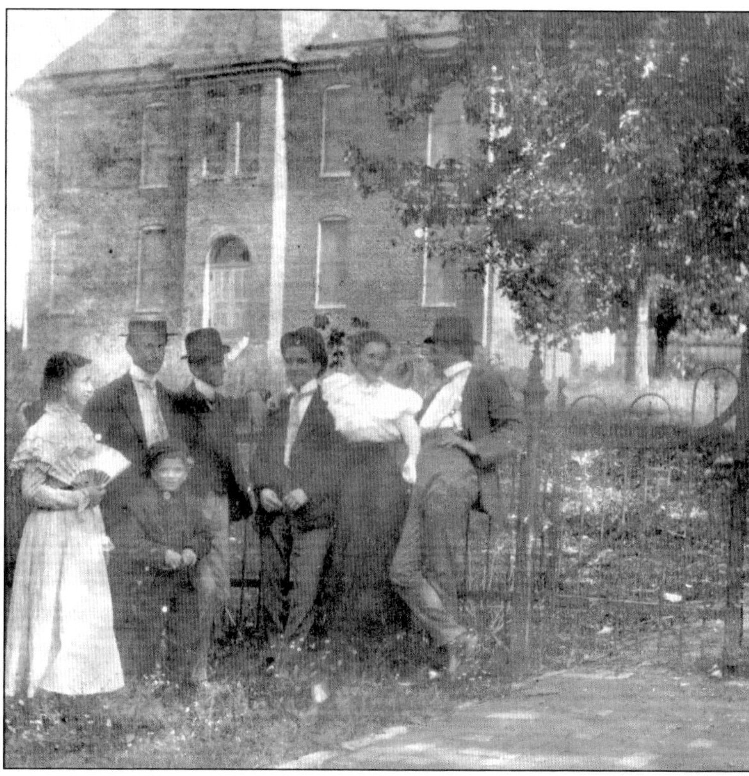

This unidentified party is near the iron double gate over the brick walkway on the Sharpsburg schools' property on East Antietam Street. The building is the "new" school. The men in high collars, ties, and suspenders seem to be enjoying a summer's day. Could this be the Eaveys with their son visiting their wedding-day picture site? (Courtesy SHS.)

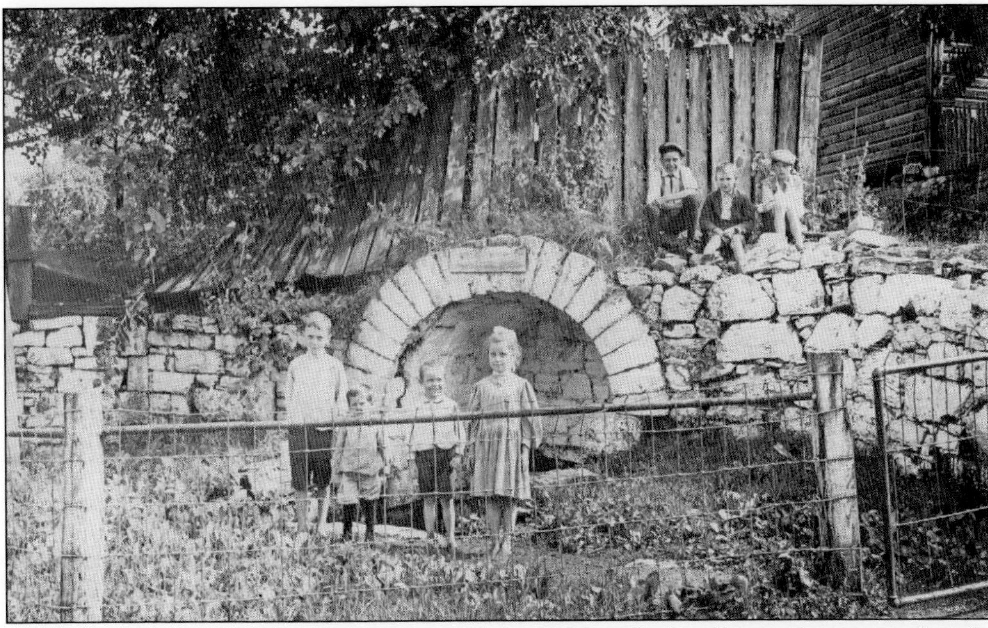

Dr. E. M. Garrott took these two pictures about 1907 at the Big Spring. It appears that the occasion's primary purpose was to photograph the 11 old-timers of Sharpsburg. Neighborhood children, some barefoot, watching the session also got to pose for a summer day's portrait. The 11 men are, from left to right, identified on the back of the photograph as R. W. Grove, Andy Snyder, Baker Wilhelm, Elie Spong, David Glass, Van Brashears, Frank DeLauney, Bill Brashears, Buddy Boyers, Martin Cramer, and Mat Spong. At the right behind the fence are Floyd Mose and ? Seaman, who later married Ernest Cramer. The children in front of the spring are, from left to right, Burnside Benner, Floyd Mose, Bruce McGraw, and Dotte McGraw. Sitting in front of the wooden fence are, from left to right, Allen McGraw, Ralph Renner, and Joe Brashears. (Both, courtesy Stephen Recker.)

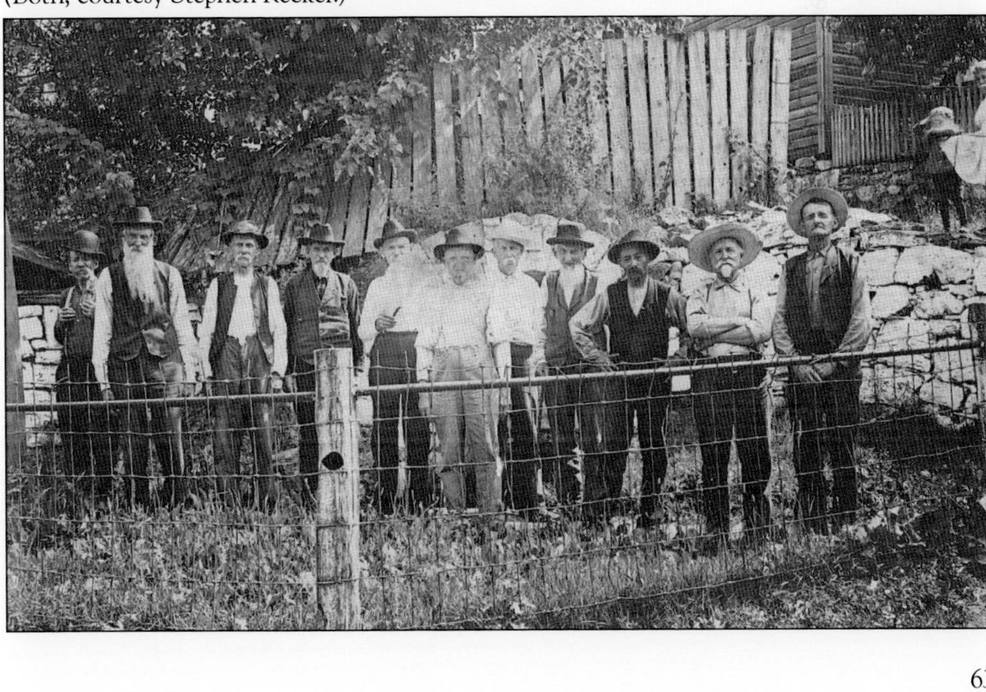

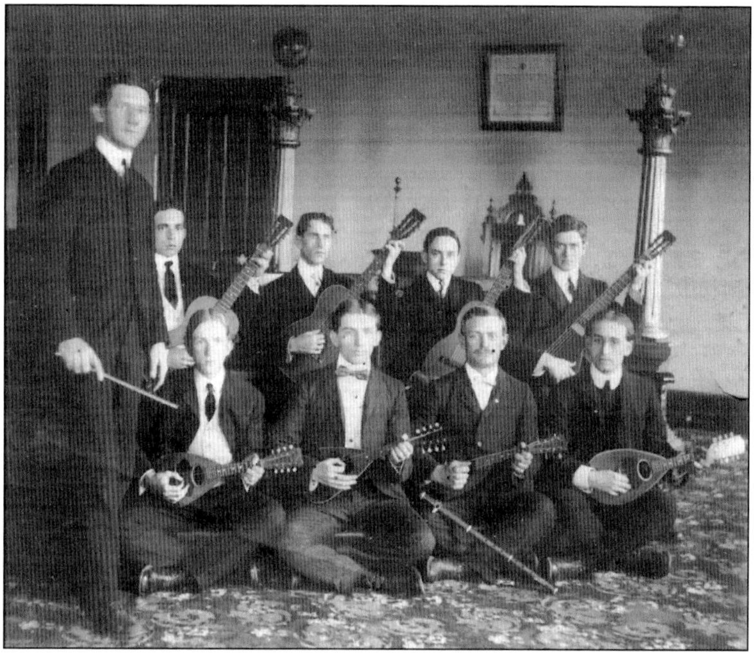

The note on the back of this photograph says it was taken about 1900 inside the Masonic lodge. The conductor and the guitar, mandolin, and flute players make up the Sharpsburg Chamber Music group. John Wesley Eavey is second from left on the back row. The others, with various styles of neckwear, are not identified. (Courtesy Linda Irwin-Craig.)

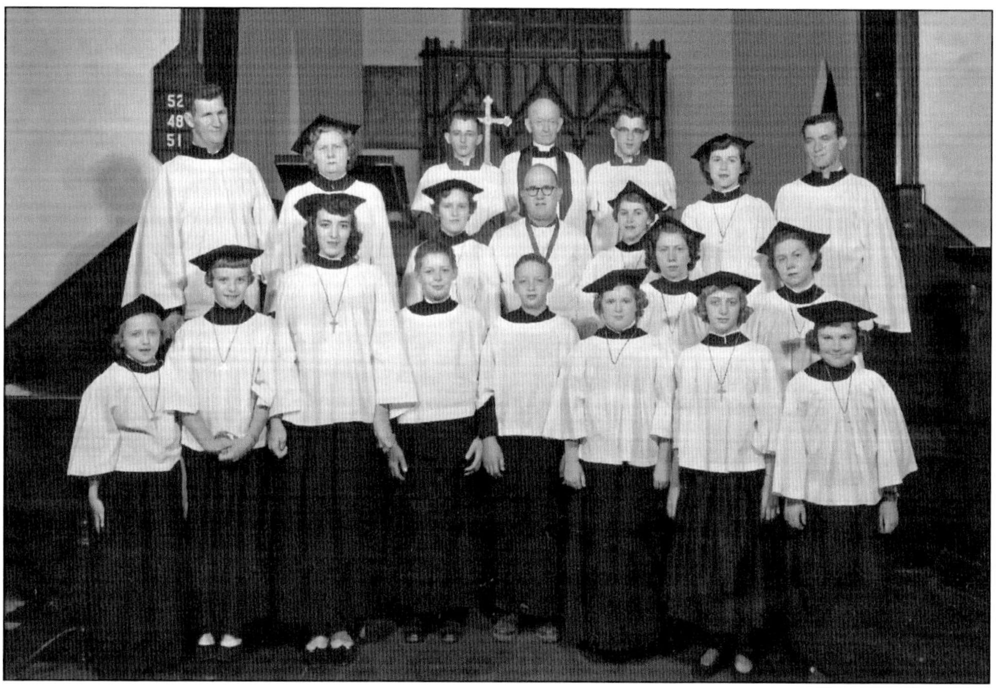

St. Paul's Choir in 1955 has boys, girls, adults, and the Reverend Walter Blaine McKinley. From left to right are (first row) Caroline Rohrer, Elizabeth Saunders, Shirley Otzelberger, Lester Ripple, Edward Rohrer, Donnalee Eyler, Grovine McGraw, and Rebecca Kretzer; (second row) Agnes Flook and Betty DeLauney; (third row) Warren Davis, Amelia Davis, MaryAnn Hoover, James Stockslager, Caroline Highberger, Patricia Highberger, and Thomas Bussard; (fourth row) rector Wayne Eyler, Reverend McKinley, and Carroll Eyler. (Courtesy St. Paul's Episcopal Church.)

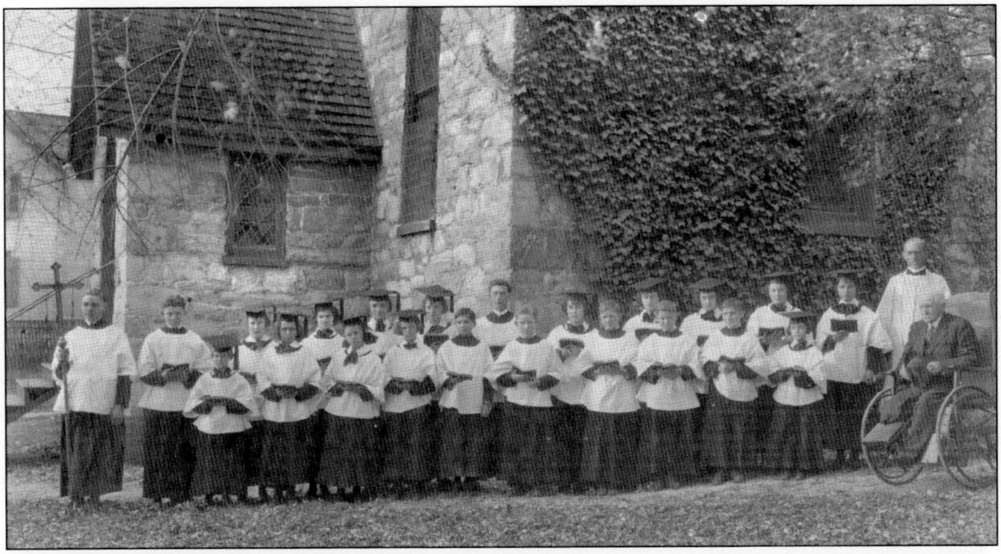

This picture of the 1925 choir was given to St. Paul's by Gussie G. Fisher. Some of the girls are identified with subsequent married names. They are, from left to right, (first row) Gussie Grove Fisher, Mildred Knode Remsburg, Blanche Hall Turner, Autella Benner Showe, Reichard Mumma, Mark Mongan, William Crampton, Raymond Grove, Calvin Mumma, Alice Grove Koontz, and Rev. Walter Blaine McKinley; (second row) Philmore Marrow (crucifer), Edward Garrot, Vera Mongan Benner, Hester Snavely Adams, Stella Benner, Margaret Garrott, Ned Crampton, Victorine Mumma Morgan, Margaret Benner Mouser, Martha Garrott, Mary DeLaundey Barkdoll, and Nettie Hemphill. Luther Piper is in the wheelchair. (Courtesy St. Paul's Episcopal Church.)

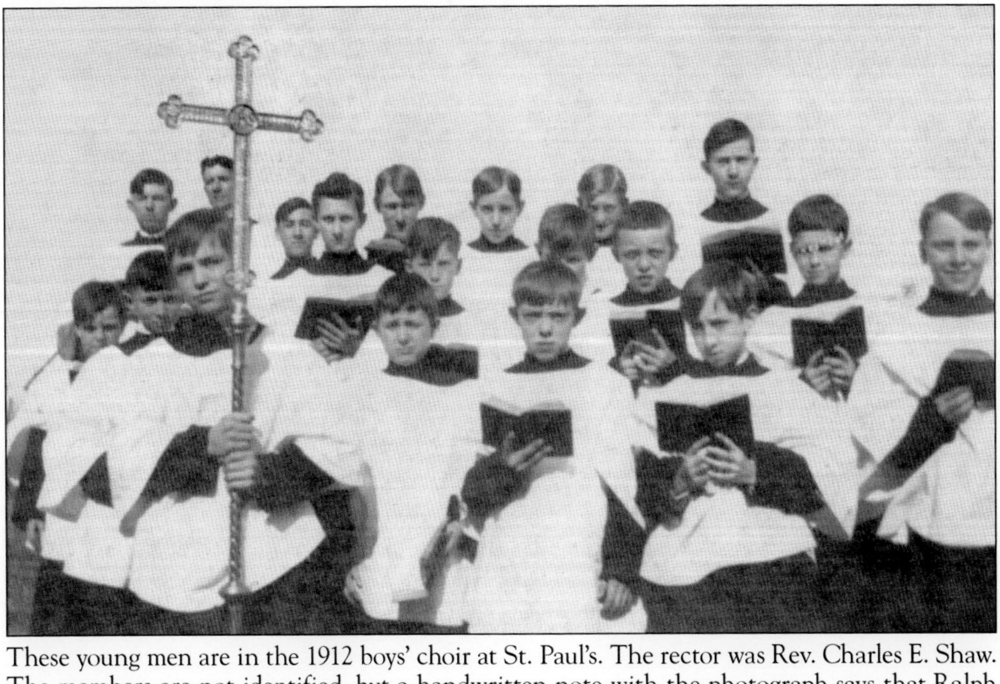

These young men are in the 1912 boys' choir at St. Paul's. The rector was Rev. Charles E. Shaw. The members are not identified, but a handwritten note with the photograph says that Ralph Sounders was absent when the picture was taken. The note is signed "Chas. McGraw, 3/6/71." (Courtesy St. Paul's Episcopal Church.)

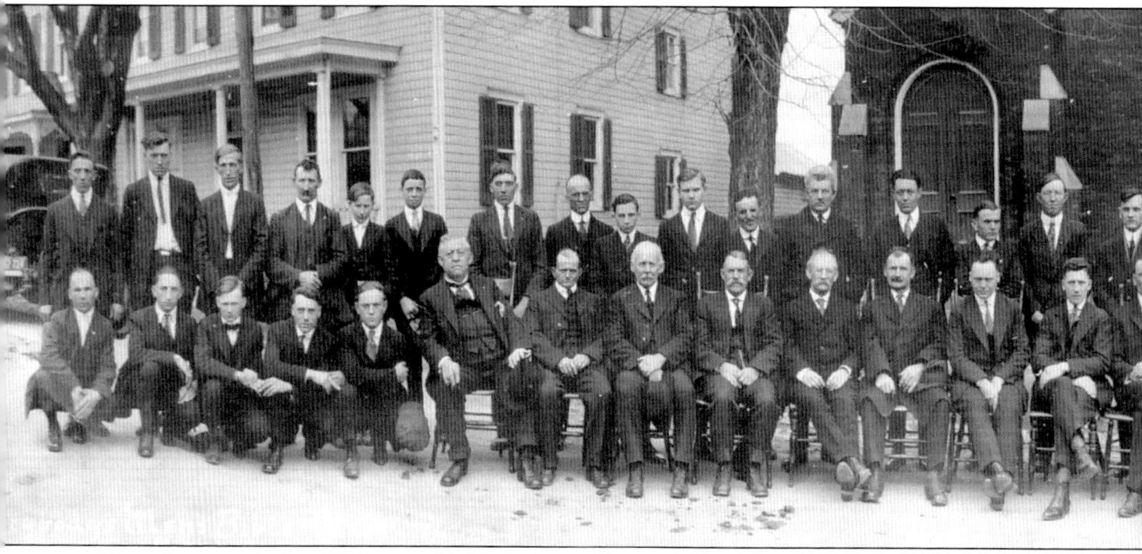

This photograph dated February 17, 1922, shows 68 members of the Everybody's Men's Bible Class of the Christ Reformed Church seated and standing on Main Street in front of the church. It

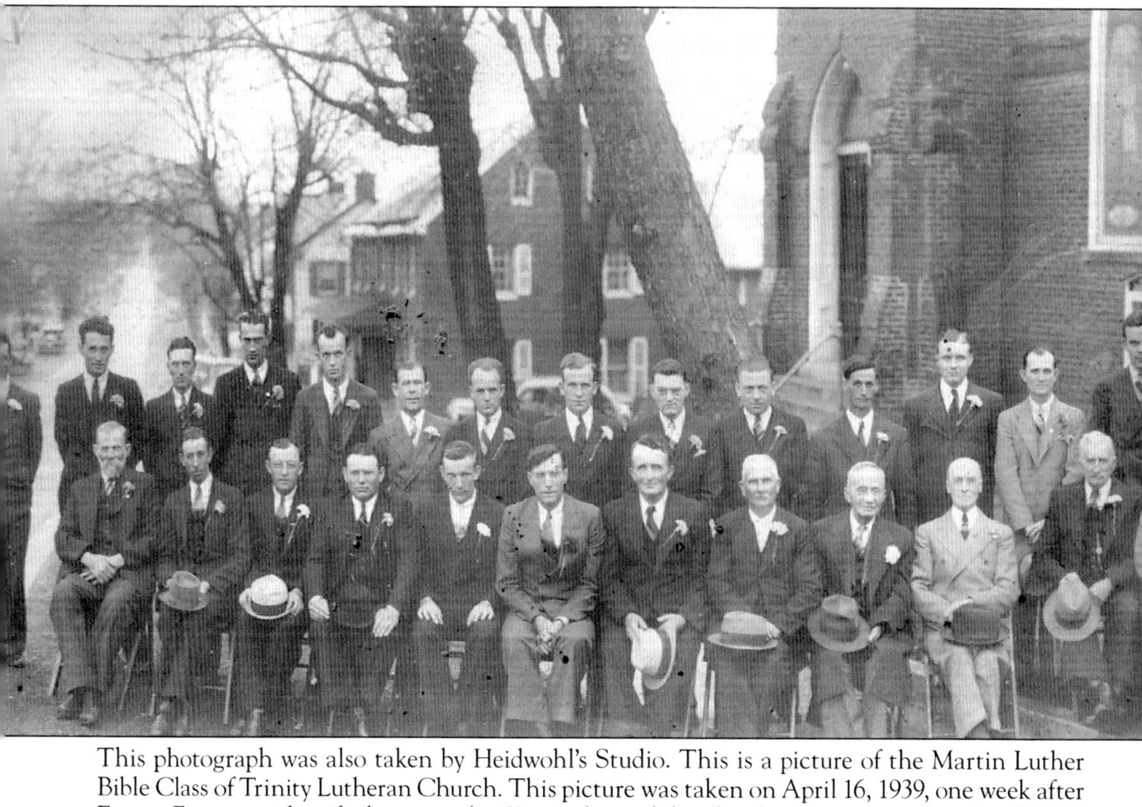

This photograph was also taken by Heidwohl's Studio. This is a picture of the Martin Luther Bible Class of Trinity Lutheran Church. This picture was taken on April 16, 1939, one week after Easter. For an unidentified reason, the 52 members of the class have carnations in their lapels.

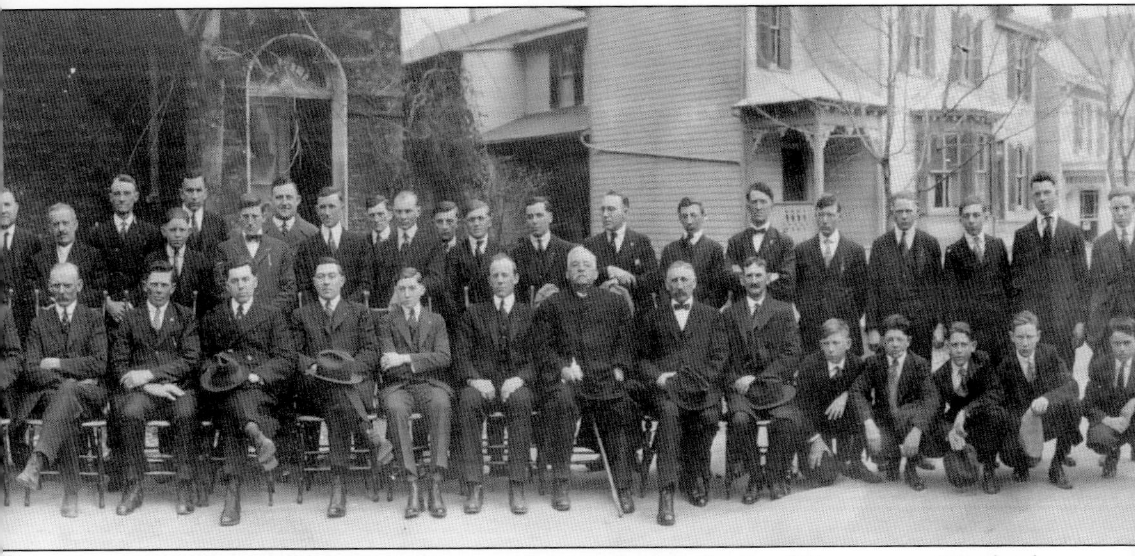

appears that about a half dozen are "young men." Heidwohl's Studio of Hagerstown, Maryland, took this photograph. (Courtesy Christ Reformed UCC.)

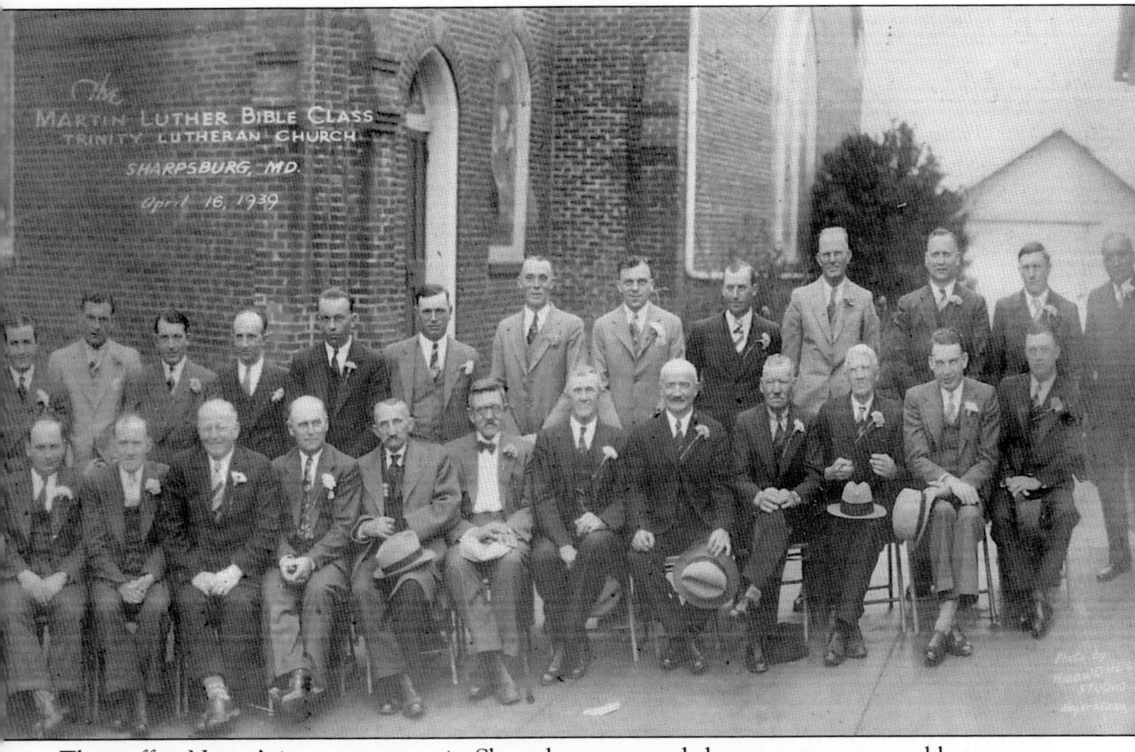

The staff at Nutter's ice cream store in Sharpsburg reported that a customer was able to name every man in the picture except for one. (Courtesy Sandra Henson.)

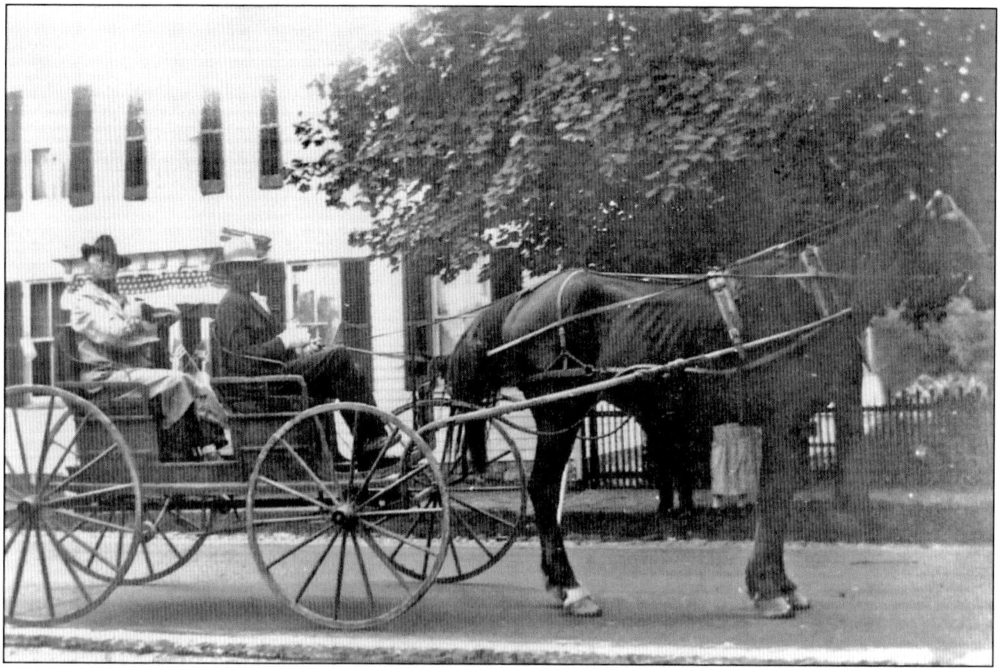

Raleigh Sherman is being driven by Emory Summers, former slave of Sherman's grandfather Henry Piper. Rev. Raymond Strine took this photograph on Homecoming Day, September 17, 1930. The carriage is in front of 132 East Main Street. Sherman died in 1931 and conveyed the Piper House to M. Victor Smith, his cousin. (Courtesy Rosita Ray.)

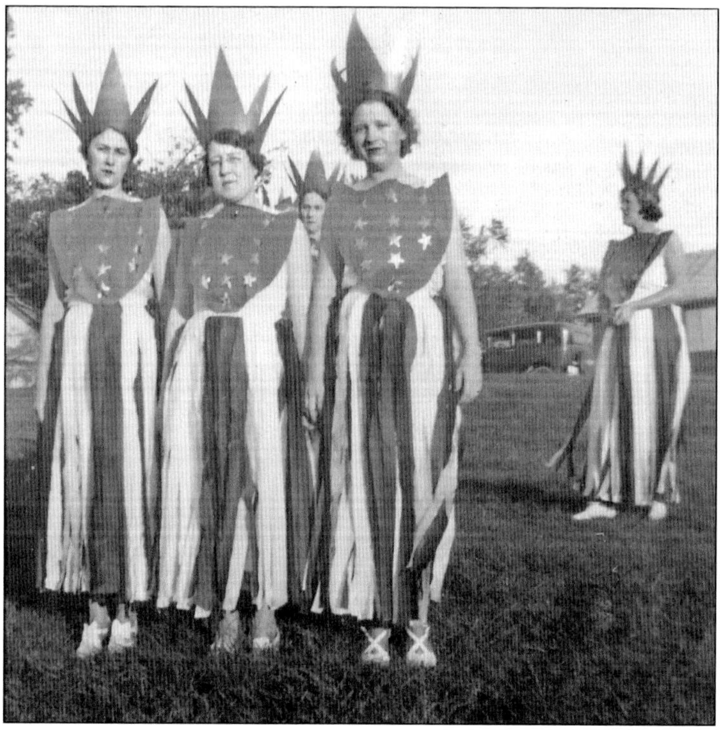

The four-day Sharpsburg Celebration in September 1937 included a parade with prizes. These unidentified women in crowns and stars and stripes won the $10 second prize in the Democratic Club section, according to the note on the photograph. The celebration came to a close on Sunday evening, September 19, with a Service of Remembrance with an address by the Honorable Theodore McKeldin of Baltimore. (Courtesy Sharpsburg Town Council.)

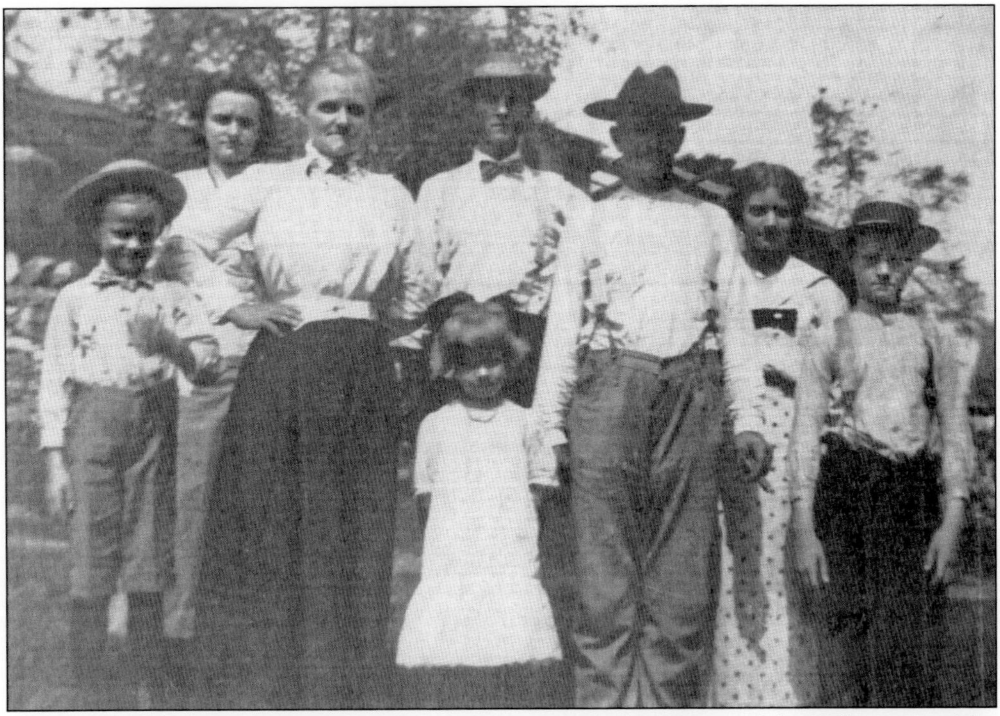

The Lumm (or Lum) family lived at Belinda Springs at the beginning of the 20th century. The earlier picture is dated about 1910. From left to right are Elias; Helen; Ella Mae (Snavely) (born 1863); Mary (born 1906); Harry, in the bow tie (born 1885); Millard Fillmore Lumm (born 1865); Mae Ruth; and Charles (born 1900). The later photograph with the massive stone chimney of the hotel at the left, has Mary, in the dark dress; Helen; Ellie; Harry, in a bow tie; Phil; Charles; Elias; and Ruth. In 1848, Jacob Snavely at public auction bought $138^{1}/_{16}$ acres of the property that had been the resort. His son, John, inherited the land and with his family of 13 lived there at the time of the Civil War. He died there in 1894; Ella Lumm bought the property in 1899. (Both, courtesy Robert Brooks, M.D.)

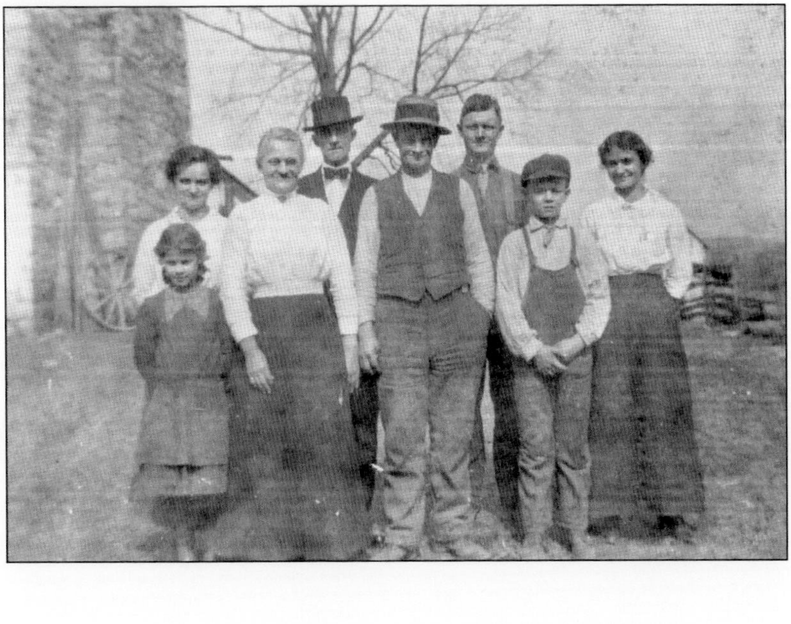

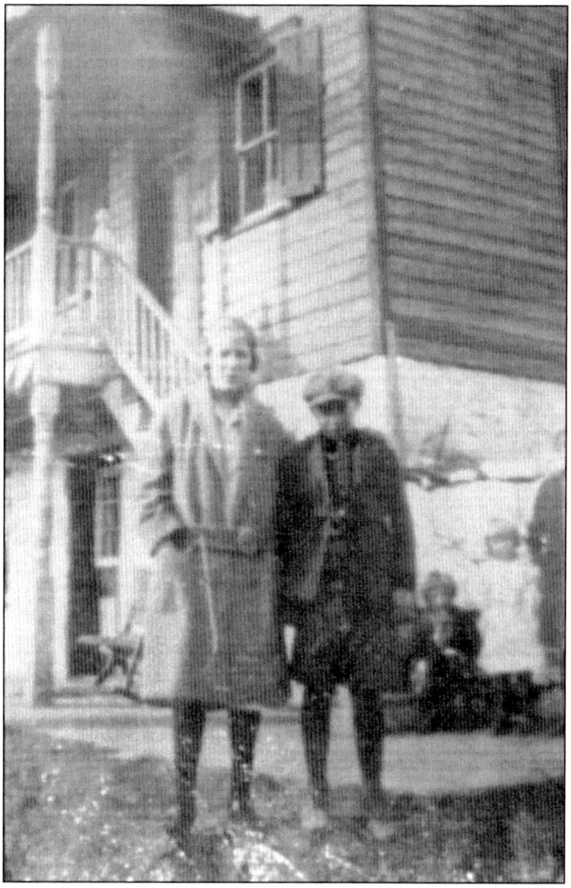

These two pictures were taken at least 10 years apart, but both are in front of Charles and Agnes Bender's home at 111 West Chapline Street. Mary Bender and her brother, William, worked on their father's canal boat (No. 55). Mary, later married to Ronald Schroeder, stands in a heavy coat. She said they were poor but had a nice home in Sharpsburg where they lived in the winter. At one point, 40 to 50 boat captains had homes in Sharpsburg, their "hailing place." She said their mules were taken to Hassetts at Four Locks at the end of boating season. Bill wears short trousers in the photograph with his sister and long trousers in the photograph with his mother, Agnes (Stull). They are standing at the west side of the house in warmer weather. The house, on Lot 74, is log, covered with clapboard siding, on an exposed stone basement. (Both courtesy William Poffenberger.)

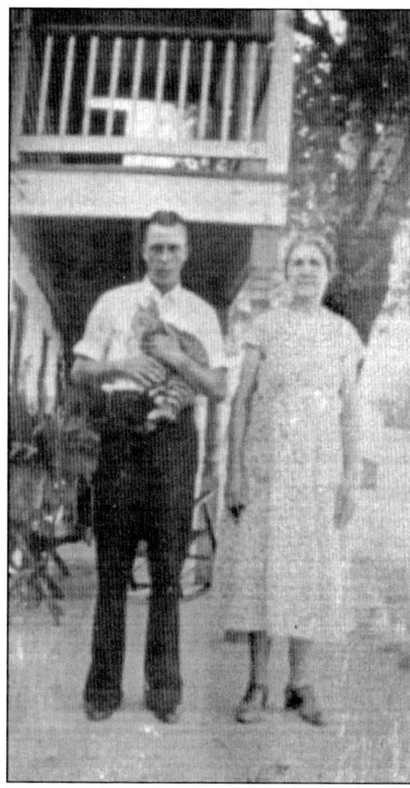

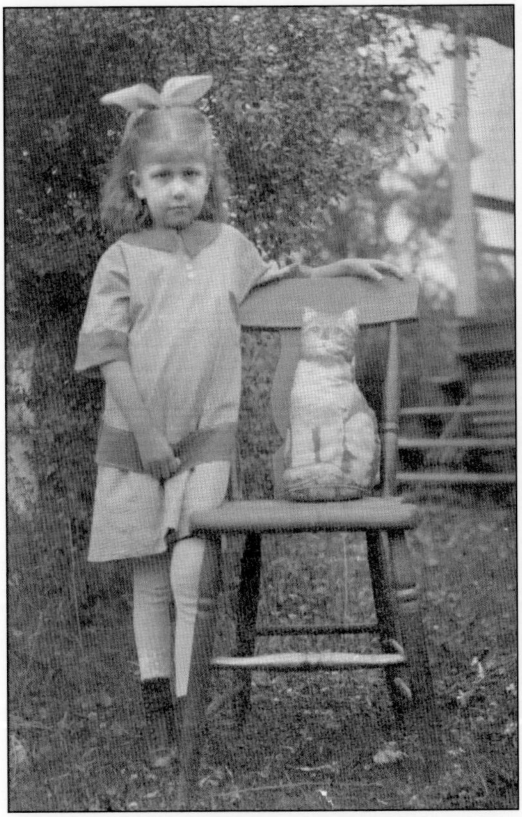

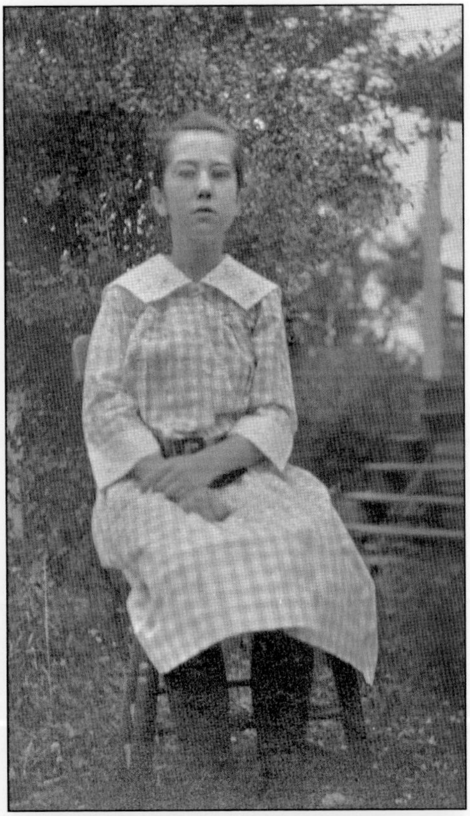

The same backyard and the same chair are used for these three photographs. It's debatable if any of the subjects are enjoying the experience. The cat even looks a bit wary. The little girl is in high-top shoes and leggings, dating the pictures to the early 20th century. The individuals and their relationships are not identified. (Courtesy Jeffrey Saylor.)

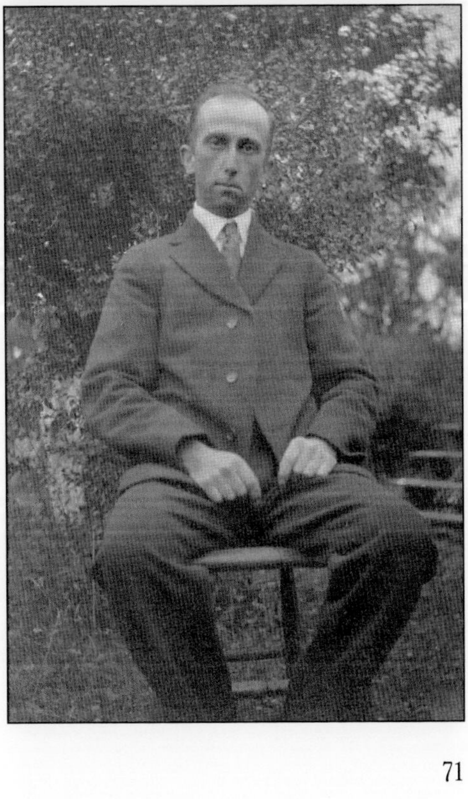

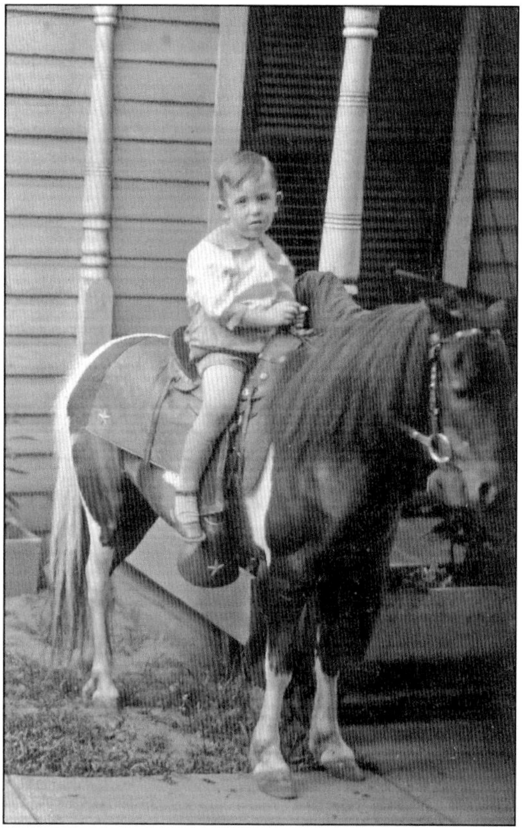

In front of the porch with its swing, Austin Myers, four and a half years old, holds on tight for his picture on the pony that looks rather resigned to picture taking. Austin's feet don't reach the stirrups, and he doesn't look too sure or pleased about his position even though a person is at his left side making sure he won't fall. Some years later, maybe 50, Austin Myers, on the far right, stands with three relatives identified as, from left to right, Granddaddy Myers, Ollie Myers, and Kim. This is four generations on another Sharpsburg porch. (Both courtesy Jeffrey Saylor.)

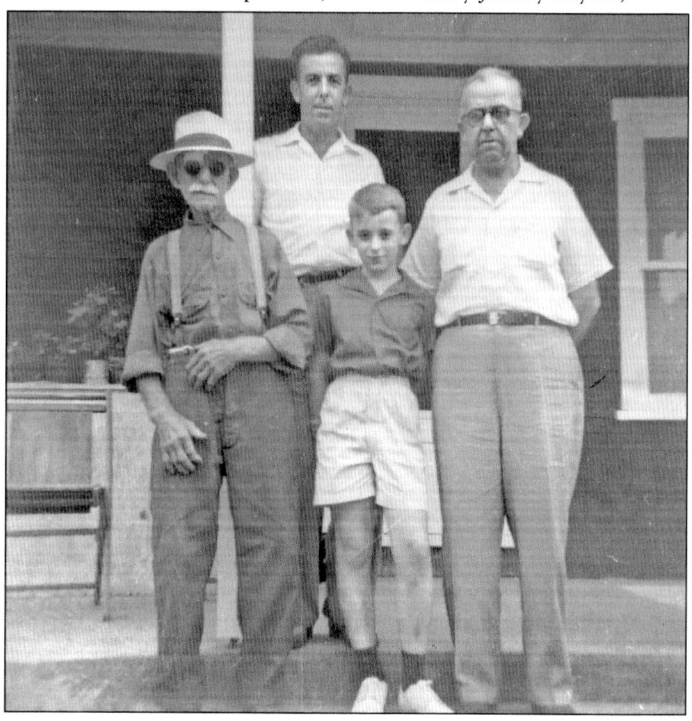

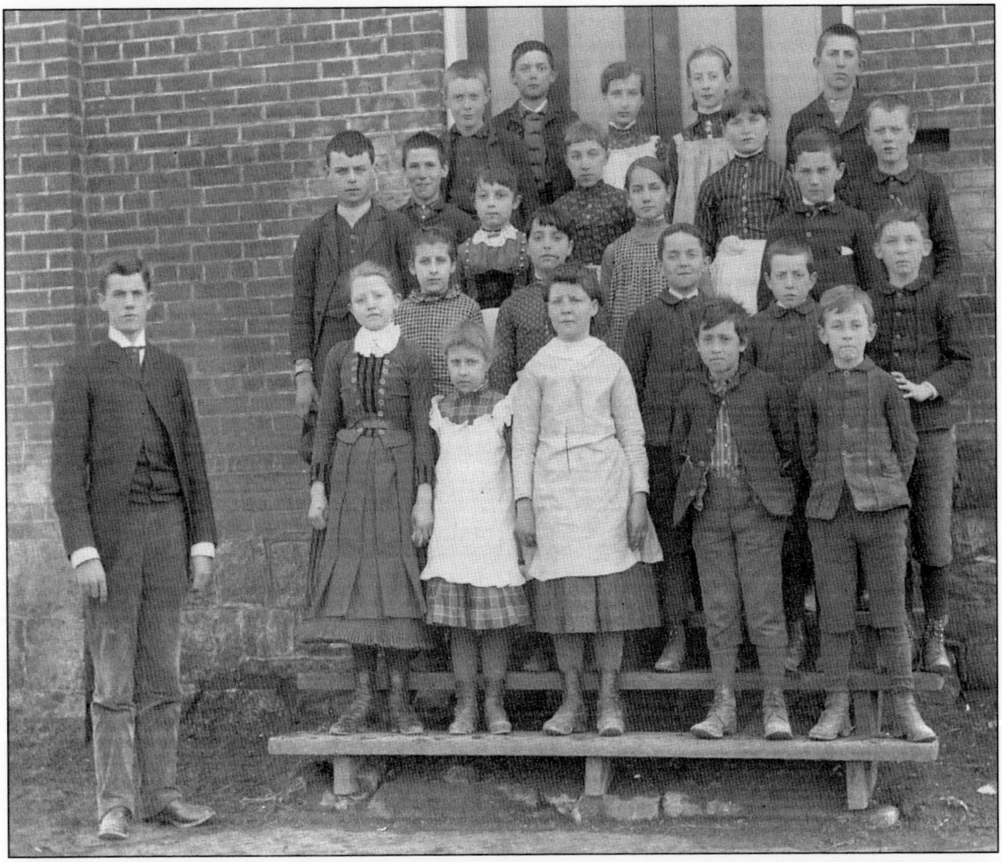

Will Little and his class of 23 students stand on the wooden steps in front of the "old" Sharpsburg school in this 1887 photograph. From left to right are (first row) Katie Marker, Edna Rohrer, Stella Highberger, Tilden Schamel, and Hayes Cronise; (second row) Bertha Mumma, Irene Smith, Hayes Miller, Roy Snavely, and Courney McGraw; (third row) John James, Frank Grove, Ethel Cramer, Helen Cronise, Bina Fisher, Fannie Hetzel, Evans Myers, and Walter Mumma; (fourth row) Clarence Snyder, Howard Edmonds, Julia Lyne, Bessie Grove, and Herbert Souders. (Courtesy Sharpsburg Town Council and Pauline Poffenberger.)

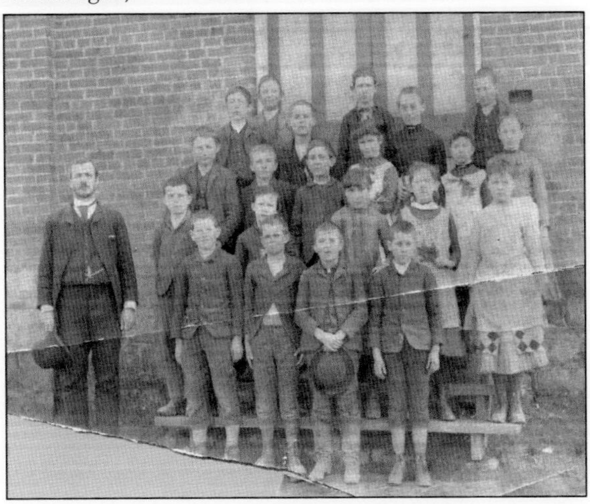

These 21 students and their teacher are unidentified. They are in front of the 1870 Sharpsburg school. Note the missing brick to the right of the door. Some of the boys are in short trousers; all have jackets, and some also wear vests. The appropriate dress for girls included a kind of jumper over a dress. (Courtesy SHS.)

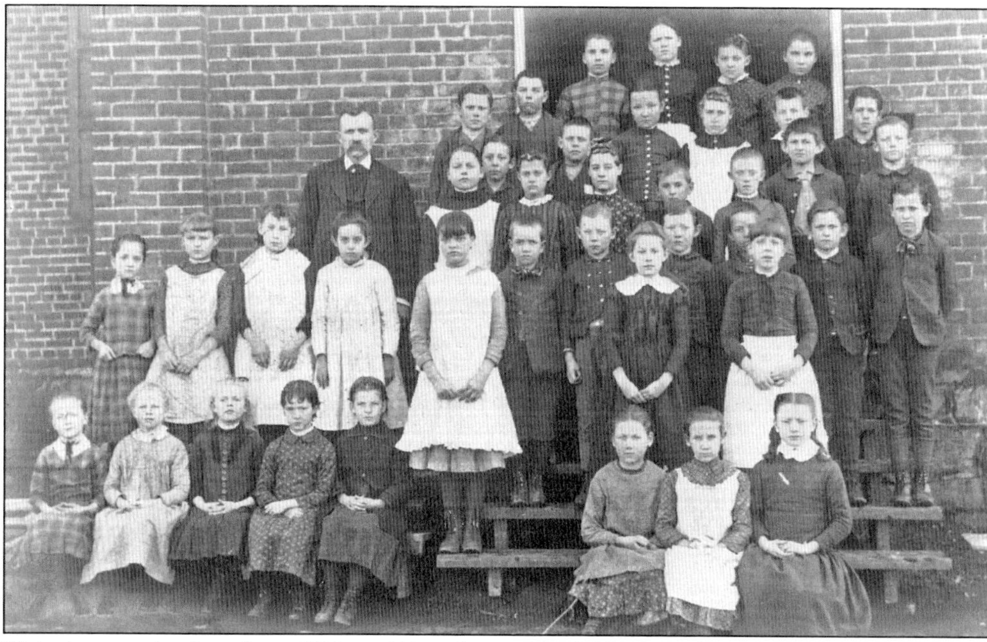

This photograph taken about 1888 is of 40 students of the "old" Sharpsburg school and their teacher, John P. Smith. The names on the back of the picture are difficult to read and are simply listed without a given order. The names are P. Miller, I. Miller, L? Marrow, M. Mumma, C? Schamel, N. Mumma, Ch? K?, Mary K?, H. Marrow, B. Moore, B. Wilson, M. Lockinbill?, L. Painter, C. Smith, H. Benner, B. Bender, G. Mongan, G. Eavey, H. Bowers?, R. Barkdoll, G. Moore, E. Swain, R. Benner?, W. Spong, A. Grove, J. Wyand, D. Snavely, H. Myers, W. Snyder, G. Mumma?, H. Reel, A. Mumma, D. Reel, H. Pennel?, L. Grove, E. Mongan, N. Swain, P. Hebb, S. Sonders, and D. Swain. (Courtesy Sharpsburg Town Council.)

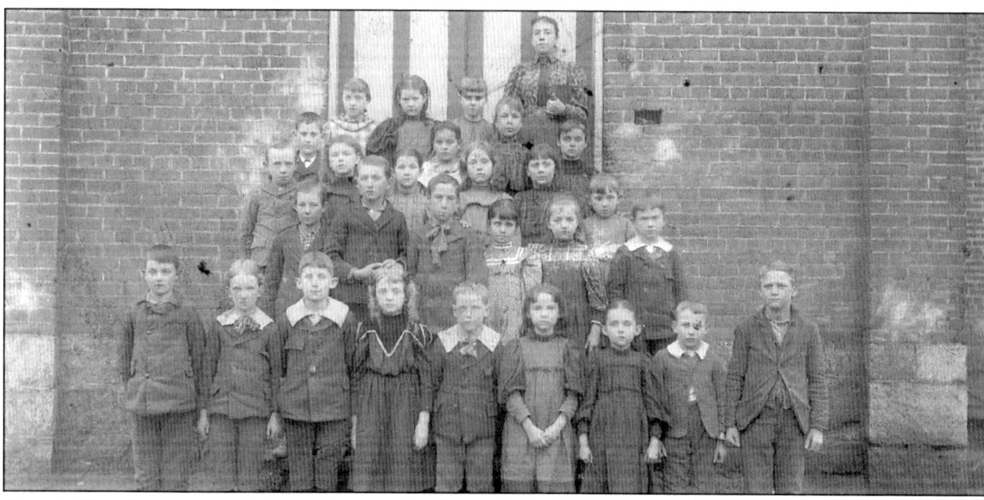

Annie Knode poses with her class at the front door of the "old" Sharpsburg school. There are fewer names on the back of the photograph than students pictured. The names are not always complete or legible. They are listed without indicating rows. ? Lumm, R. Grove, H. Wilson, M. Renner, H. Marker, A. Edmonds, N. Delauney, L. Otto, E. Salior, L. Swain, H. M?, U. Mose, D. Remsburg, ? Marker, R. R?, E? Jackson, J. S?gger, M. Schamel, M. McGraw, ? Thomas, ? Painter, ? Underdunk, M. Snavely, M. Stouffer, and V. Swain. (Courtesy WCFL/WMR.)

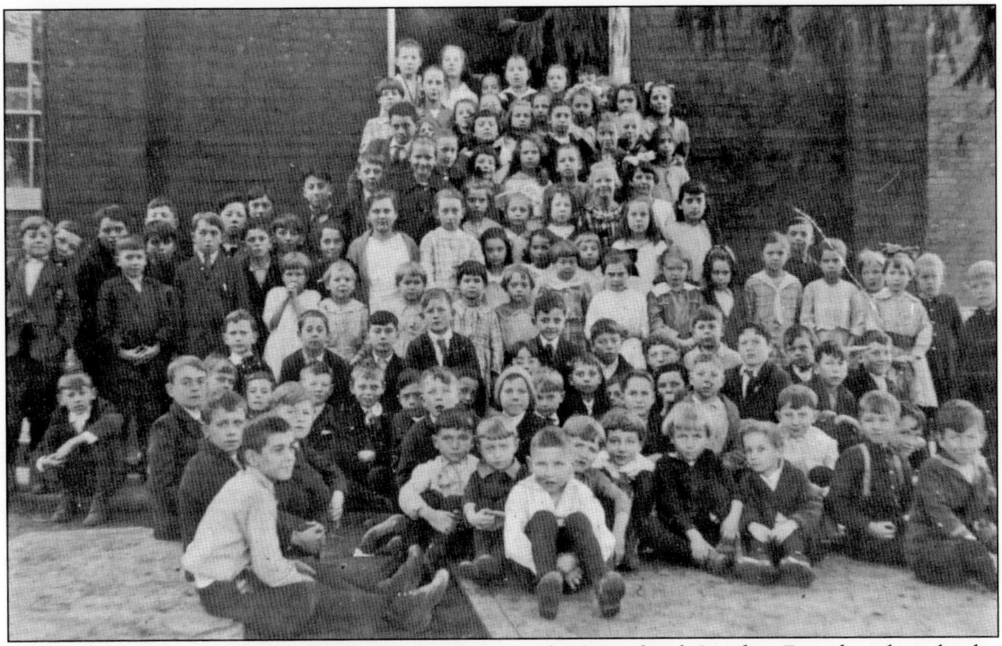

Pearl Virginia (Line) Kaetzel lent this picture to the *Maryland Cracker Barrel* with only the information that it was the Sharpsburg School in 1920. The 113 children might have been the entire school body of the "old" 1870 school, where they are gathered around the front door. Most of the boys are dressed with coats and ties. Several of the girls have bows in their hair. It must have been an important portrait. A grinning boy at the right salutes the photographer, while others show various states of apprehension and attention. (Courtesy *Maryland Cracker Barrel*.)

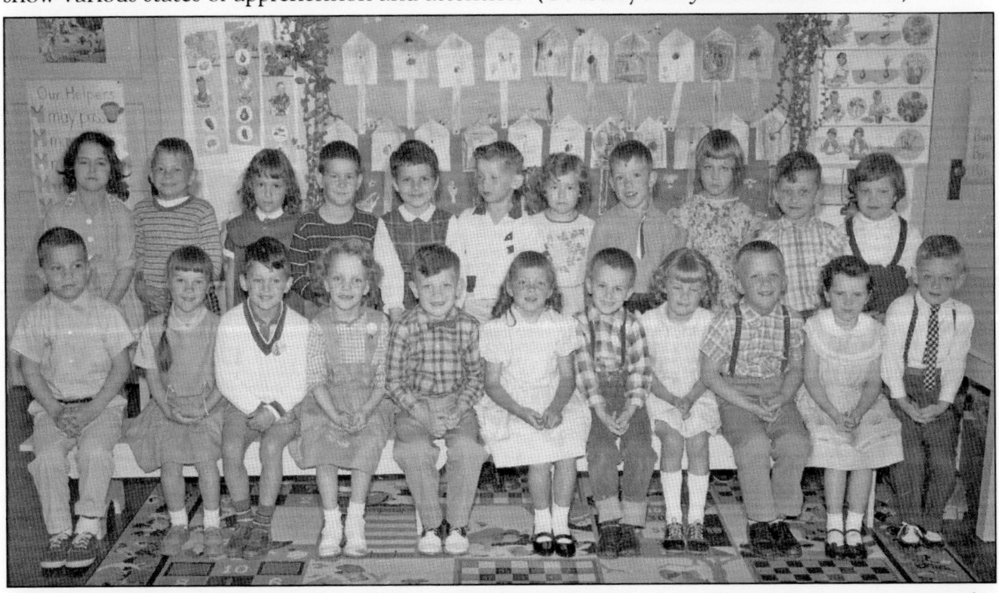

Charlotte Davis was the teacher of this 1962 kindergarten class. Their classroom was in the Sharpsburg Elementary School on West Main Street. Jeff Saylor, current vice mayor of Sharpsburg, is in the center of the back row. These 20th-century children are dressed much less formally than 19th-century girls and boys. Only one of the boys has short trousers, and none of them wear jackets. (Courtesy Jeffrey Saylor.)

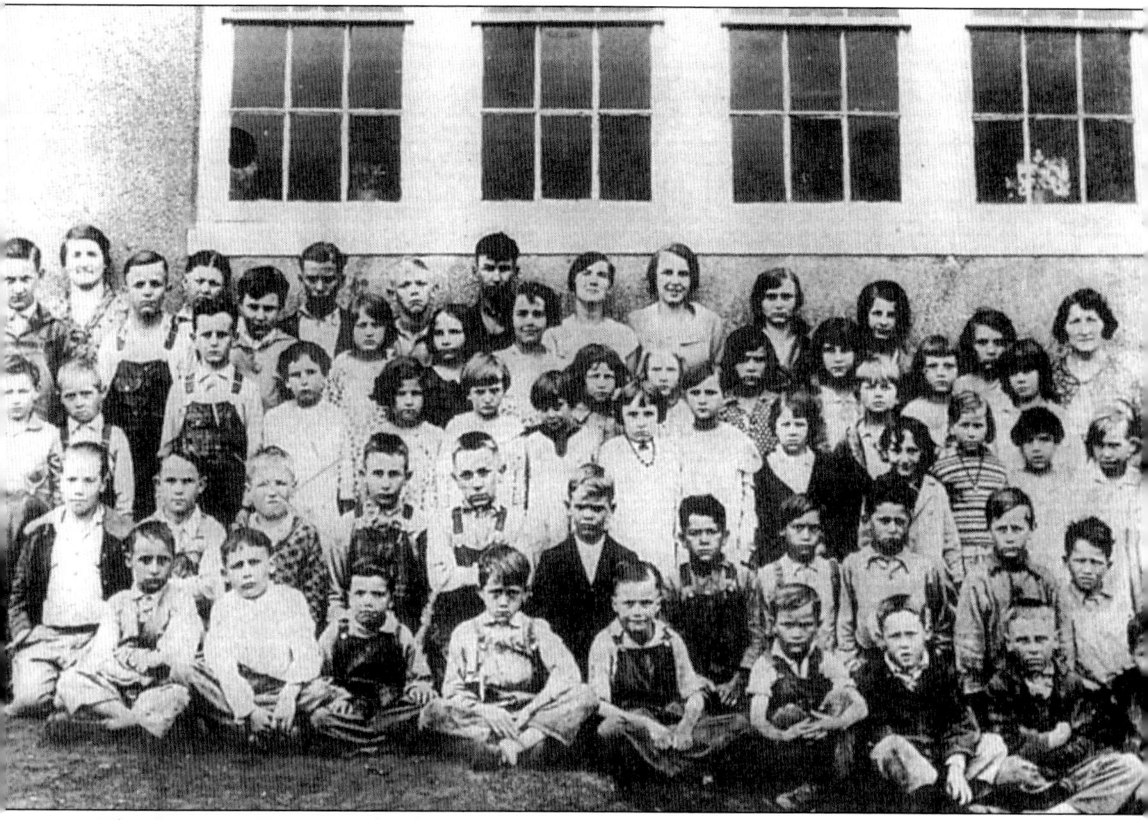

The Antietam Furnace School was on Harpers Ferry Road about 3 miles south of Sharpsburg. The two-room school contained grades one through eight. These are the 57 students of 1932 with their two teachers. Twenty-one different family names appear in the class. From left to right are (first row) Charles Pierce, Jack Tucker, Theodore Byrd, Pete Bussard, Gardner Byrd, John Hetzel, Hollis Shoemaker, Earl Hetzel, and Charles Boyer; (second row) Carl Byrd, Mel Crampton, Charles Myers, Malcolm Hetzel, Don Hetzel, Allen Marshall, Bernard Otzelberger, Howell Pierce, Thomas Ecton, John Campbell, Bruce Ecton, and Pete Ebersole; (third row) Allen Myers, John Hetzel, Alice Burgan, Doris Jamison, Mary Burgan, Anna Bussard, Isabel Ecton, Sis Hetzel, May Otzelberger, Louise Tucker, Arbutus Jamison, Irene Hetzel, Alicia Otzelberger, Ruth Hetzel, Bertie Otzelberger, Francis Jamison, and Ethel Hetzel; (fourth row) Lester Burgan, Mary Kretzer, Jame Campbell, Ruth Byrd, Pauline Ebby, Naomi Jamison, Leoda Crampton, Ardelia Jamison, and Jessie Hammond (teacher); (fifth row) Donald Otzelberger, Lottie Houser (teacher), Buddy Jamison, George Kretzer, Bobby Sadler, Ken Byrd, Layton Jamison, Toots Otzelberger, Thelma Byrd, Clara Marshall, Geraldine Hetzel, and Anna Hutson. (Courtesy WCHS.)

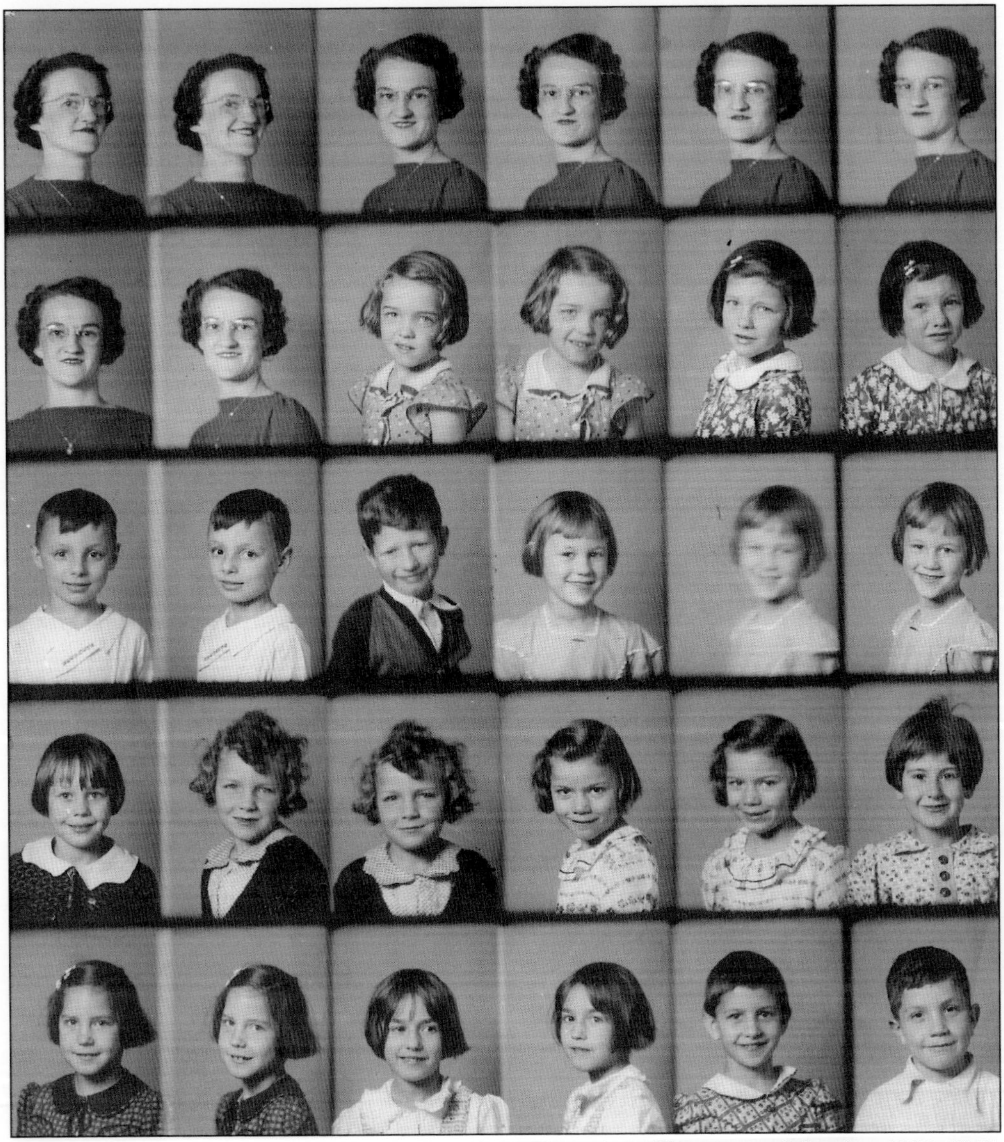

These are some of the pupils in the third grade at Sharpsburg Elementary School in 1939–1940. No longer are classes lined up in front of the school building. Some of the students had more than one picture taken, but none had so many as their teacher, Mary Cox Smith. (Courtesy Sharpsburg Elementary School.)

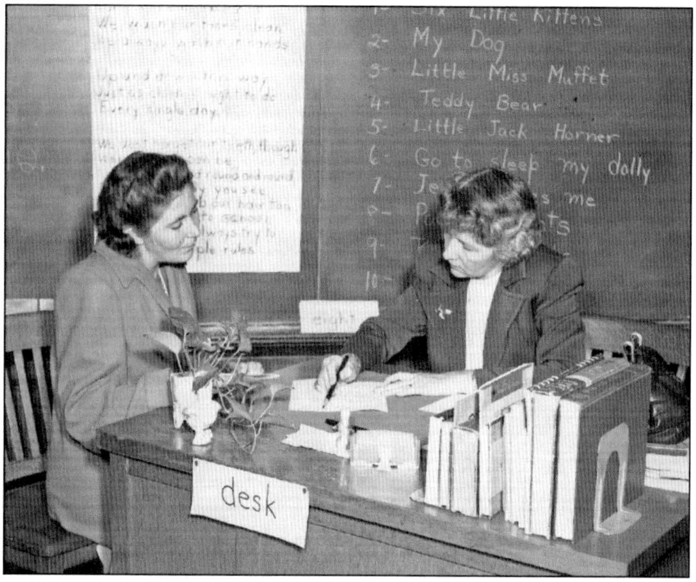

This parent-teacher conference took place at the elementary school on Main Street. Based on the vocabulary help desk and the number flash cards on the rail, the student being discussed was most likely in the first grade. It looks as if the teacher is using one of those big fat first-grade pencils. (Courtesy Sharpsburg Elementary School.)

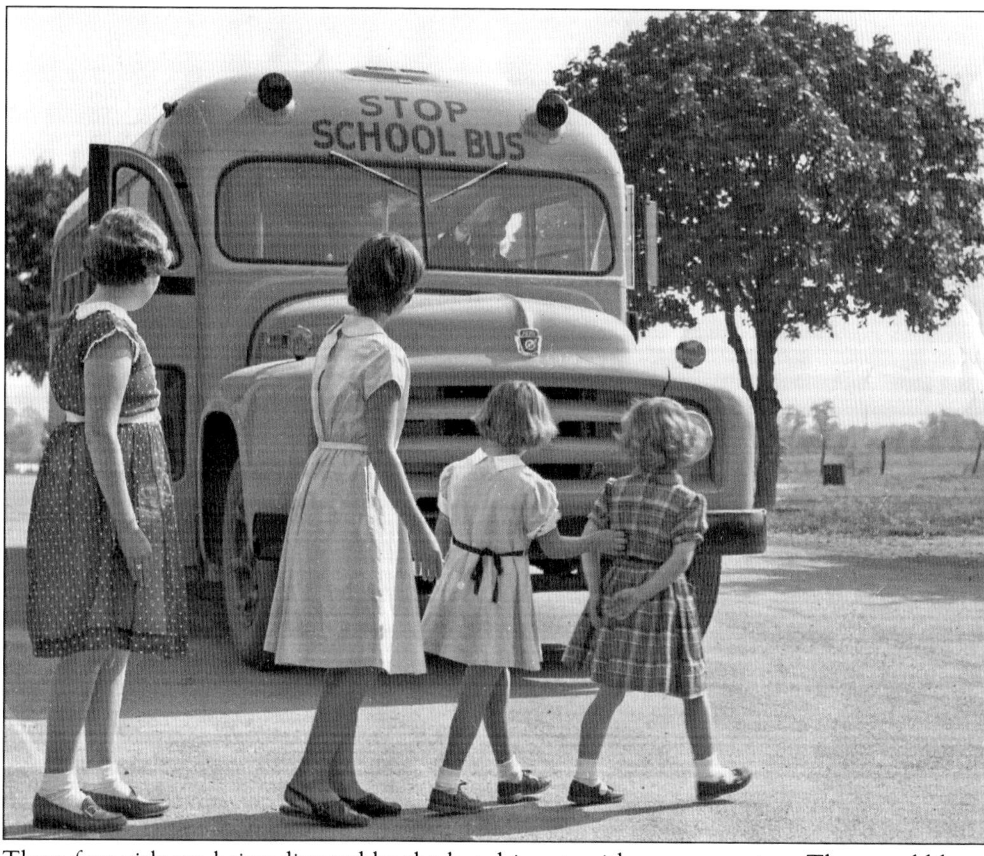

These four girls are being directed by the bus driver to either cross or stop. They would have understood his hand signal, and they certainly are paying attention to him. This picture dates from the mid-1950s. The students were attending Sharpsburg Elementary School. (Courtesy Sharpsburg Elementary School.)

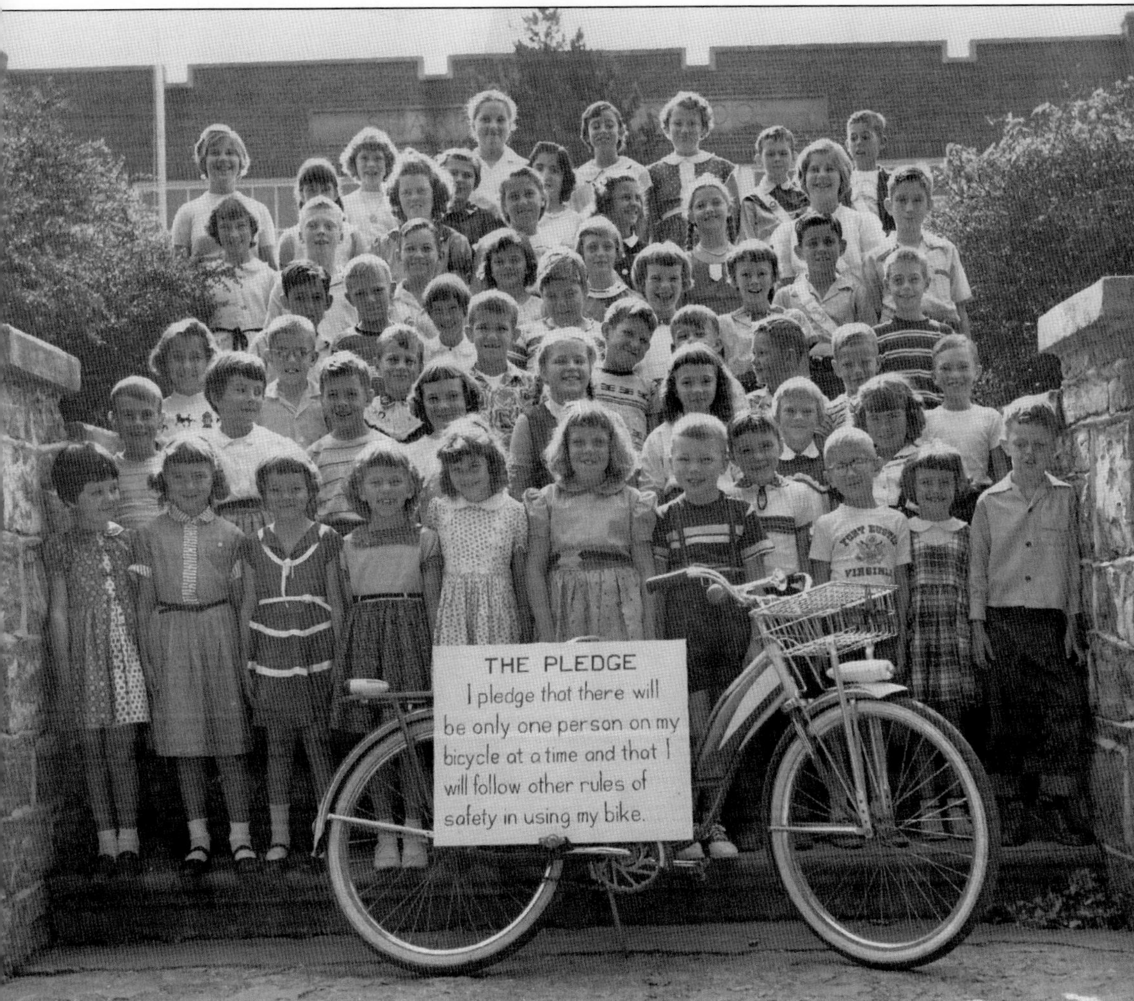

Fifty-seven students take a bicycle safety pledge on the front steps of Sharpsburg Elementary School in this *c.* 1954 photograph. The 57 safety program participants are, from left to right, (first row) Sharon Sagle, Elizabeth Ann Rebb, Barbara Ann Lumm, Alice Roulette, Mary Lulu Grove, Harriet Reel, Victor Smith, Gregory Churchey, Jere Fournier, Connie Mason, and an unidentified boy; (second row) Dennis Carahan, Mary Ann Waters, Gary Churchey, Rebecca Ann Kretzer, Donnalee Eyler, Joyce Grim, Donna Culler, and Christine Kauffman; (third row) Beverly Myers, Nevin Renner, Jerry Otzelberger, Jackie Rohrer, Charles Canfield, Johnny Hammond, Jeffry Gladhill, Gary Slaughter, and Gary Benner; (fourth row) Larry Saylor, Franklin Hammond, Norma Wilson, Jimmy Myers, Elizabeth Saunders, Vicki Sweeney, and Bobby Easterday; (fifth row) Jerry Sweeney, Dallas Churchey, Valerie Cline, Groveine McGraw, Sonny Knode, and Dale Bussard; (sixth row) Janice Crampton, Jo Ann Roulette, Maetta Rhodes, Ann Vickers, Sue Kelley, and Ruth Myers; (seventh row) Naomi Myers, Connie Bussard, Doris Ann Marshall, and Phyllis Eichelberger; (eighth row) Patricia Knight, Mary Ann Hoover, Janet McCoy, Judy Byrne, Eugene Eichelberger, and Raymond Saylor. (Courtesy Sharpsburg Elementary School.)

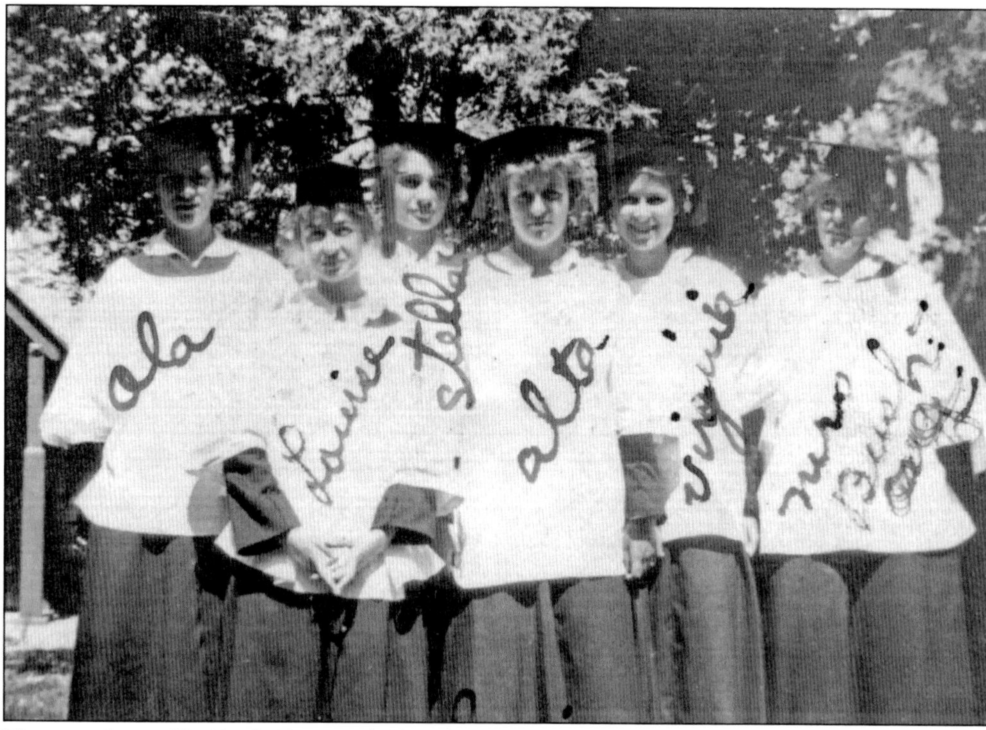

This is a choir of St. Paul's Episcopal Church pictured about 1910. The members are, from left to right, Ola ?, Louise Grove, Stella Benner, Alta Crampton, Virginia Mumma, and Mrs. Bushong, who was, according to the note on the photograph's back, maybe the organist and/or the choir mistress. They are standing near the church office. (Courtesy St. Paul's Episcopal Church.)

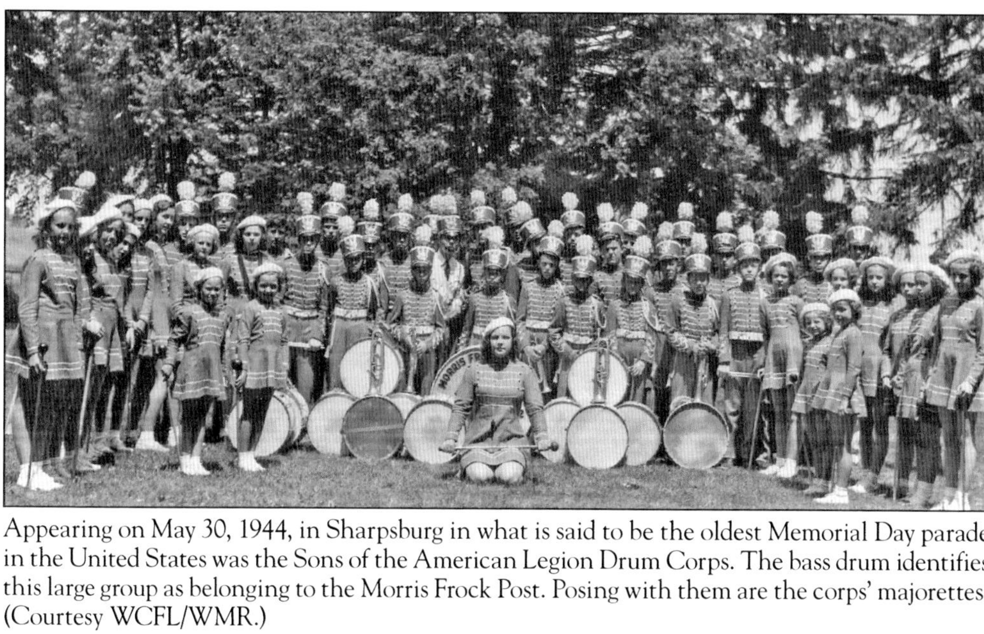

Appearing on May 30, 1944, in Sharpsburg in what is said to be the oldest Memorial Day parade in the United States was the Sons of the American Legion Drum Corps. The bass drum identifies this large group as belonging to the Morris Frock Post. Posing with them are the corps' majorettes. (Courtesy WCFL/WMR.)

This is "Uncle Dent" Hoffmaster in the early 1900s. The outdoor photograph has the note, "Papa for Aunt Sis." Uncle Dent holds a pipe in his left hand, and chickens stand around the yard. Chickens and pigs were common in many Sharpsburg backyards. Because the trees and fields are bare, the background is clear, and it looks as if a railroad track runs alongside the field. The railroad tracks are just beyond the western edge of Sharpsburg. (Courtesy Jeffrey Saylor.)

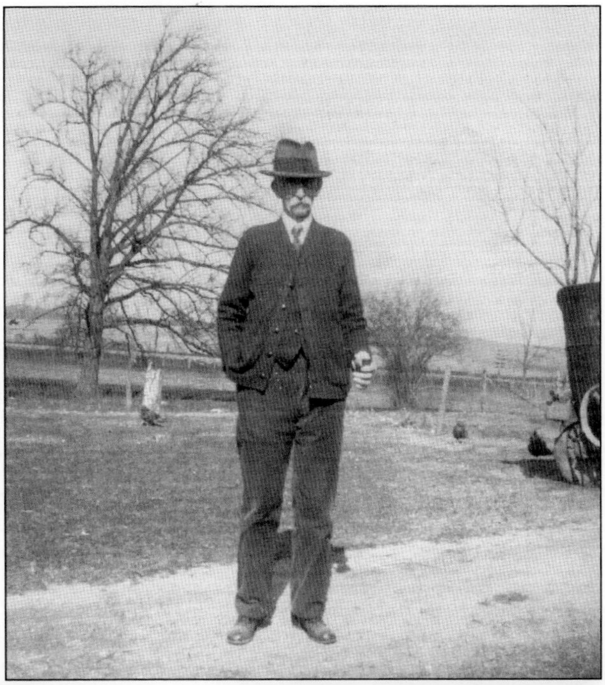

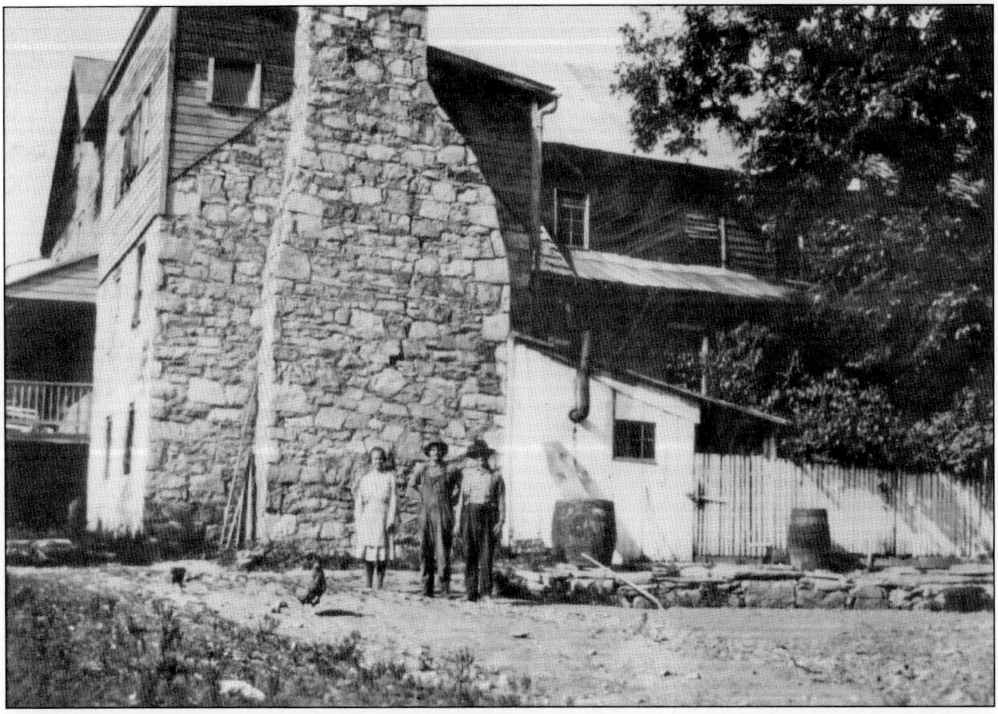

Phil Lumm, right, stands in his usual hat and suspenders. He and his family, and some chickens, lived on the Belinda Springs property until 1929, when it was sold at foreclosure. A November 1929 newspaper report said the hotel building, recently purchased by R. K. Baker on the Belinda Sulphur Springs farm, was to be razed. A private residence is now on the property along Antietam Creek. (Courtesy Robert Brooks, M.D.)

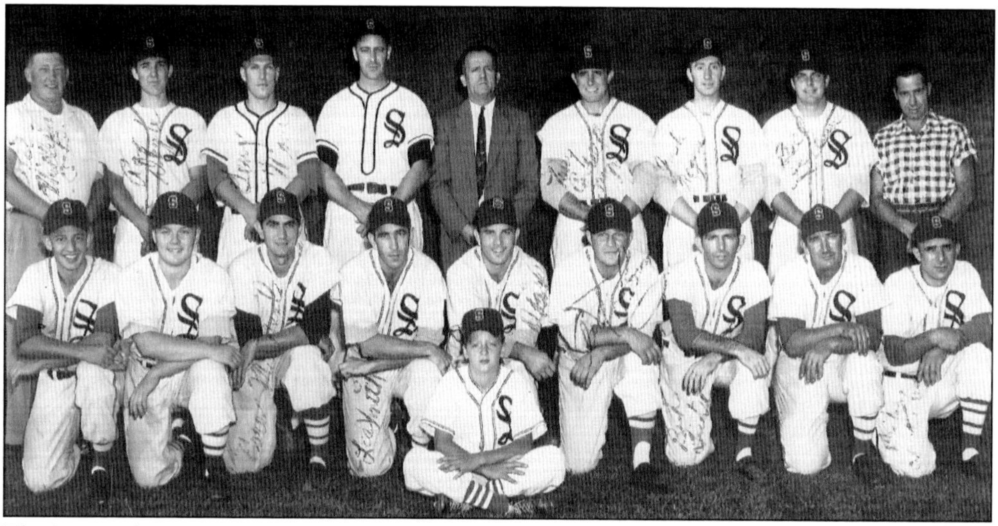

The league champion 1956 Sharpsburg Bluebirds semi-professional baseball team included, from left to right, (first row) Jim Jennings, Ted Byers, Paul McNeal, Les Smith, Dick Parks, Ott Long, Bob Tritch, Harry Schlotterbeck, and Dick Schlotterbeck; (second row) Vice Pres. William Phillips, Ray Doyle, Terry Mose, Al Bennett, Pres. Elmer Koontz, manager Tony Cordell, Jack Rogers, Bill Green, and business manager Roland McKinsey. Batboy Eddie Rohrer is in front. (Courtesy *Maryland Cracker Barrel*.)

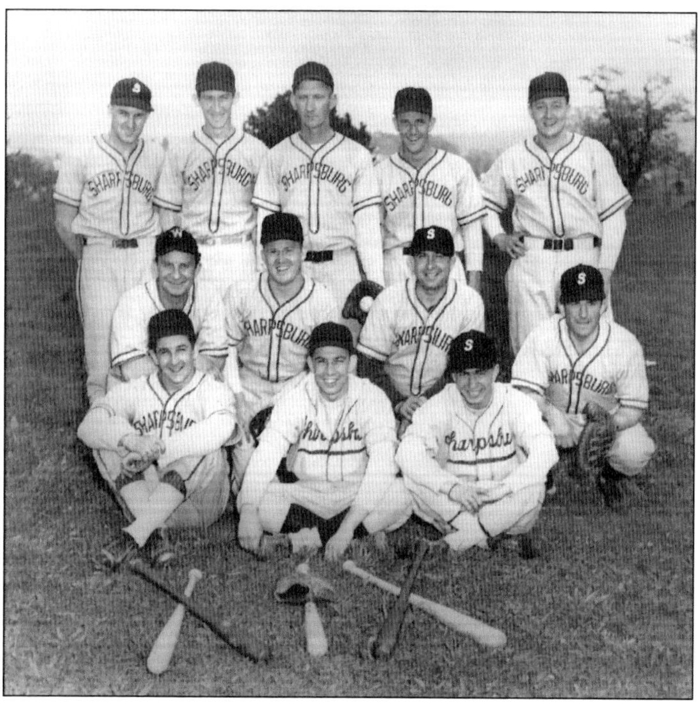

Handwriting on the back of this picture identifies these 1930s Sharpsburg "Blue Bird" baseball team members as, from left to right, (first row) Henry DeLauney, Bodie Brashears, and Jack Snipe Benner; (second row) Petey Brashears, Bricky Stockslager, Goat Bender, and Shotgun Grove; (third row) Kitty Kauffman, a player named Mentzer, Cocky Brashears, Cal DeLauney, and William Rohrer. The Bluebird team was one of 10 amateur Washington County League teams. (Courtesy Jeffrey Saylor.)

The only things identified in this photograph are Bill Bender, on the right, and about 30 fish. Bender, son of a canal boat captain, lived on West Chapline Street. The cap Bender is wearing might be from the Sharpsburg Bluebirds. It appears that the men are in a backyard where laundry hangs on a line and two children stand in the garden. (Courtesy Nellie Kline.)

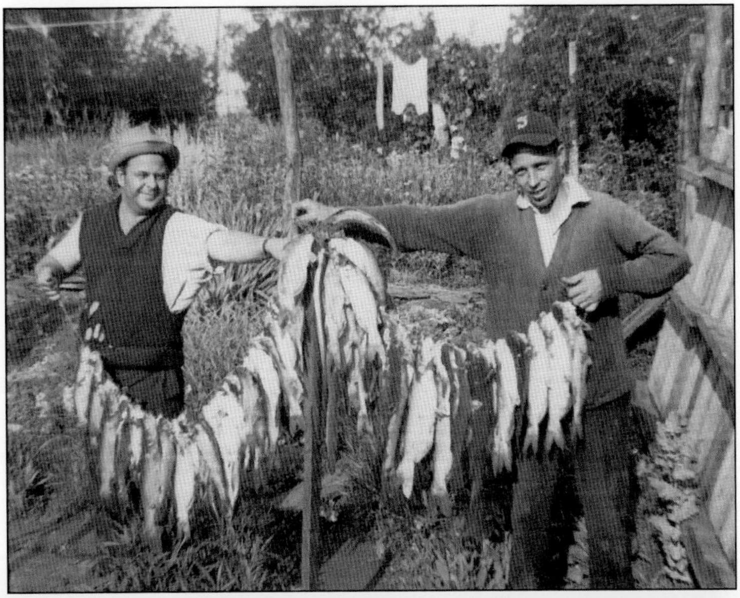

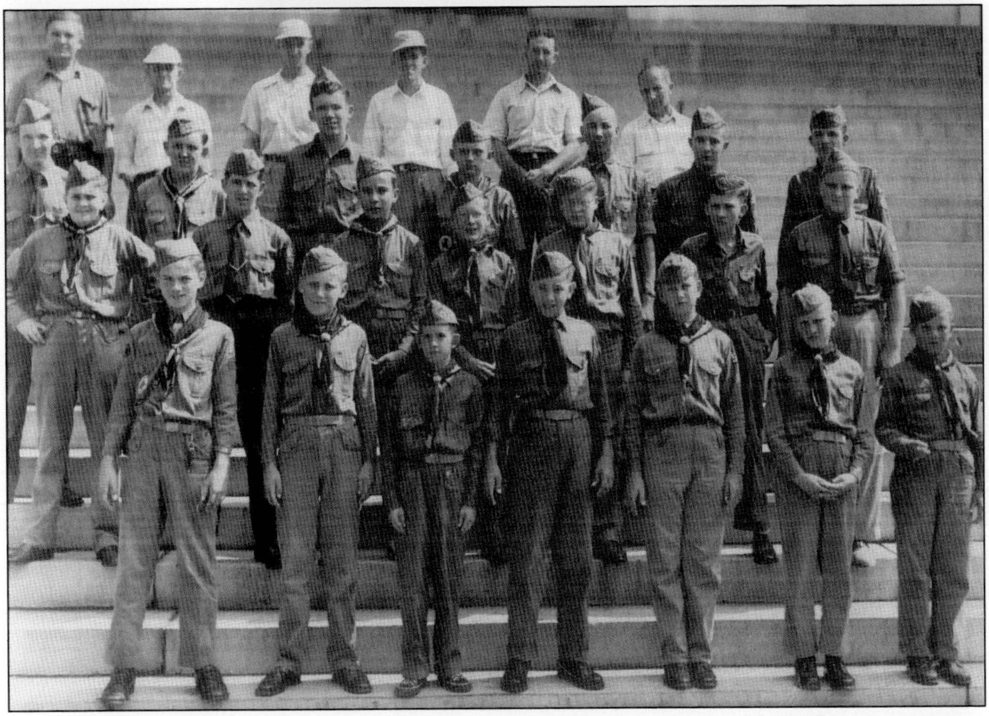

St. Paul's Episcopal Church and the other Sharpsburg churches sponsored this Boy Scout troop, which appears to be on the steps of the Capitol in Washington, D.C., in 1949 or 1950. From left to right are (first row) James Poffenberger, Roy Semler, Clinton Smith Jr., Charles Stottlemyer, Jerry Bender, Elwood Crampton, and George Churchey; (second row) Joseph Shealy, Jacob Bender, David Cline, Tony Gift, Ted Hebb, Bobby Knootz, and Phillip Conner; (third row) Richard Poffenberger, Bill Welsh, Jack Early, John Dorsey, Bill Poffenberger, Marvin Brashears, and Jack Arundt; (fourth row) Ted Hebb, Albert Bowers, Henry Poffenberger, Harry Holmes, Argle Grove, and Ronald Otto. (Courtesy St. Paul's Episcopal Church.)

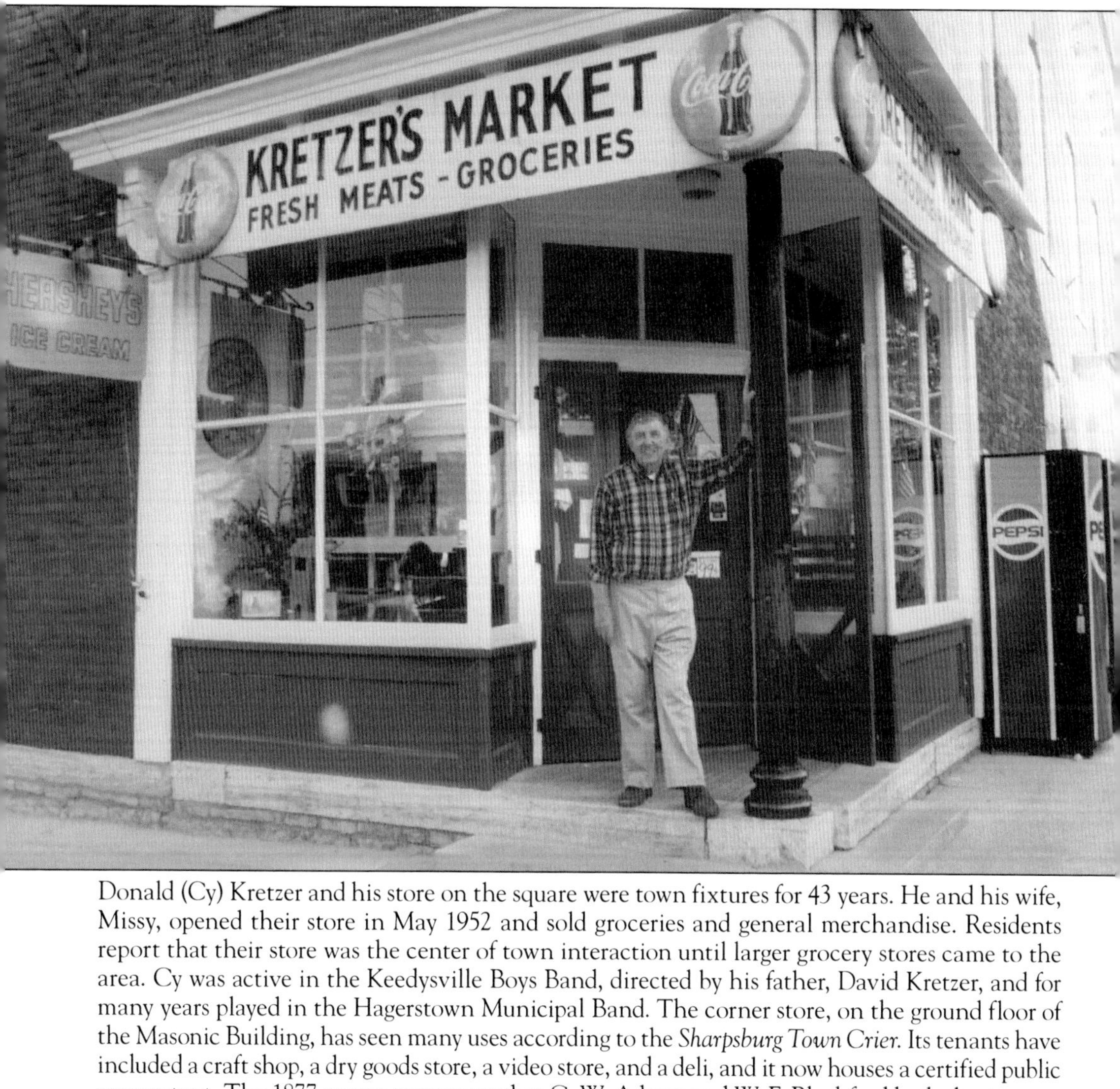

Donald (Cy) Kretzer and his store on the square were town fixtures for 43 years. He and his wife, Missy, opened their store in May 1952 and sold groceries and general merchandise. Residents report that their store was the center of town interaction until larger grocery stores came to the area. Cy was active in the Keedysville Boys Band, directed by his father, David Kretzer, and for many years played in the Hagerstown Municipal Band. The corner store, on the ground floor of the Masonic Building, has seen many uses according to the *Sharpsburg Town Crier*. Its tenants have included a craft shop, a dry goods store, a video store, and a deli, and it now houses a certified public accountant. The 1877 survey map notes that C. W. Adams and W. F. Blackford had a business at this corner of Public Square. They were dealers in "Dry Goods, Notions, Hardware, Queensware, Groceries, Hats, Caps, and Carpets." Barron's *History of Sharpsburg* reports that U. S. Myers and Charley Gross also operated stores at this location. (Courtesy Sharpsburg Town Council.)

Three

The Battlefield

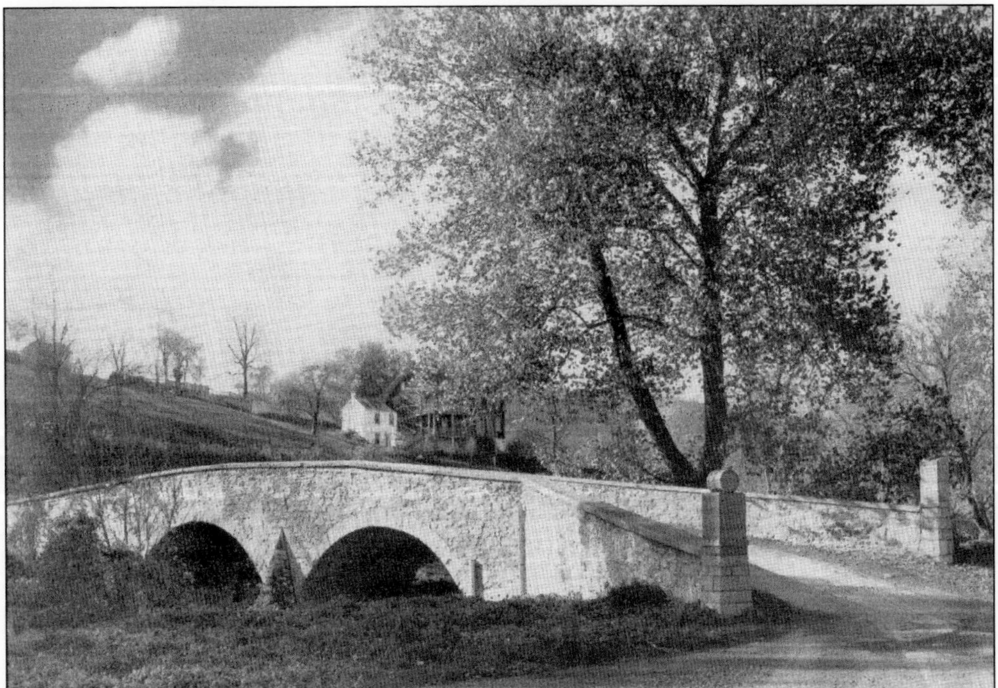

The sun shines on Burnside Bridge in this September 1937 *Southern Spectator* magazine cover photograph for the 75th anniversary of the Civil War Battle of Antietam. Known as Rohrback Bridge before the 1862 battle, the span was erected according to an 1834 Maryland law authorizing the construction "of a stone bridge across the Antietam Creek, where the road from Sharpsburg to the Maple Swamp crosses said creek." The road also was called Old Monocacy Road. (Courtesy Frank Hammond.)

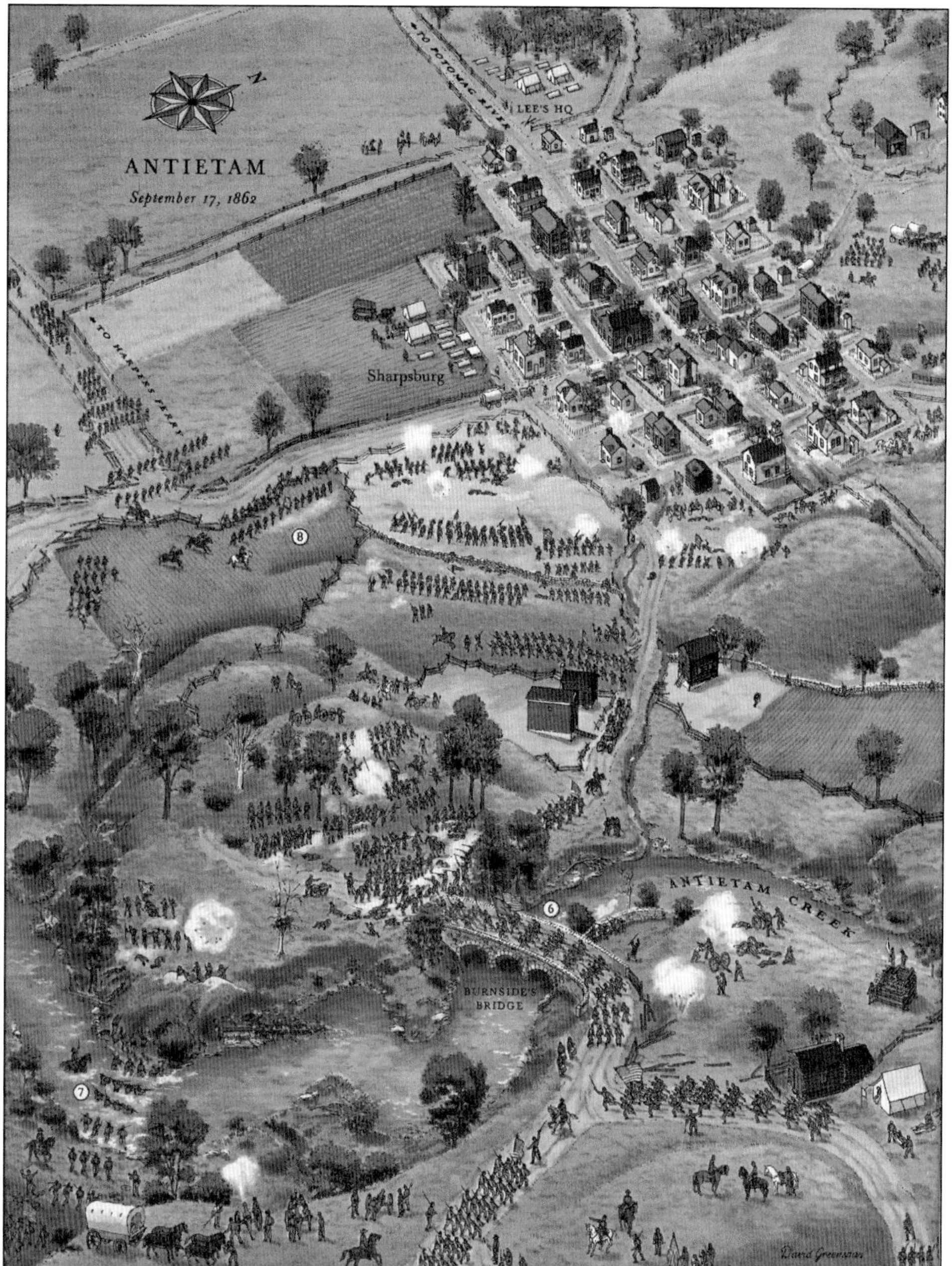

This 100th anniversary program back cover illustration from the *American Heritage Picture History of the Civil War* shows Battle of Antietam morning and afternoon action near Burnside Bridge (lower center). The Confederate commander, Gen. Robert E. Lee, was able to reinforce his battle line because it took Union general Ambrose Burnside until 1:00 p.m. to cross Antietam Creek on the bridge that bears his name. Then Gen. Isaac Rodman crossed the creek below the bridge and Federal troops began advancing toward Sharpsburg and Lee's tent headquarters (top center). At 4:30 p.m., however, Gen. A. P. Hill arrived from Harpers Ferry (upper left) to drive back the Northerners, rescue Lee's army, and end the battle. Historian James M. McPherson estimates that 6,000 soldiers were dead or dying at day's end. (Courtesy authors' collection.)

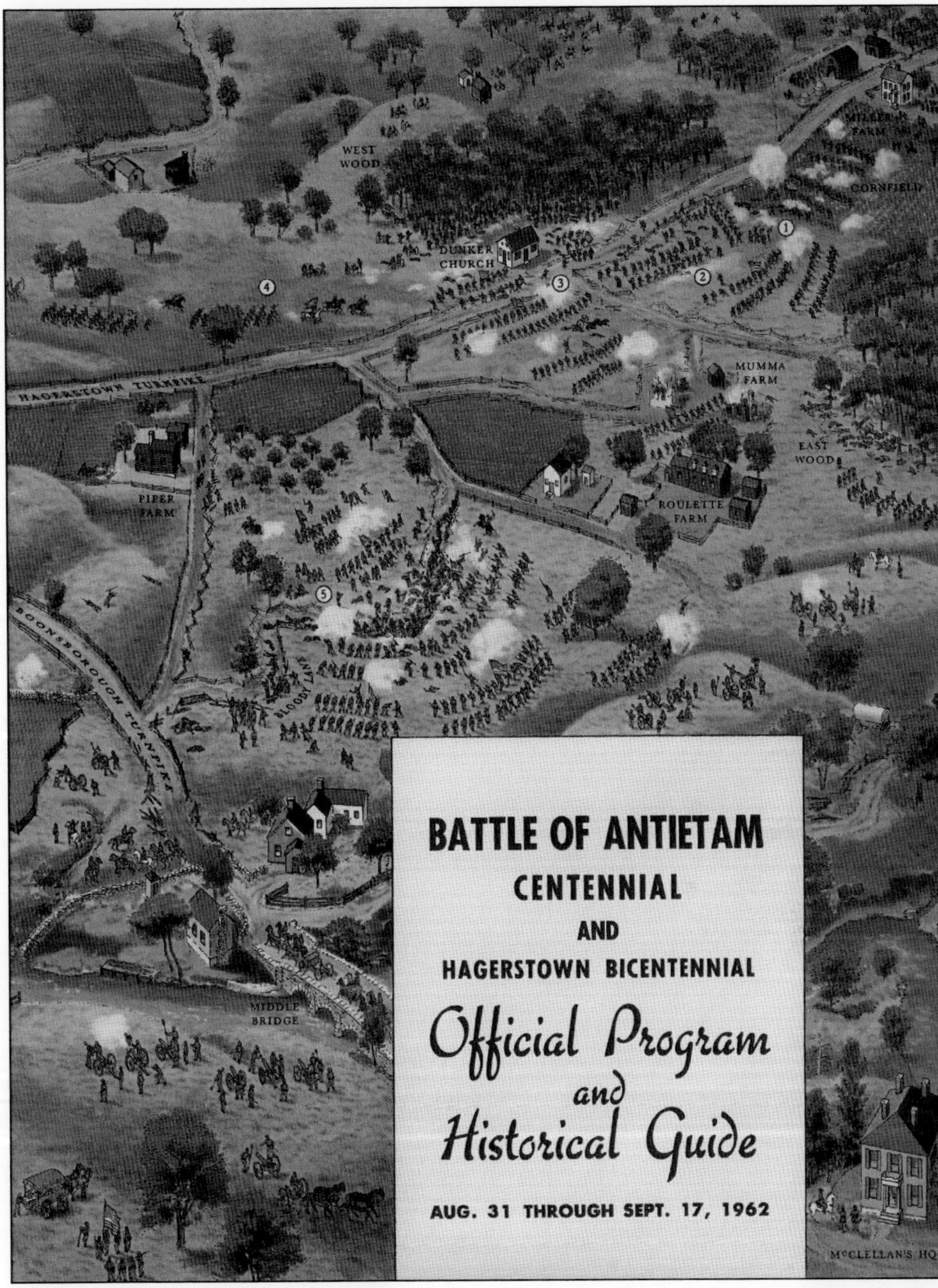

Featuring an illustration from the *American Heritage Picture History of the Civil War,* this Battle of Antietam 100th anniversary program cover shows how the battle began at dawn when Union general Joseph Hooker moved south to attack the left flank of the Confederate commander, Gen. Robert E. Lee. The battle raged in the David H. Miller cornfield (upper right) until Confederate general John Bell Hood counterattacked from the West Wood. Union general Joseph Mansfield then drove through the East Wood to the Dunker church, but Gen. Edwin Sumner was caught in a cross fire and routed by the Confederates at 9:00 a.m. Gen. D. H. Hill later was pushed out of Bloody Lane (center left), but the Union commander, Gen. George B. McClellan, did not attack the center of the Confederate line. (Courtesy authors' collection.)

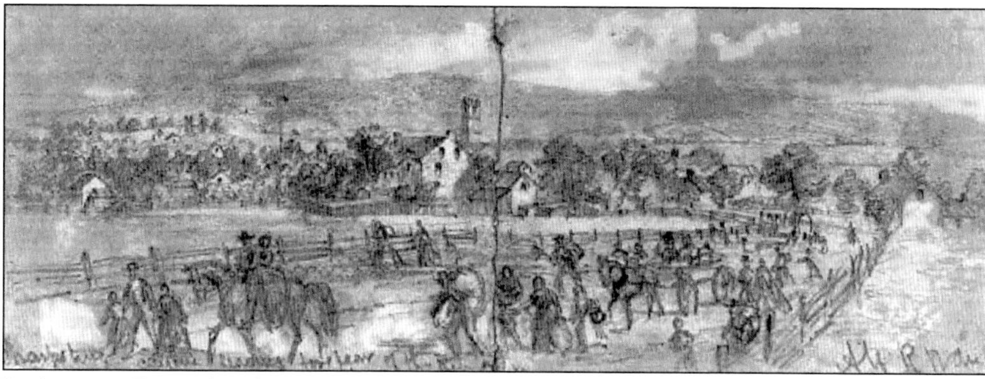

In *Antietam Remembered*, Virginia Mumma Hildebrand reported that a "short stout man with curly hair" went through Sharpsburg warning residents of an impending battle. Some residents stayed in their own homes, but many left to take shelter away from town. Alfred Rudolph Waud's illustration "Sharpsburg Citizens Leaving for Fear" of the Rebels dated September 15, 1862, shows individuals carrying sacks as they walked or rode out of town. The Episcopal church tower is clearly depicted under an ominous-looking sky. (Courtesy Library of Congress.)

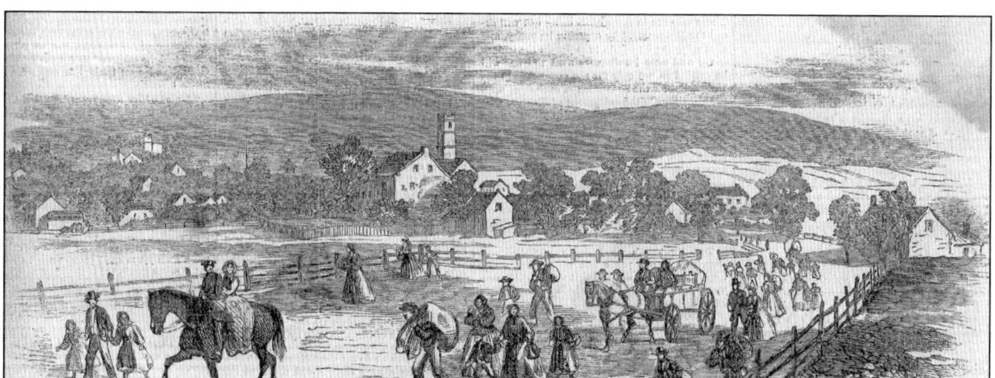

This etching of Alfred Rudolph Waud's drawing appeared in the October 11, 1862, issue of *Harper's Weekly*. Waud reported in that issue that Sharpsburg's population was 2,000 and mostly Union. A correspondent for the weekly reported, "All who did not leave sought shelter in the cellars, and were uninjured." In this etching, the tower of the Lutheran church, soon to be used as a Confederate signal tower, can be seen at the upper left. (Courtesy Phil Wingert.)

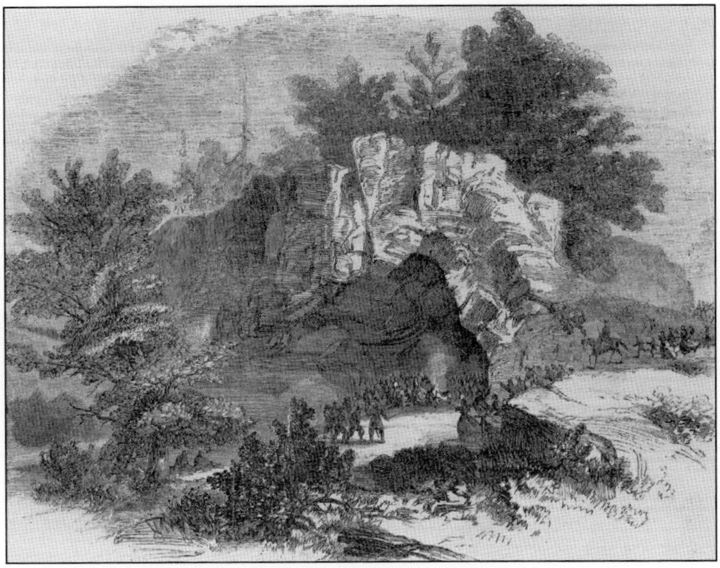

Killiansburg Cave (also Killings or Killingsburg) along the C&O Canal about 2 miles from town reportedly sheltered 100 to 200 civilians during the battle. Others who left their homes found shelter at Snyder's Landing, in farms and mills near Keedysville, at the Manor church, and at the home of a Parson Adams on Harpers Ferry Road. This illustration is from a sketch by F. H. Schell. (Courtesy NPS/ANB.)

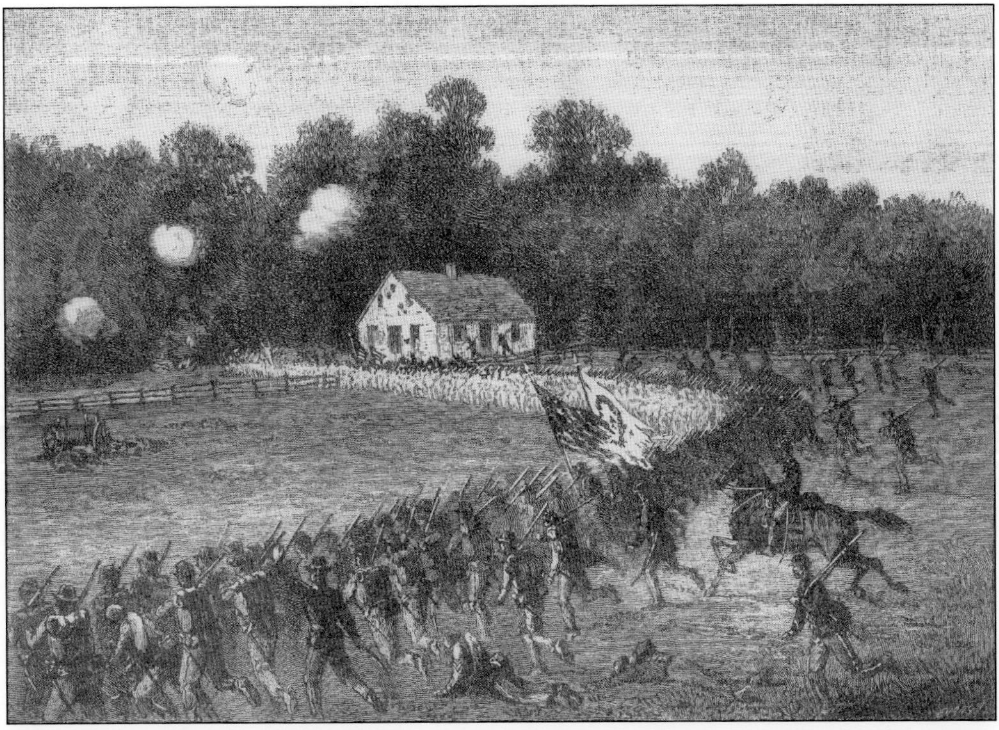

Union troops attack Confederate positions near the Dunker church in this Battle of Antietam sketch by Civil War artist Edwin Forbes. The church was the focal point of repeated clashes on the morning of September 17, 1862, as both armies sought to occupy and hold the high ground around it. Leveled by a storm in 1921, the church was rebuilt with some of its original materials in 1962. (Courtesy NPS/ANB.)

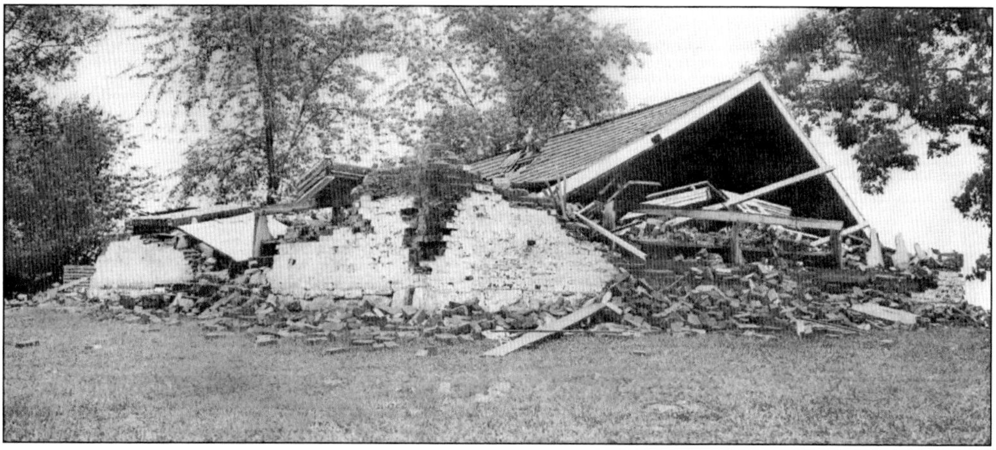

On May 23, 1921, a violent wind-and-hail storm demolished the Dunker church in a way warring armies did not. Elmer Garfield Boyer of Sharpsburg bought the land and the church ruins at a public sale for $800. He stored the ruins on his property on Chapline Street until the salvaged pieces were incorporated in the rebuilt church. (Courtesy NPS/ANB.)

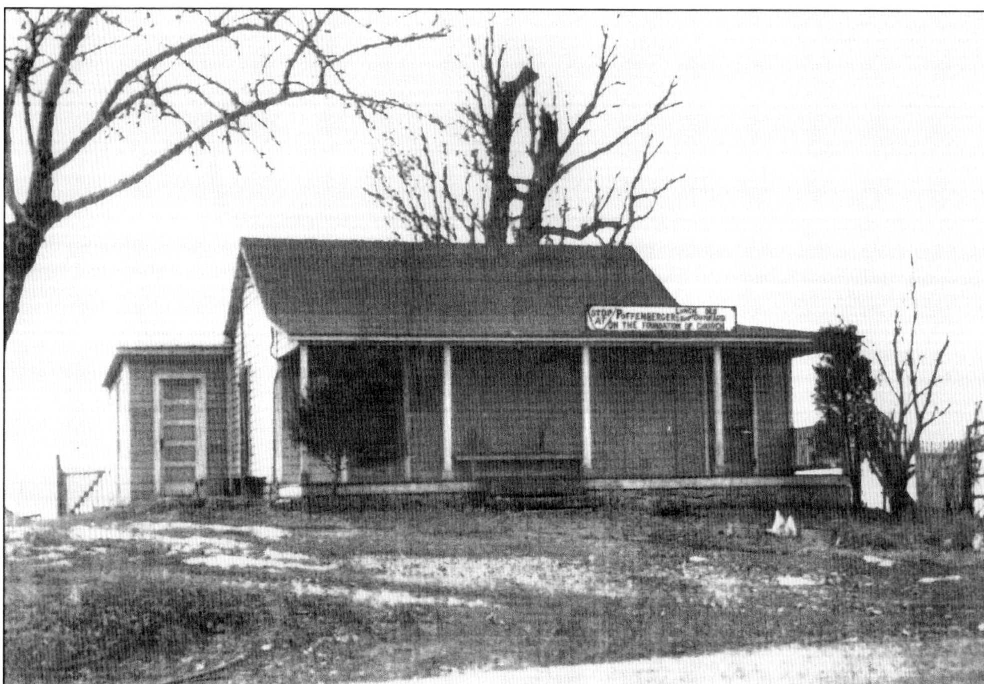

During the 1930s and 1940s, this lunch stand stood "on the foundation of Old Dunkard Church," according to the sign above the porch. The church (Dunker or Dunkard) got its name from their practice of baptism by immersion or dunking. Before being baptized, members promised not to own slaves or take part in war. (Courtesy NPS/ANB.)

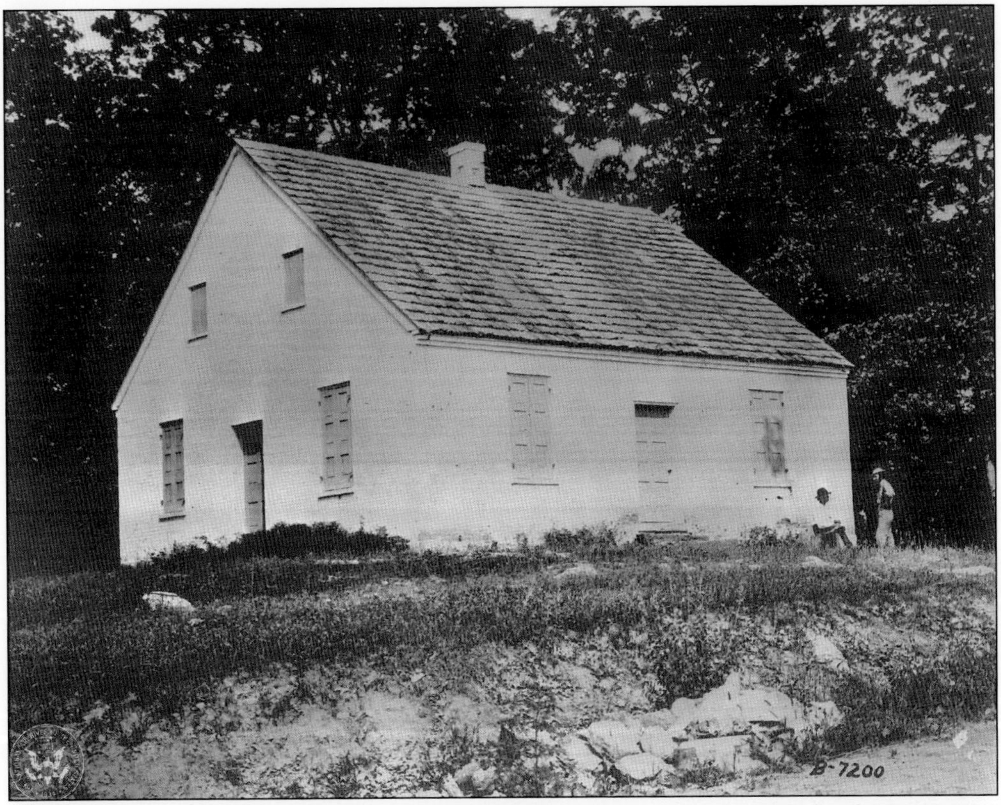

This undated photograph shows the Dunker church repaired after the 1862 battle. By 1864, it was again being used for worship. Before the original church was built in 1853, the congregation used the second floor of Daniel Miller's farmhouse for services. Samuel Mumma Sr. and his wife, Elizabeth (Daniel Miller's daughter), deeded land to seven deacons of the German Baptist Brethren Church for a church. The deed specified that the Brethren, in order to retain ownership of the land, must conduct public worship there. (Courtesy NPS/ANB.)

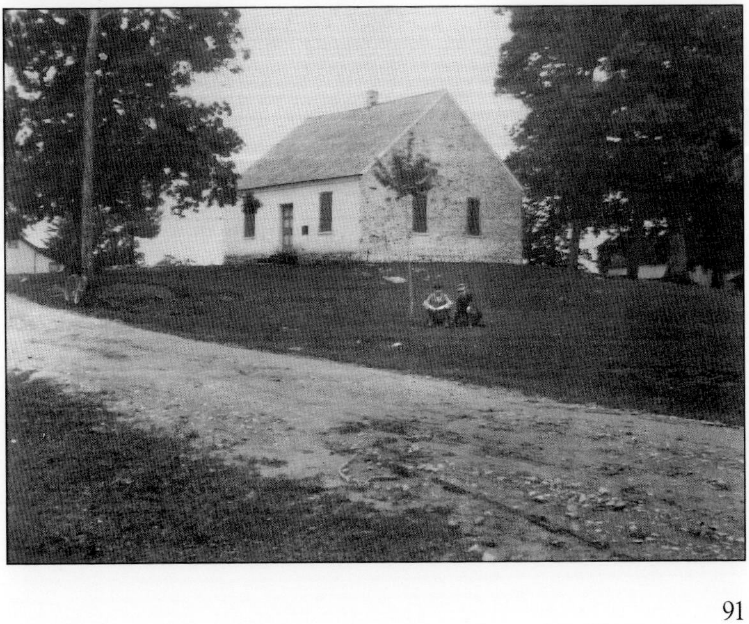

This June 1, 1903, photograph of the rebuilt Dunker church shows visitors to the church. At least one of them, it seems, was traveling by bicycle. The road in front of the church is the old Hagerstown Pike. A note with the photograph says the building was almost demolished in the battle. (Courtesy NPS/ANB.)

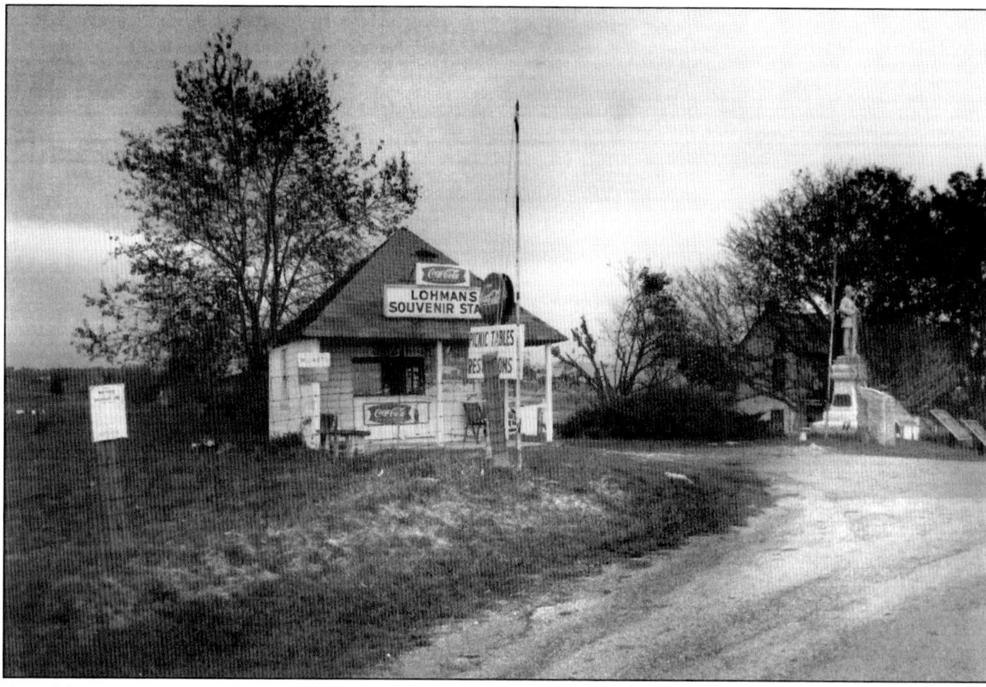

A public notice is attached to a fence post (left) near Lohman's Souvenir Stand, another building, a Civil War statue, and several Antietam National Battlefield markers in this photograph from 1965, when Lohman's Souvenir Stand was considered one of several "obtrusions near Bloody Lane." Today the 3,200-acre battlefield houses 96 monuments to those who fought in the bloodiest single-day battle of the American Civil War. (Courtesy NPS/ANB.)

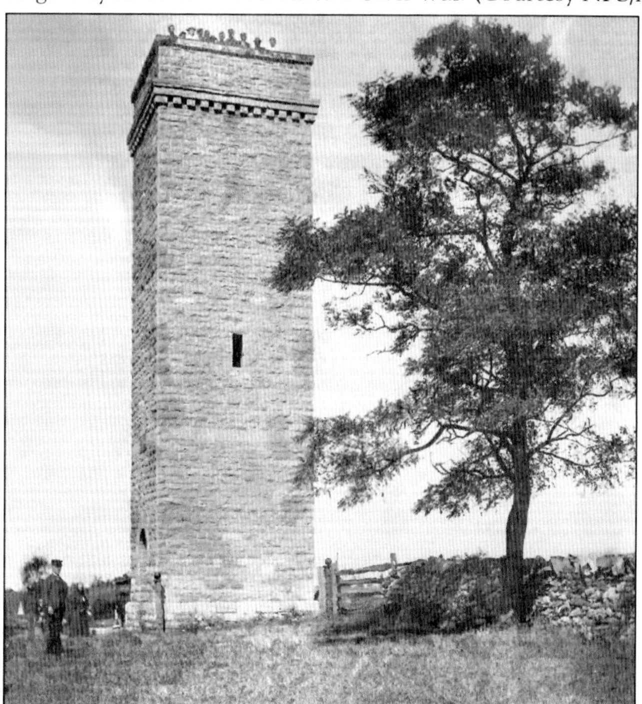

While their Chesapeake and Ohio Canal excursion boat captain stands firmly on the ground below them, members of an early-20th-century Cumberland, Maryland, tour group take in the view from atop a roofless Antietam National Battlefield observation tower. A roof has since been added to the top of the tower near Bloody Lane northeast of Sharpsburg. (Courtesy NPS/C&O Canal NHP.)

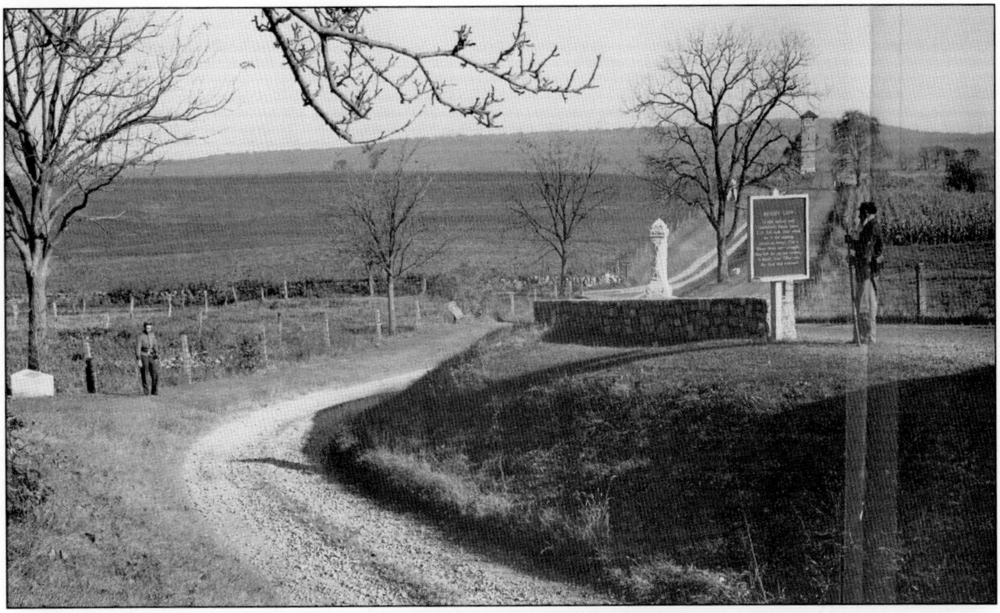

A Union reenactor (right) faces a Confederate reenactor (left) near a plaque and a monument marking Bloody Lane on the on the Antietam National Battlefield northeast of Sharpsburg. The battlefield's stone observation tower stands in the southeastern distance of this late-20th-century image produced by Raup Photography in Hagerstown, Maryland. Bloody Lane fighting on September 17, 1862, highlighted the midday phase of the American Civil War's bloodiest single-day battle. (Courtesy WCHS.)

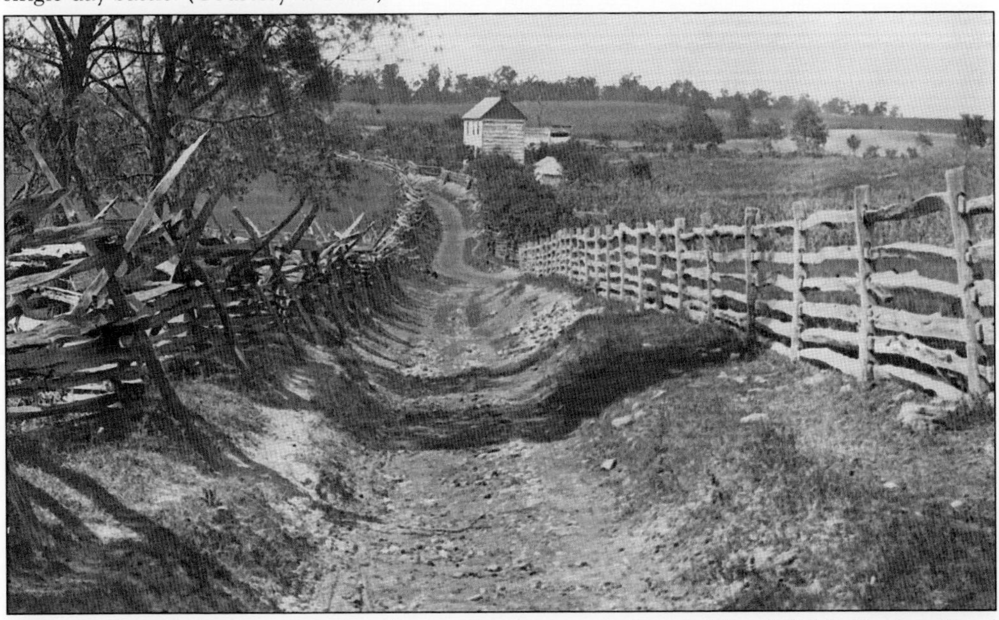

Protected by two kinds of wooden fences, the Antietam National Battlefield's Sunken Road stretches northeast toward a log house in this 1877 photograph. The Sunken Road became Bloody Lane after 5,000 casualties were recorded there in midday fighting during the Civil War Battle of Antietam on September 17, 1862. The Sunken Road was called Hog Trough Road by farmers who used it as a shortcut to Orndorff's Mill east of Sharpsburg. (Courtesy WCHS.)

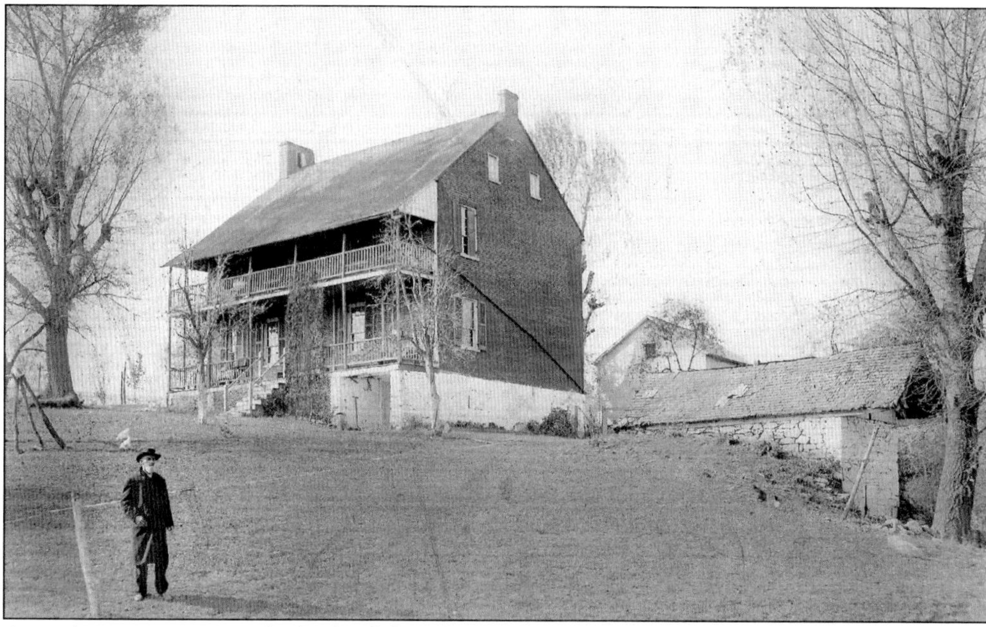

According to a note on the back of this photograph, Sam Jennings is standing in front of the Henry Rohrback home near Burnside Bridge in a picture Jennings had taken in 1906. Burnside Bridge was known as Rohrback Bridge before the 1862 Civil War Battle of Antietam, when Union general Ambrose Burnside took three hours to cross the Antietam Creek span only to be turned back by Confederate general A. P. Hill. (Courtesy NPS/ANB.)

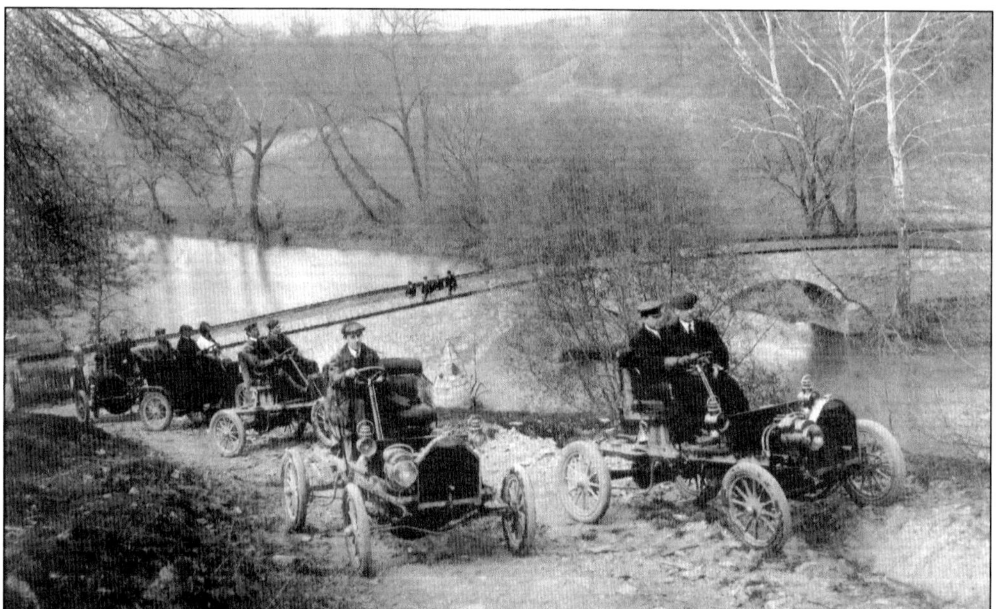

Five Crawford automobiles made in Hagerstown, Maryland, are test driven above the Antietam National Battlefield's Burnside Bridge in this early-20th-century photograph. Twelve hundred Confederate soldiers firing from above this same bridge kept 14,000 Union troops from crossing the Antietam Creek for three crucial hours during the Civil War Battle of Antietam on September 17, 1862. (Courtesy NPS/ANB.)

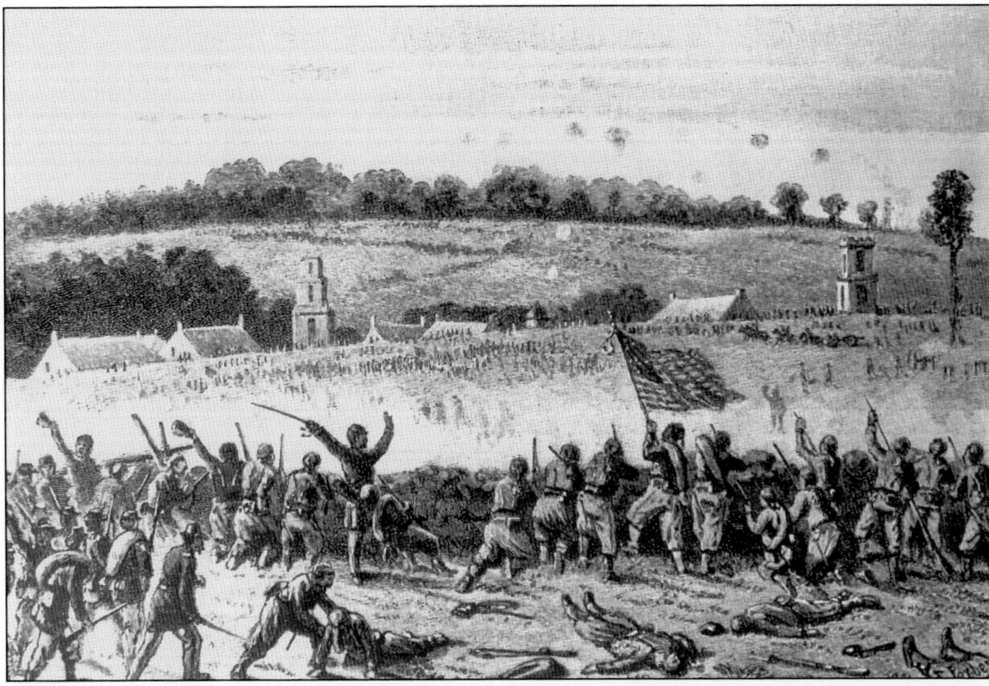

With Sharpsburg rooftops and church steeples visible over a ridge, Union troops fire from behind a stone wall in this Battle of Antietam final attack sketch by Civil War artist Edwin Forbes. Union general Ambrose Burnside's troops had begun moving toward Sharpsburg, but Confederate general A. P. Hill's troops arrived in time to turn back the Union advance. The three-phase September 17, 1862, battle, the bloodiest single day of the war, left 23,110 casualties. (Courtesy WCHS.)

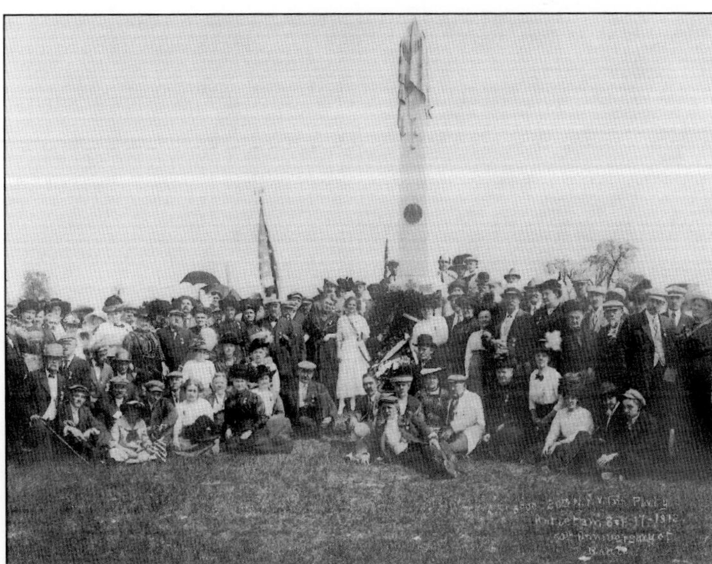

Veterans, family members, and friends gather around the Antietam National Battlefield's 20th New York Volunteer Infantry monument on September 17, 1912, for the 50th anniversary of the Battle of Antietam. A total of 96 battlefield monuments salute the Union and Confederate soldiers who fought at Antietam on September 17, 1862, the bloodiest day of the American Civil War. (Courtesy NPS/ANB.)

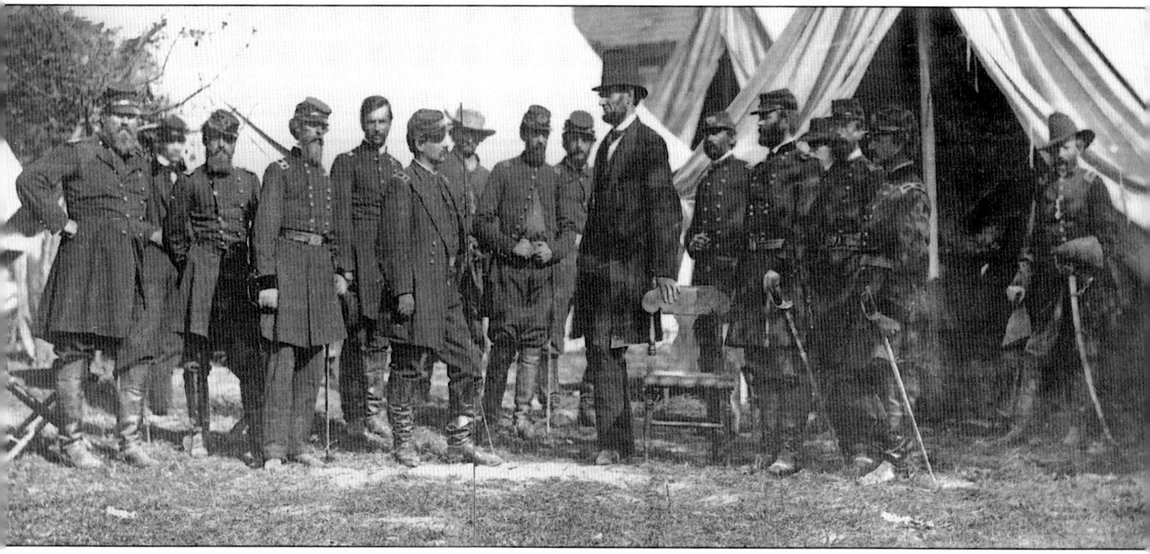

Library of Congress records identify the men in this October 3, 1862, Alexander Gardner photograph as, from left to right, Col. Delos B. Sacket, inspector general, Army of the Potomac; Capt. George Monteith, Fifth Corps, aide-de-camp to Gen. Fitz John Porter; Lt. Col. N. B. Sweitzer, aide-de-camp to Gen. George B. McClellan; Maj. Gen. George W. Morrell, Fifth Corps; Lt. Col. A. S. Webb, Fifth Corps, commissary of subsistence; Gen. George B. McClellan, commander of the Army of the Potomac; Scout Adams; Johnathan Letterman, medical director, Army of the Potomac; Capt. George A. Custer, aide-de-camp to General McClellan; Pres. Abraham Lincoln; Brig. Gen. Henry J. Hunt, chief of artillery, Army of the Potomac; Maj. Gen. Fitz John Porter, commander of the Fifth Corps; Col. G. K. Warren, Fifth Corps; Lt. Col. Fred T. Locke, Fifth Corps, assistant adjutant general to General Porter; Brig. Gen. A. A. Humphreys, Fifth Corps; and Lt. George A. Batchelder, Fifth Corps acting ordinance officer. The group gathered west of Sharpsburg at Mount Airy, the Civil War home of Stephen Grove, where some 400 soldiers were recuperating or dying from wounds received in the September 17, 1862, Battle of Antietam. (Courtesy NPS/ANB.)

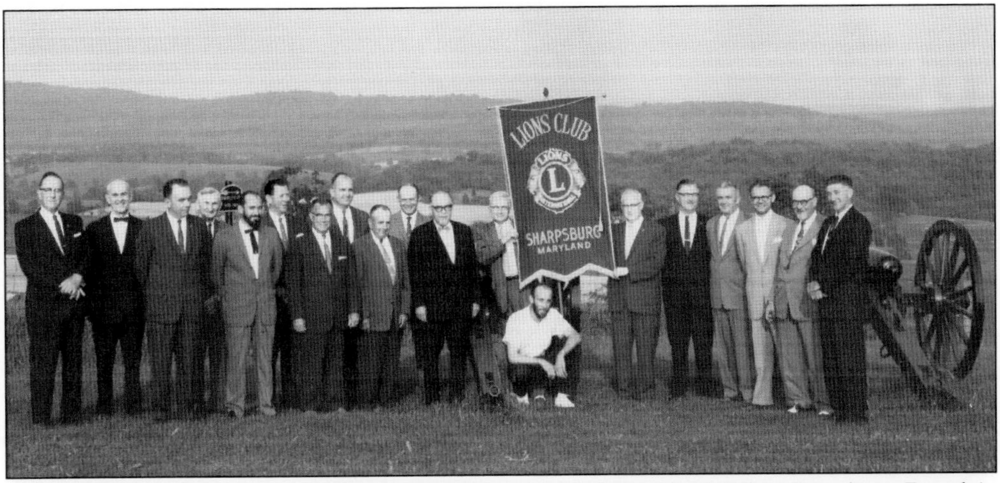

This 1962 Sharpsburg Lions Club lineup includes, from left to right, J. Edgar Remsburg; David A. Gross; John J. Roulette; Roger E. Moore; Clifton E. Smith; William Wyand; Theodore Poffenberger; Thomas E. Crampton; Fred O. Flook; Albert E. Davis; Walter H. Shealy, M.D.; J. Keith Meyers; William T. DeLauney; Samuel H. Lohman; M. Howell Davis; Theodore H. Hebb; Raymond F. Munch; Edward Q. Carter; and Herbert F. Myers. (Courtesy Jeffrey Saylor.)

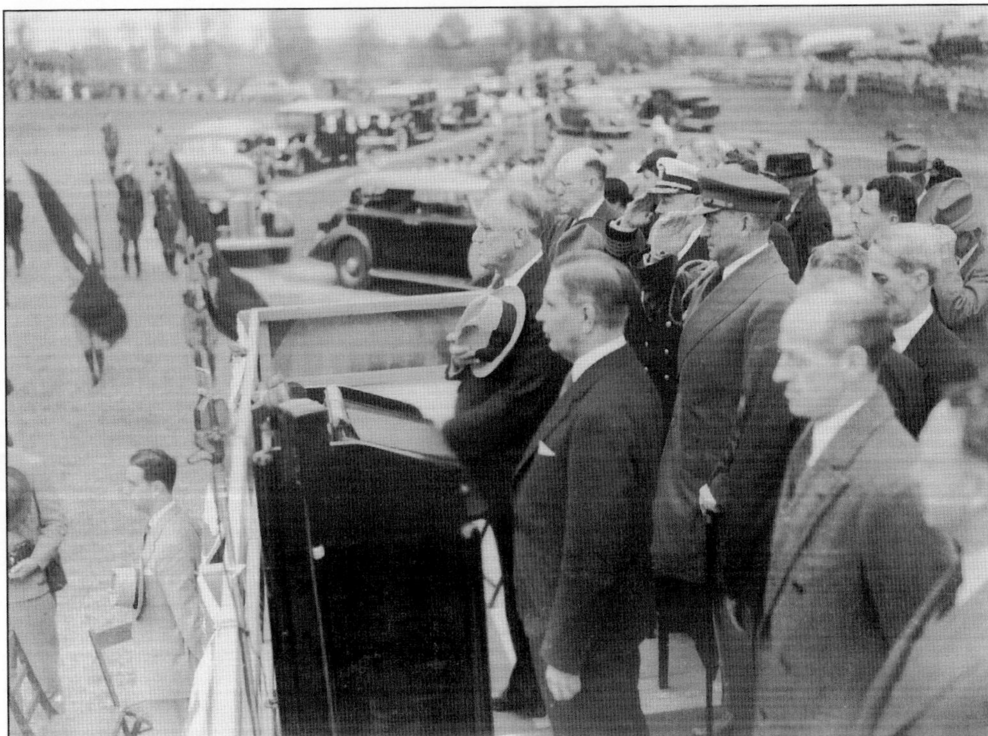

Pres. Franklin Delano Roosevelt holds his hat over his heart during his 1937 address at the Antietam National Battlefield near Sharpsburg for the 75th anniversary of the Battle of Antietam. More people were killed or wounded at Antietam on September 17, 1862, than on any other single day of the American Civil War. Federal losses were estimated at 12,410, and Confederate losses were set at 10,700. (Courtesy Sharpsburg Town Council.)

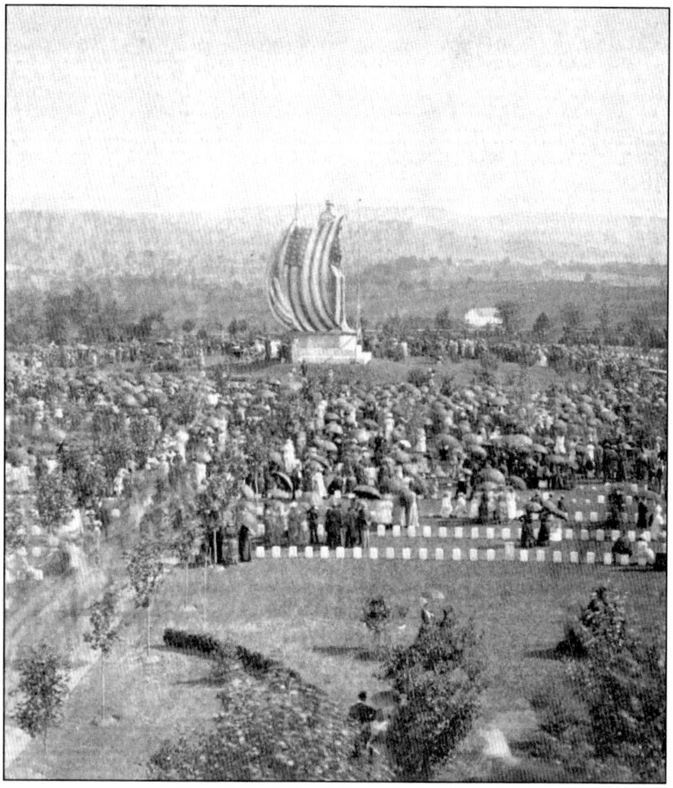

In this photograph by Elias Marker Recher of Hagerstown, Maryland, a large crowd gathers around the Soldiers' Monument for the September 17, 1867, dedication of the Antietam National Cemetery. The cemetery dedication was held five years after the 12-hour Civil War Battle of Antietam created a record 23,110 casualties. The remains of 4,776 Federal soldiers, including 1,836 unknowns, are buried in the national cemetery on the eastern edge of Sharpsburg. (Courtesy WCHS.)

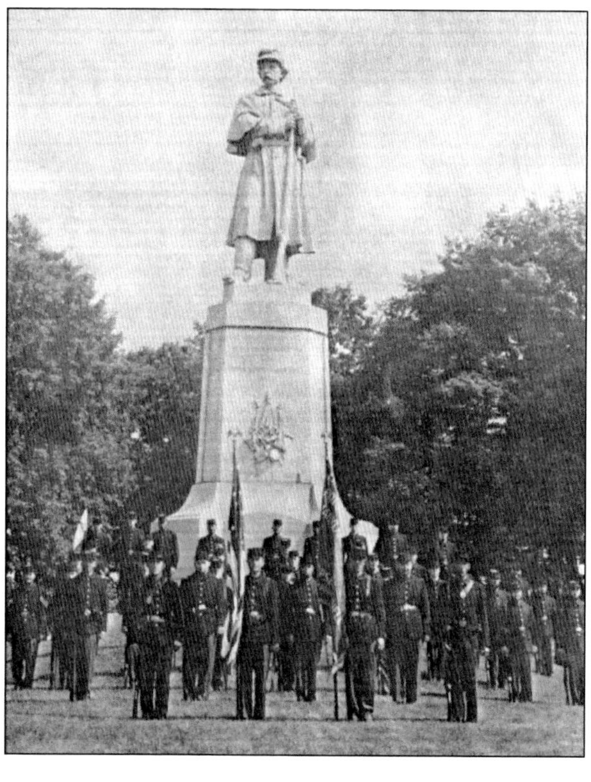

The 45-foot-tall Soldiers' Monument statue of a Union army private known as Old Simon stands above members of the Sharpsburg Rifles at Sharpsburg's Antietam National Cemetery in this 1959 Ament Studios photograph. The picture appears on the cover of Virginia Mumma Hildebrand's *The Sharpsburg Rifles, First Maryland Regiment, Potomac Home Brigade, Maryland Volunteers*. The Potomac Home Brigade was formed to protect Maryland's boundaries during the Civil War. (Courtesy Sharpsburg Public Library.)

Four

THE CANAL

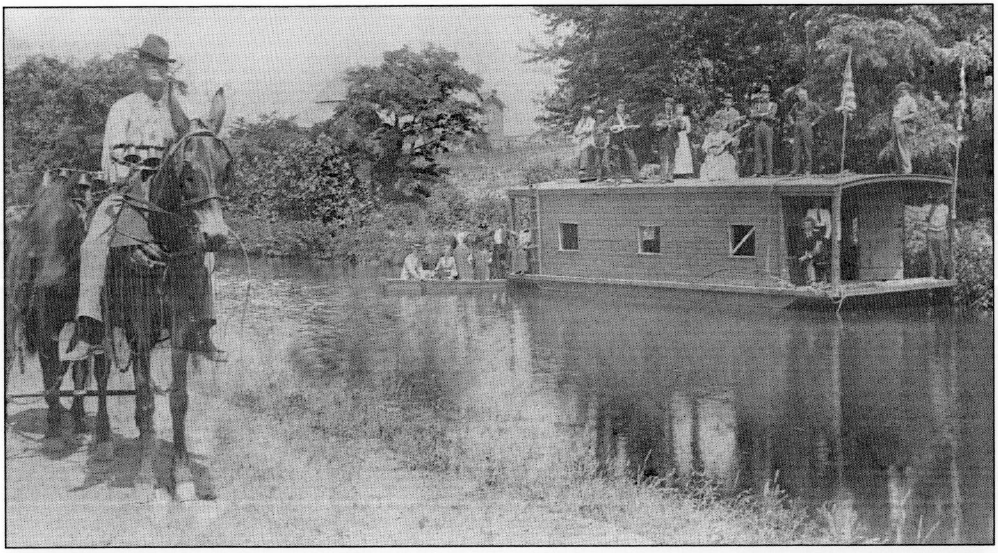

Complete with crew, musicians, mule driver, and two mules wearing their distinctive calming bells, this dance boat has stopped on the Chesapeake and Ohio Canal near Sharpsburg. In Thomas Hahn's book *The C. & O. Canal Boatmen*, William Frank "Cotton" Zimmerman says mules loved to hear the bells: "When they had them stabled and fed good and then we put the bells on them, they would walk proud." (Courtesy NPS/C&O Canal NHP.)

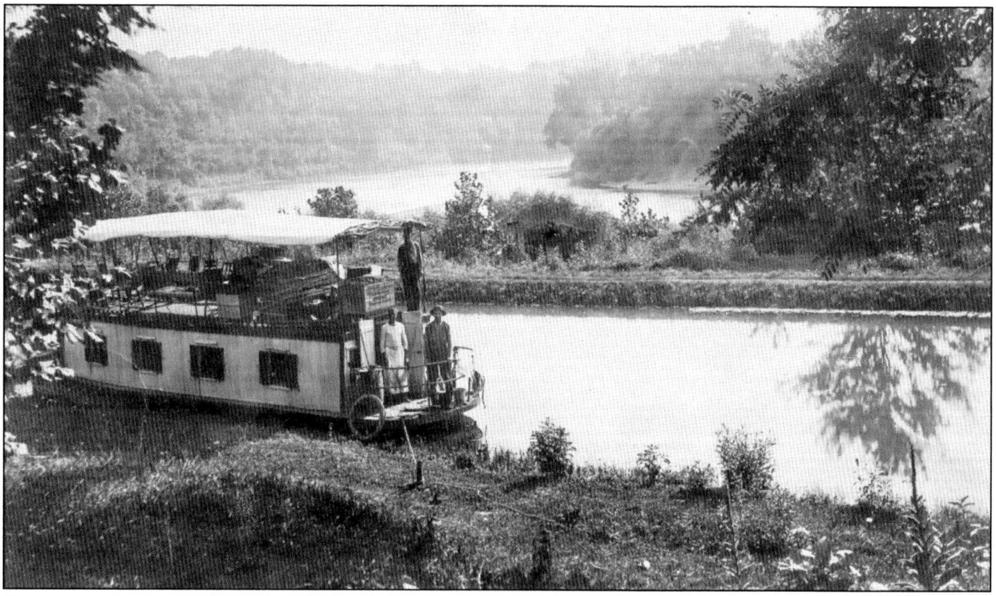

Crew members stand on the deck of their motorized touring houseboat during a stop at Snyder's Landing on the C&O Canal at the edge of the Potomac River west of Sharpsburg in 1916. "I used to vacation at the Landing in 'The Enchanted Barn,' a renovated barn named after a novel by G.J. Hill," said Marylou Schwartz, whose parents were passengers on this 1916 excursion. (Courtesy WCHS.)

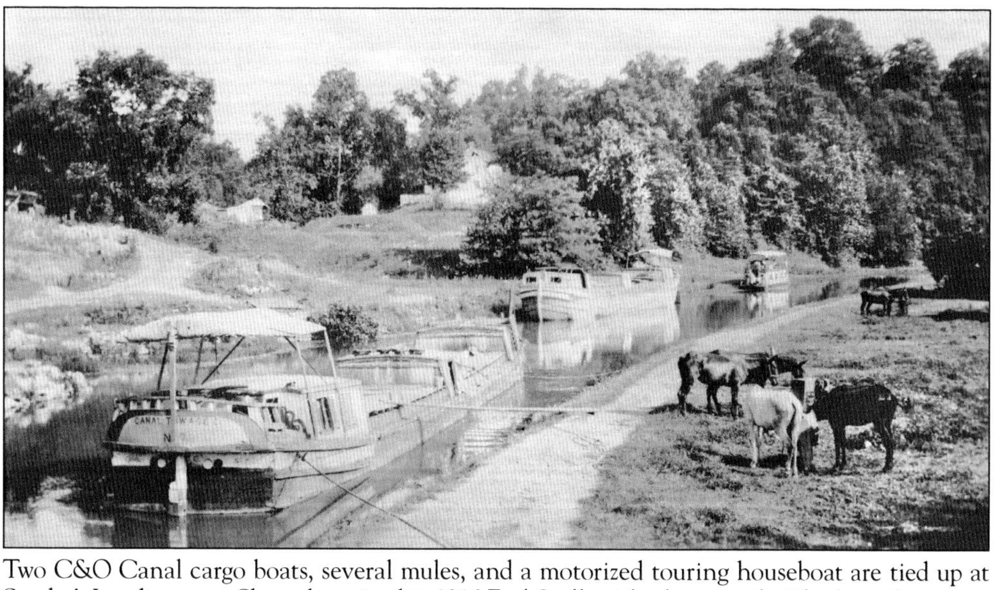

Two C&O Canal cargo boats, several mules, and a motorized touring houseboat are tied up at Snyder's Landing near Sharpsburg in this 1916 Earl Stallsmith photograph. The houseboat tour group included Mr. and Mrs. Paul L. Spangler of Gettysburg, Pennsylvania, whose daughter, Marylou Schwartz of Gettysburg, in 1999 gave the Washington County Historical Society a series of photographs from her parents' 1916 canal adventure. (Courtesy WCHS.)

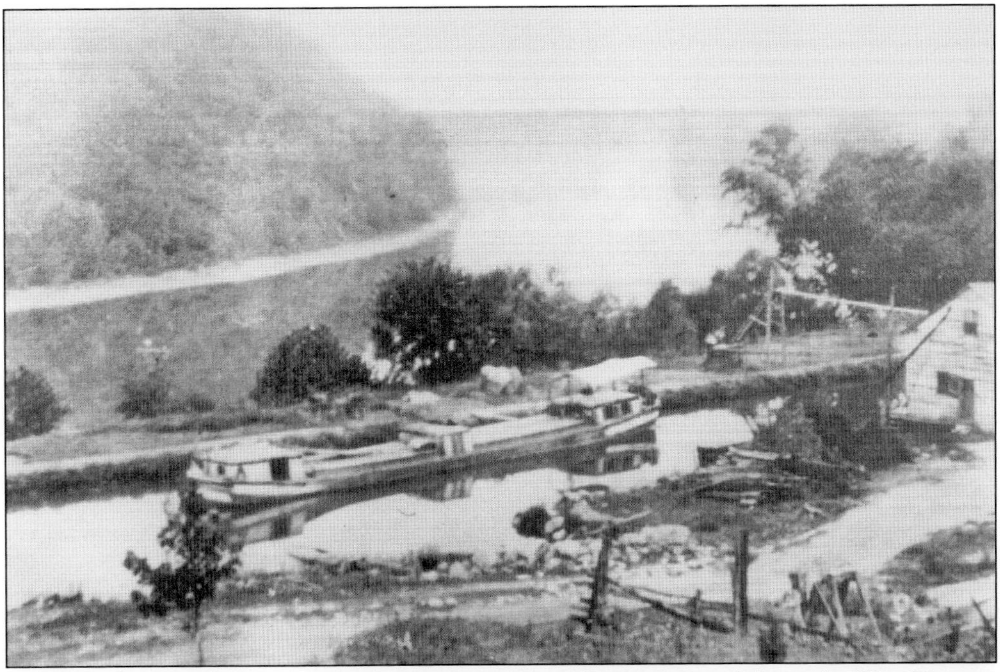

This overview of Snyder's Landing at milepost 76.6 on the C&O Canal shows the West Virginia shore of the curving Potomac River, mules on the towpath, a loaded boat sitting low in the water, the pedestrian bridge over the canal, a coal pile next to Jim Snyder's warehouse, and, in the foreground, Snyder's Landing Road, which goes to Sharpsburg, 1.7 miles to the east. (Courtesy WCFL/WMR.)

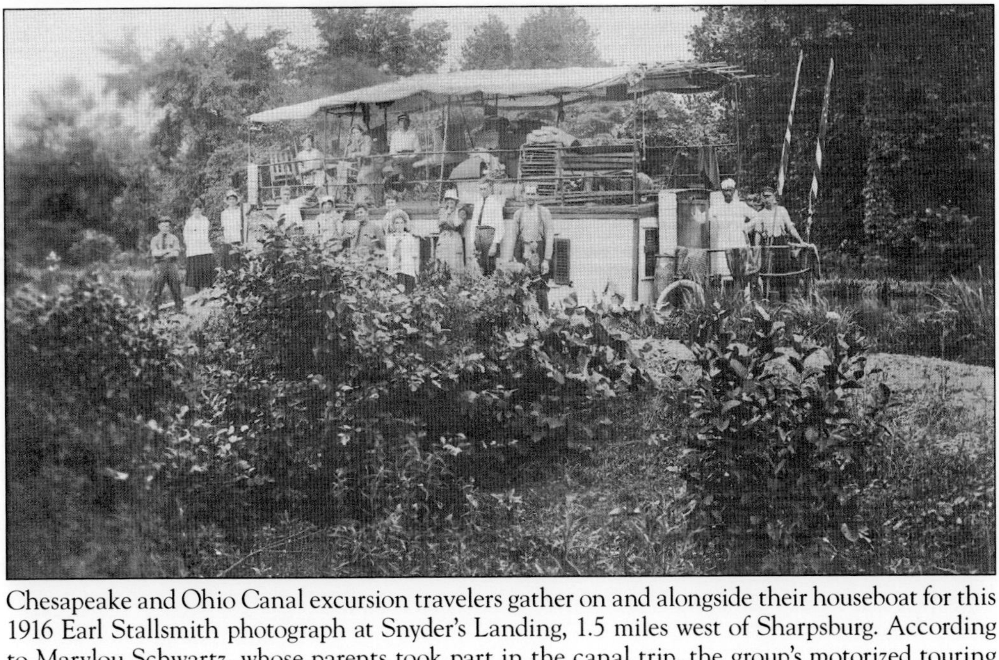

Chesapeake and Ohio Canal excursion travelers gather on and alongside their houseboat for this 1916 Earl Stallsmith photograph at Snyder's Landing, 1.5 miles west of Sharpsburg. According to Marylou Schwartz, whose parents took part in the canal trip, the group's motorized touring houseboat was based in Williamsport, Maryland, and was owned by Harry and Alice Snook, who also operated a grocery/general store in nearby Halfway, Maryland. (Courtesy WCHS.)

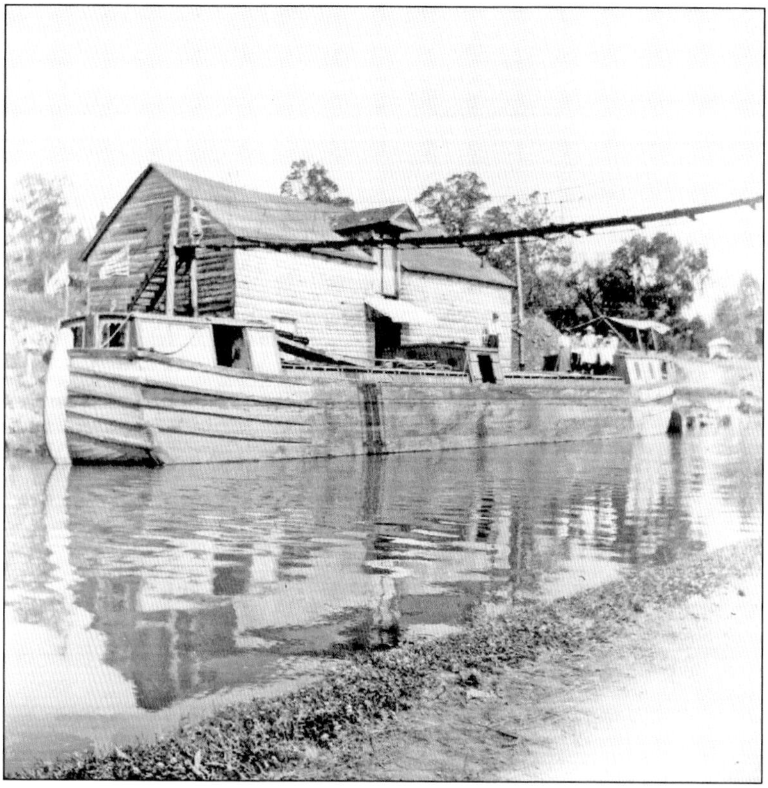

This empty boat docked at the Snyder Coal and Grain Warehouse sits high in the water. The footbridge allowed pedestrian access to both sides of the canal. It was built high so that boats could pass or park underneath it. The person on the bridge might have been a member of what appears to be a family crew standing next to the boat's living quarters. (Courtesy WCFL/WMR.)

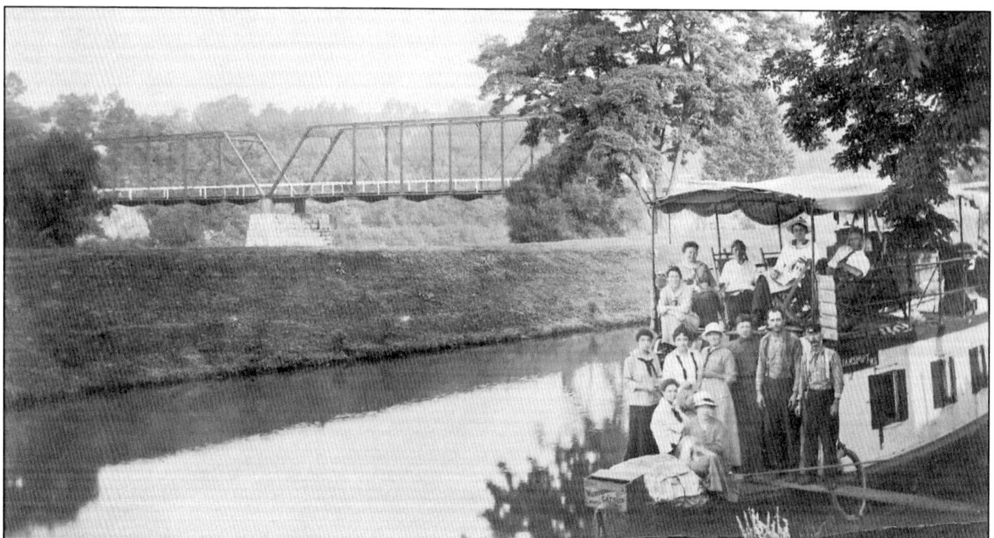

Chesapeake and Ohio Canal excursion travelers gather on their motorized houseboat near Lock 38 on the Maryland side of the Potomac River about 3 miles southwest of Sharpsburg. The Potomac River bridge to Shepherdstown, West Virginia, is visible above the mule towpath berm in this Earl Stallsmith photograph. An estimated 2,000 mules pulled 500 cargo barges up and down the 184.5-mile canal during its heyday. (Courtesy WCHS.)

In fancy hats and ties, two men, four women, and a boy pose on the steps of the swinging pedestrian bridge at Snyder's Landing. Behind them are the canal, a corner of the warehouse, a pile of coal, and the road to Sharpsburg. The photograph is undated; the canal ceased operation in 1924, following a flood. (Courtesy WCFL/WMR.)

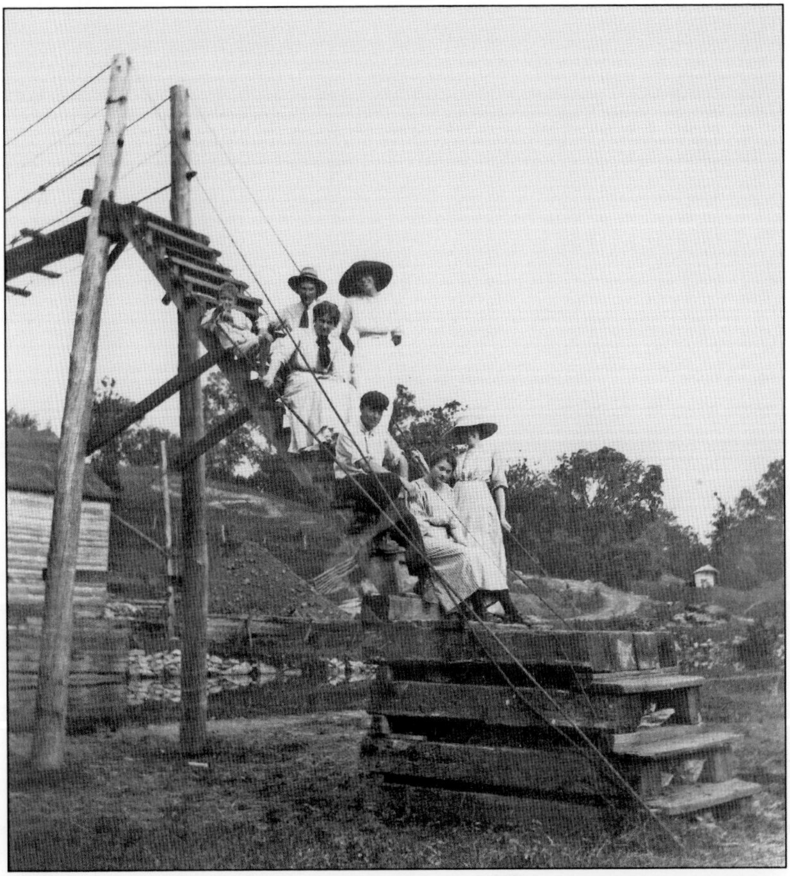

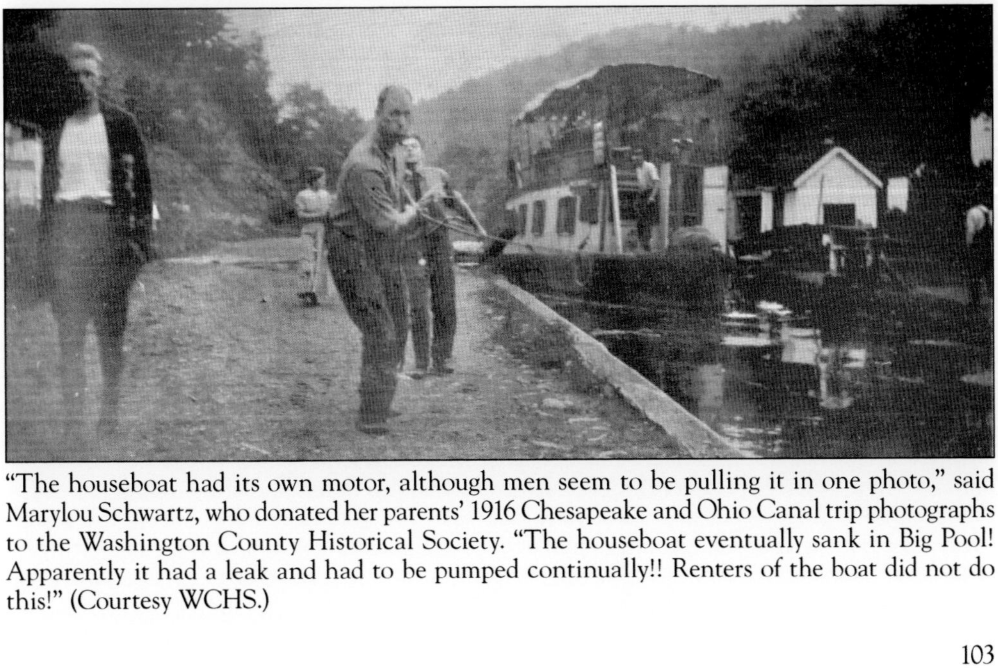

"The houseboat had its own motor, although men seem to be pulling it in one photo," said Marylou Schwartz, who donated her parents' 1916 Chesapeake and Ohio Canal trip photographs to the Washington County Historical Society. "The houseboat eventually sank in Big Pool! Apparently it had a leak and had to be pumped continually!! Renters of the boat did not do this!" (Courtesy WCHS.)

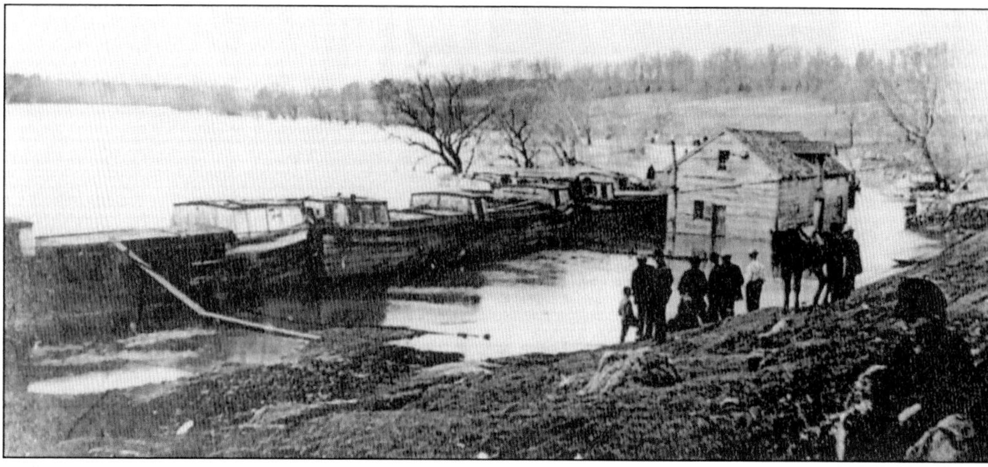

A boy plays with his dog (lower right) while others watch the Potomac River flooding along the Chesapeake and Ohio Canal at Snyder's Landing west of Sharpsburg. Differing sources record the year of the flood as either 1902 or 1910. In his *Historic Resource Study: Chesapeake & Ohio Canal*, Harlan Unrau recounts 43 significant water and ice freshets in the canal's history from 1828 to 1924. (Courtesy Betty Lou Rinn.)

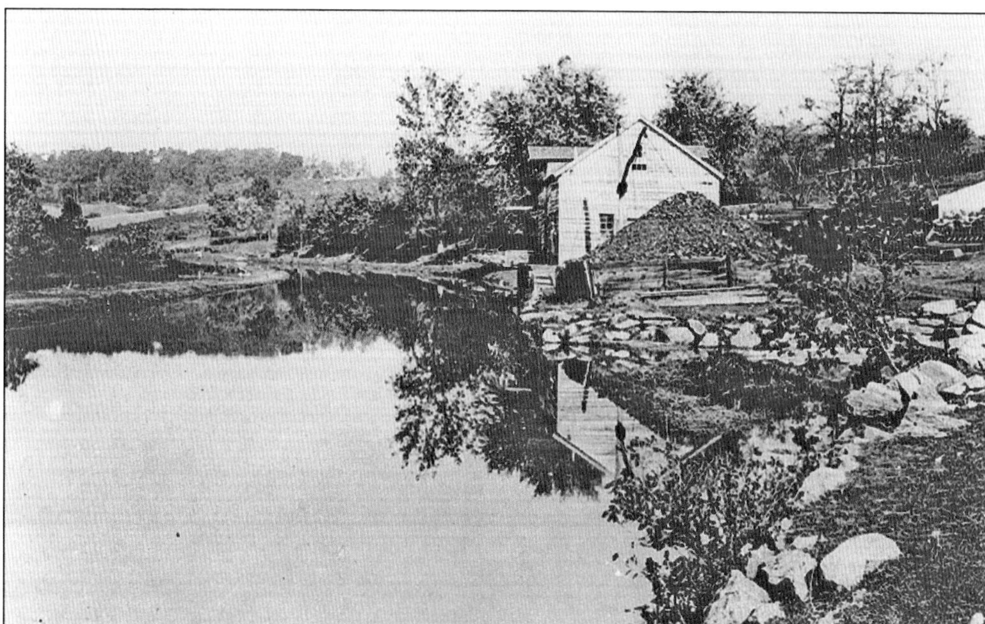

This photograph, taken between 1850 and 1875, shows Snyder's warehouse and its coal pile reflected in a calm, empty canal. Some 200 Sharpsburg residents sought refuge here from the Battle of Antietam in September 1862. Before Snyder built his warehouse, this landing was called Sharpsburg Landing, a spot popular with boatmen for tying up their boats during the winter season. Lee Barron reported that almost half of the boats operating in 1910 wintered here. Snyder closed the warehouse when the canal stopped operating after the flood of 1924. The warehouse was washed away in the flood of 1936. (Courtesy Bonnard J. Morgan Sr. and WCFL/WMR.)

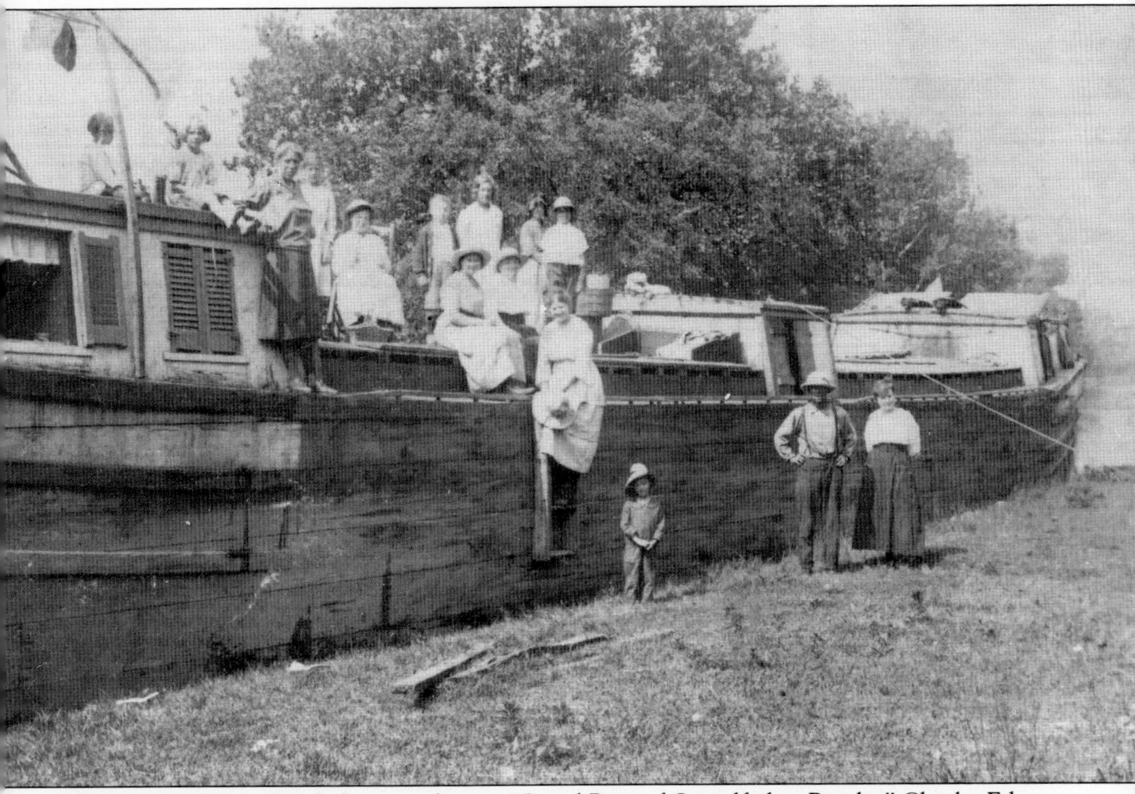

The note on this undated photograph says, "Canal Boat of Grandfather Bender." Charles Edgar Bender, captain of Boat No. 55, is shown with his boat and an outing probably made up of friends and family. The woman next to him might be his wife, Agnes May (Stull). They had eight children: seven daughters—Mary, Rachel, Etta, Flo, Geneva, Julia, and Betsy Ross—and one son, William E. His oldest daughter, Mary, went to work on his boat when she was nine, and her brother, William, went on the boat when he was seven. Mary (Bender) Schroeder, quoted extensively in Thomas F. Hahn's *The C&O Canal Boatmen, 1892–1924*, tells of the hard work and dangers of working on a canal boat. According to the National Park Service, Charles Bender was a captain from about 1900 to 1923. His father, Benjamin, had worked as a boatman, and his brother Raleigh was the captain of Boat No. 1. (Courtesy William Poffenberger and Nellie Kline, grandchildren of Charles Bender.)

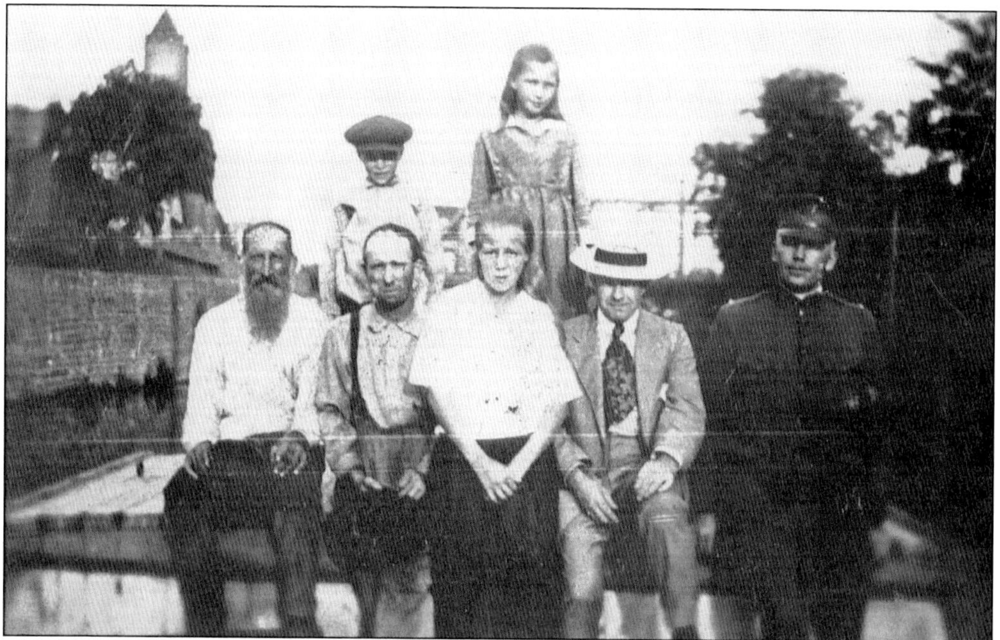

Sharpsburg resident Capt. Charles E. Bender (seated second from left) pauses in Georgetown with his daughter Mary (center front) and his son William (back left). Captain Bender operated Chesapeake and Ohio Canal towage Boat No. 55. The other persons are not identified. The girl might be one of Bender's other daughters. The 184.5-mile trip from Cumberland to Georgetown usually took seven days. (Courtesy Nellie Kline.)

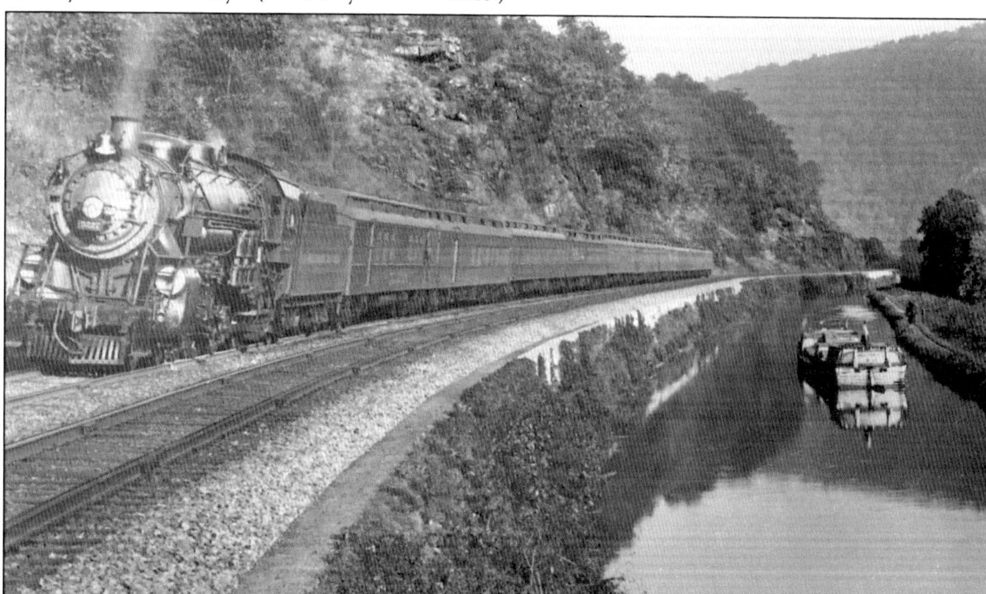

A westbound Baltimore and Ohio Railroad Capital Limited train passes Capt. George Bowers's eastbound Chesapeake and Ohio Canal Boat No. 49 with Lloyd Lemen as mule driver and "Mr. Eversole" steering in about 1920. In 1880, a Captain Bowers of the *Adam Sherman* was fined $1.50 for pumping his boat one-and-half days at $1 per day. Canal boats were pumped to prevent sinking. (Courtesy WCHS.)

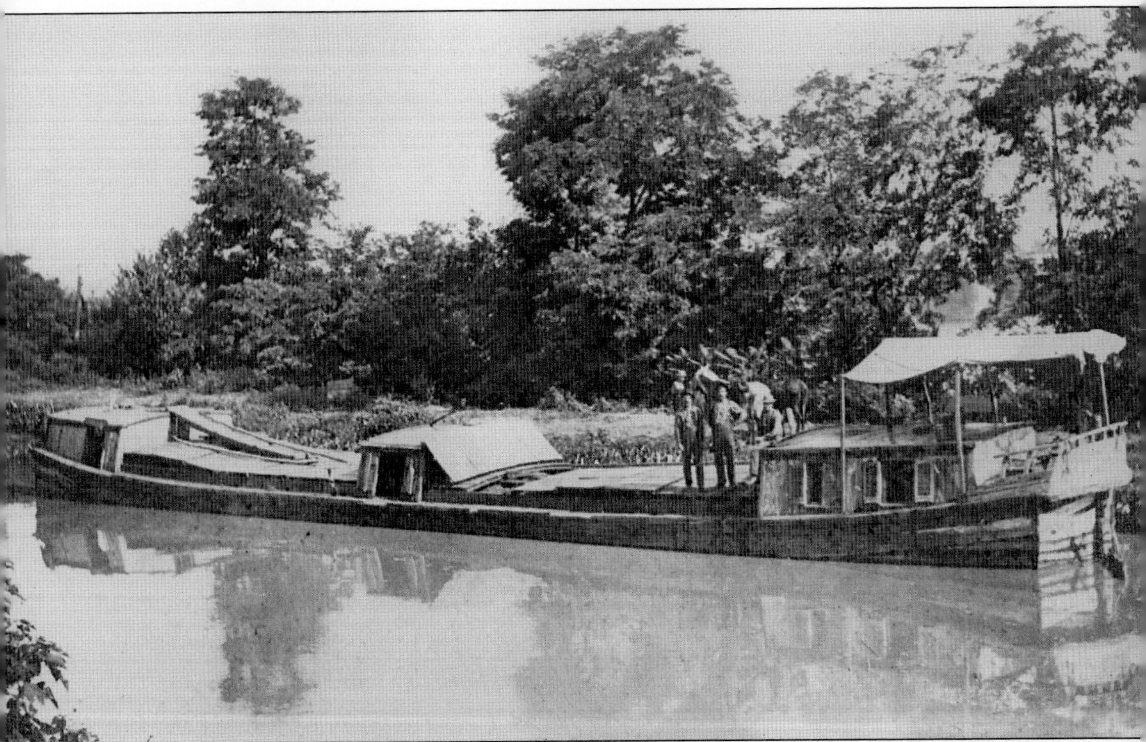

The note on the back of this photograph says, "I searched for this photo for 25 years. It was found on September 30, 2000, at Barron's C&O Canal Trail Store at Snyder's Landing outside Sharpsburg, Maryland. The photo was taken about 1905 (a guess based on an average boat lasting 20-25 years, and the fact that this one had not been painted the 'new' canal company colors) somewhere between Cumberland and Georgetown and full of coal. Capt. Raleigh Bender is in the center with the mustache and has his hands on his hips. His son, Ray Bender, is standing with the mules, wearing a straw hat. I thought you would like to have a copy to hang in 'his' (your) tavern. I hope you enjoy looking at it as much as I enjoyed finding it. Sincerely, Randy Leatherman (great grandson of Raleigh Bender)." Raleigh Bender's boat was No. 1. He was also called "Riley Bender" and "Raleigh Painter." Bender's father, Benjamin (known as Bender as well as Painter), was a boatman; his brother Charles was captain of Boat No. 55. (Courtesy John and Renay Tyler and Captain Bender's Tavern.)

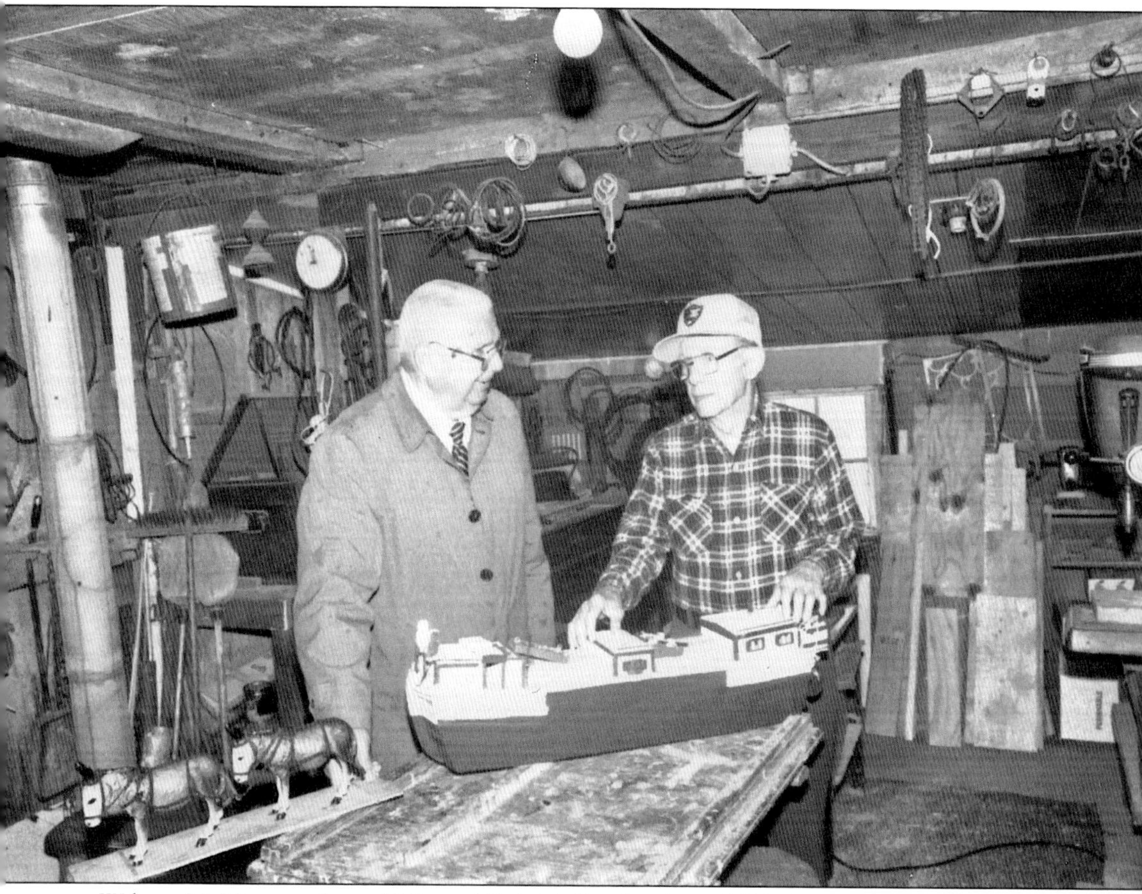

Wilmer M. Mumma, born 1920, and Raleigh Bender, born 1874, discuss the model of Captain Bender's canal Boat No. 1 in the basement of Bender's Sharpsburg home. Another picture of a younger Bender with his model appears in the March 1960 *National Geographic*. He was not alone in thinking that his mules Jack, Kate, and Rock were the best. Thomas Hahn quotes another boatman, "Captain Bender had the best mule team on the canal. He'd put the bells on them and crack that big old blacksnake wagon whip and them mules was as steady as a clock tickin' and keep it up." Bender held several records with the C&O Canal. He worked the longest, 36 years, many as a captain; held the record of 62 hours for the fastest time for an unloaded boat from Georgetown to Cumberland (timed by George L. Nicholson, canal general manager); and brought the last load of coal from Cumberland through the Paw Paw Tunnel in 1925. After his canal days, he operated Bender's Tavern (still on Main Street) and reportedly told many stories about the canal and town. (Courtesy Stephen Recker.)

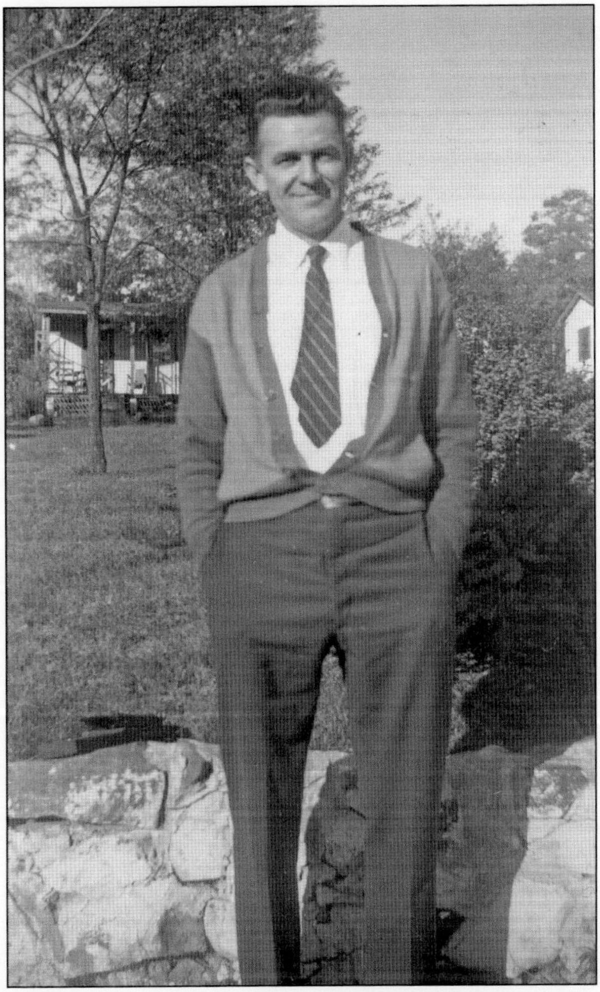

This is Ronald Schroeder, who as a boy was a mule driver on the C&O Canal. He became captain of Canal Boat No. 2. He married Mary Bender who worked on her father's (Charles Bender) boat. Schroeder made this replica, which is trimmed in red, of that canal boat, No. 55. The canal boats were about 90 feet long and only 6 inches narrower than the 15-foot-wide locks they passed through. At the front of the boat was the mule shed or stable. A mule in the model is standing at the opening. An awning was rigged over the living quarters, about 10-foot-by-12-foot, at the back of the boat, which was where the steersman or steerswoman stood. The middle of the boat had 14 covered hatches and a hay shed where workers might sleep. (Both, courtesy Abby Draper and Nellie Kline.)

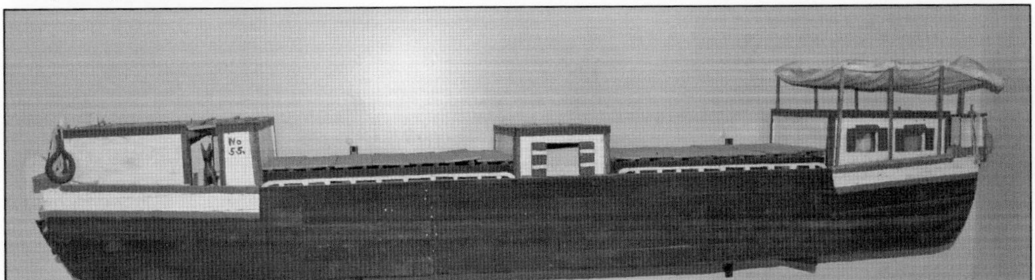

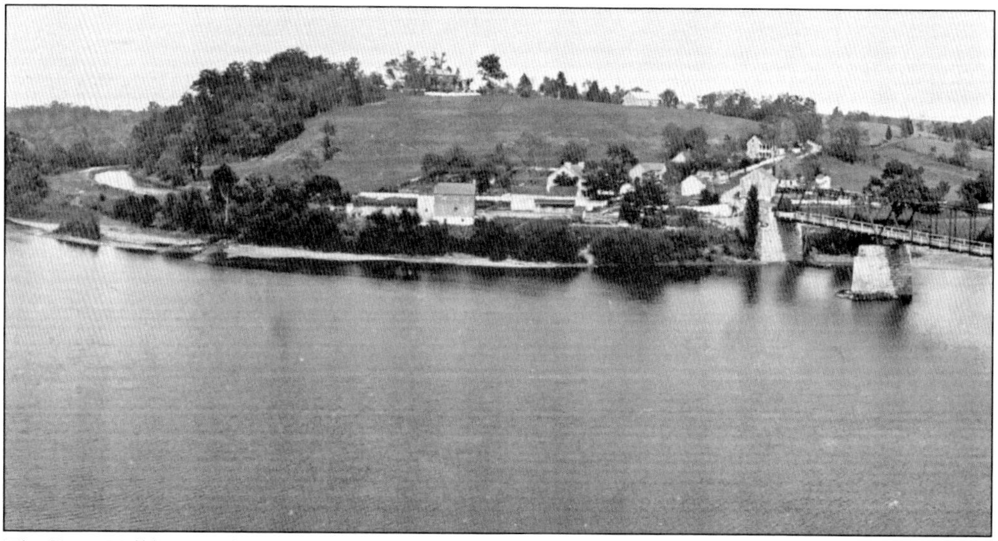

The Ferry Hill home of Confederate Civil War officer Henry Kyd Douglas, the Lock 38 community of Bridgeport, and a Potomac River bridge destroyed in the 1936 flood all are shown in this photograph from Thomas Hahn's *Chesapeake and Ohio Canal Old Picture Album*. Thomas Van Swearingen is said to have begun a ferry at this location southwest of Sharpsburg in 1765. Confederate troops burned a wooden toll bridge here in 1861. (Courtesy WCHS.)

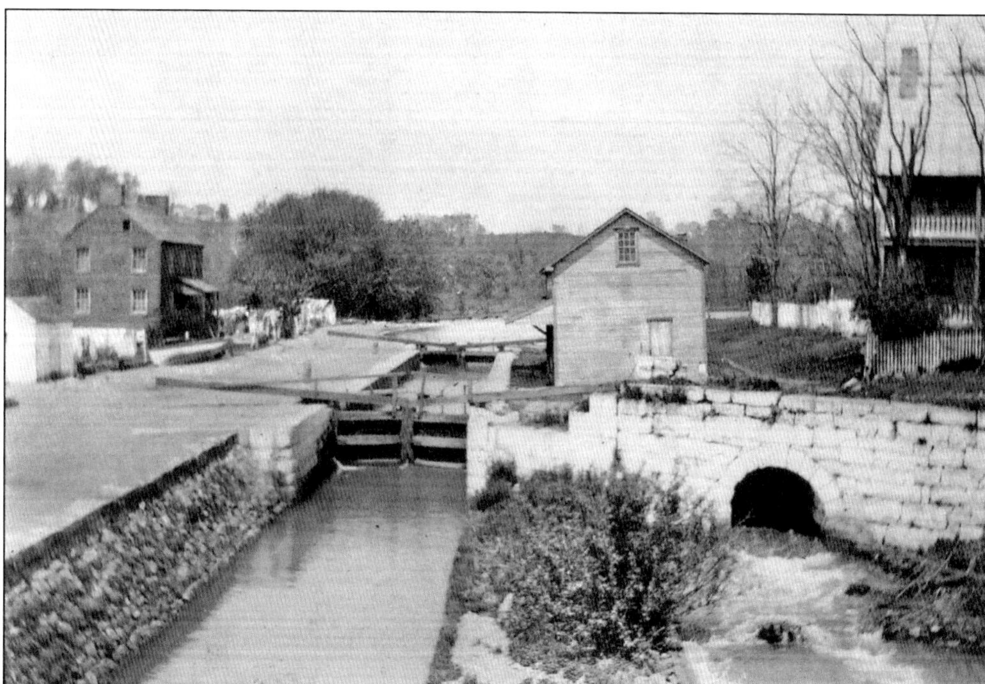

Following its 1828 ground-breaking in Washington, D.C., the Chesapeake and Ohio Canal awarded contracts in 1832 for the construction of Lock 38 (above) near Sharpsburg, Lock 37 near Dargan, and the Antietam Creek Aqueduct near the village of Antietam. "Go view those magnificent aqueducts, locks and culverts of hewn stone," said William Price of Cumberland, Maryland, at the official opening of the completed canal in 1850. (Courtesy WCHS.)

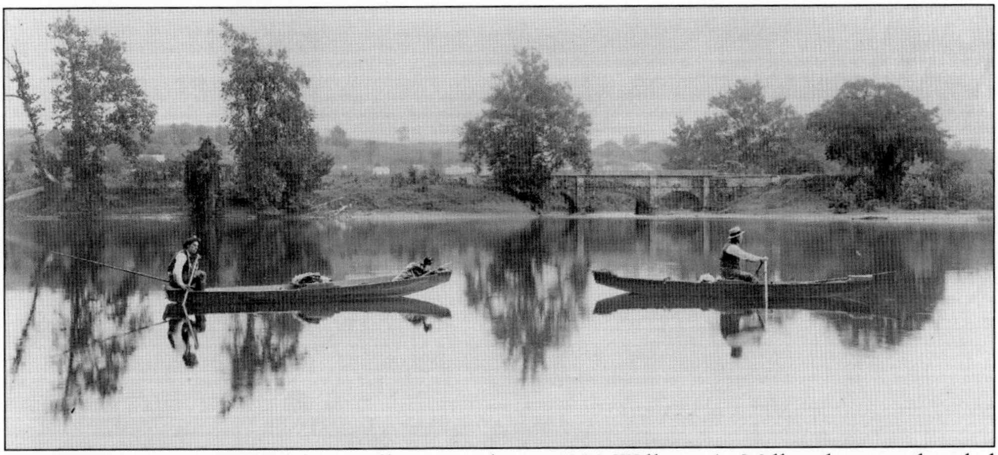

Two boaters appear headed for a collision in this *c.* 1900 William A. Miller photograph titled "Mouth of the Antietam." The Chesapeake and Ohio Canal Antietam Aqueduct crosses behind the boaters near the village of Antietam where the Antietam Creek joins the Potomac River south of Sharpsburg. The canal featured 11 aqueducts, 74 lift locks, 7 dams, 150 culverts, 1 tunnel, and a 12-foot-wide towpath. (Courtesy WCHS.)

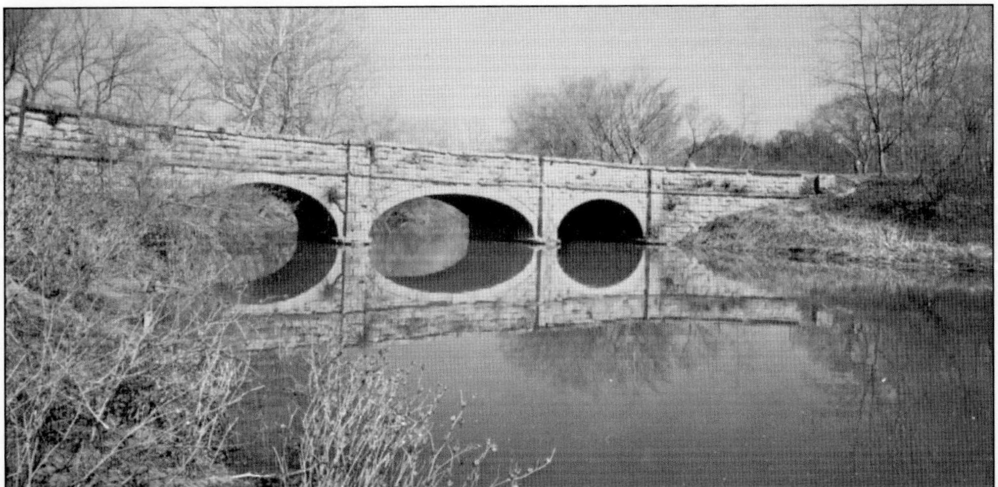

The Antietam Creek Aqueduct casts its reflection on its namesake creek 3 miles south of Sharpsburg in this 1961 Historic American Buildings Survey photograph from Thomas Hahn's 1976 book *Chesapeake and Ohio Canal Old Picture Album*. Constructed in 1834 as the fourth of 11 stone aqueducts on the canal, the 140-foot-long Antietam Creek Aqueduct sustained serious damage in 1864 during the American Civil War. (Courtesy WCHS.)

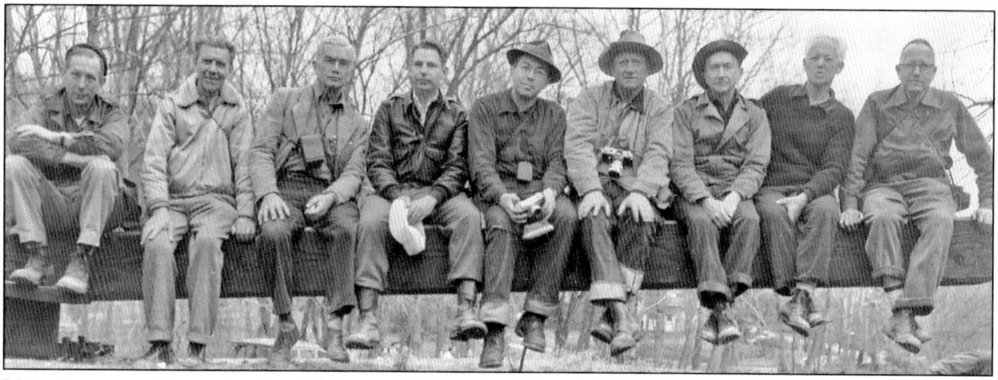

U.S. Supreme Court justice William O. Douglas (fourth from right) rests on a lock gate swing beam during his 1954 Chesapeake and Ohio Canal "Douglas Hike" from Cumberland, Maryland, to Washington, D.C. Douglas's well-publicized hike helped thwart an effort to turn the canal towpath into a paved highway. After ending commercial operations in 1924, the 184.5-mile canal became a national historical park in 1971. From left to right are Grant Conway, Olaus Murie, John (Jack) Permain, Colin Ritter, Albert Farwell, Douglas, Harvey Broome, George Miller, and Constant (Connie) Southworth. (Courtesy WCHS.)

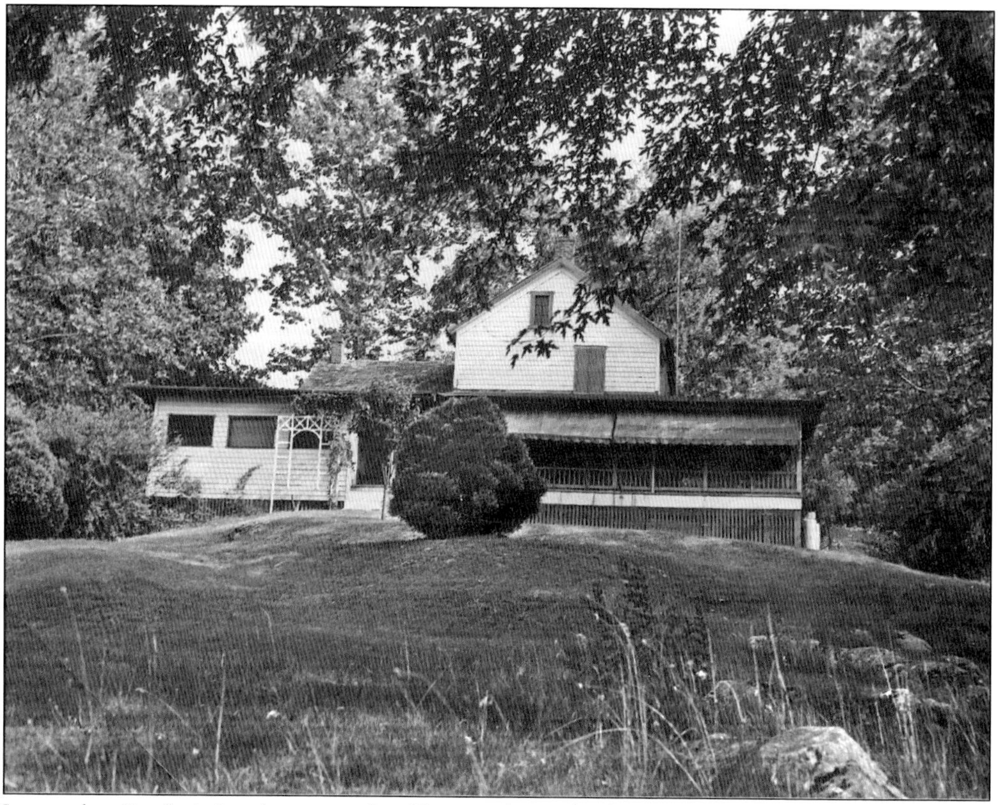

Located at Snyder's Landing near the Chesapeake and Ohio Canal towpath 1.5 miles west of Sharpsburg, this house was the Betts and Sinn home from 1945 to 1962. "In the early 1930s, Snyder's Landing was a large park and recreation area," says local historian Lee Barron. "It was not unusual to see 500 persons out for a Sunday outing and swim in the summer." (Courtesy Betty Lou Rinn.)

Five

The Area

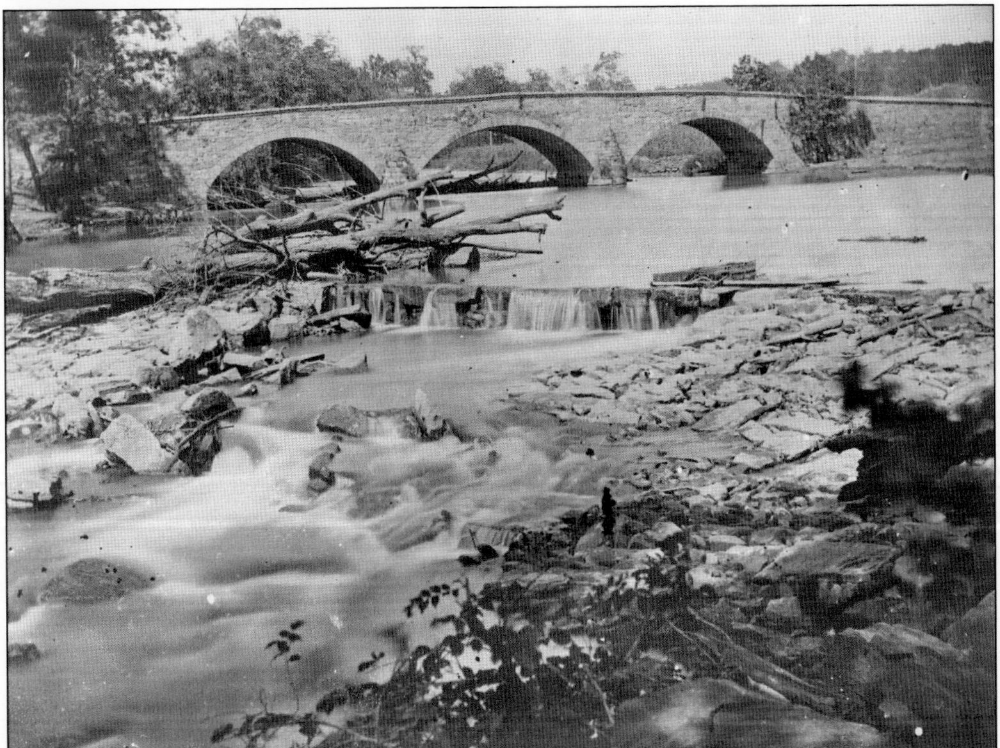

This bridge built by Silas Harry in 1824 was last seen in 1889. The Johnstown flood affected the Antietam Creek, which wrecked the Middle Bridge, already unstable because of a construction flaw. The General Assembly of Maryland in 1822 authorized a levy of $1,800 to build this "bridge over Antieatam Creek, at the place where the road leading from Boonsborough to Sharpsburg crosses said creek, near Mumma's Mill." Remains of the mill's dam are in the foreground of the photograph. (Courtesy NPS/ANB.)

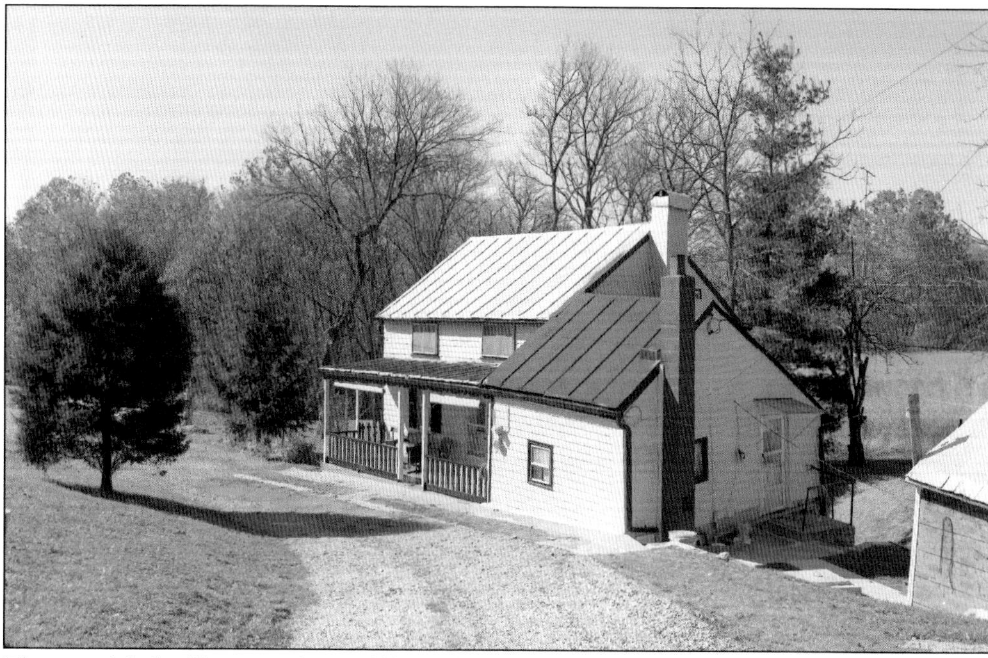

The remodeled tollhouse at the Middle Bridge was given a covered porch and an addition on its east side. The long overhanging roof was cut back to the south-facing wall. A metal roof replaced the original, which probably was made of wood shingles. The original chimney was capped and was probably used for a stove, not a fireplace. (Courtesy SHS and Library of Congress.)

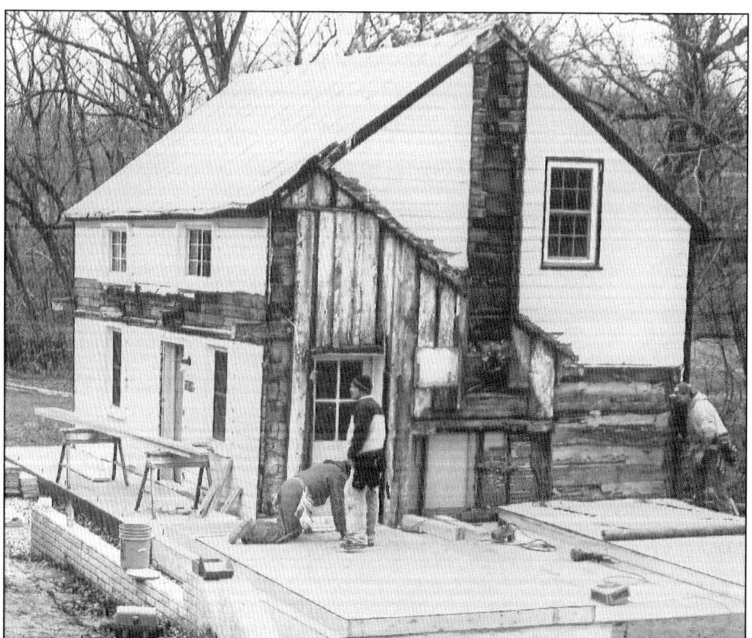

In December 2008, the tollhouse was sold at a foreclosure auction. When the new owner removed the porch and addition, the original log structure was revealed. Board-and-batten siding had covered the logs. It was then covered with clapboards. The lintel of the original fireplace is in place, and the hole in the chimney for a stovepipe is visible about 3 feet above the lintel. (Photograph by Tim Doyle.)

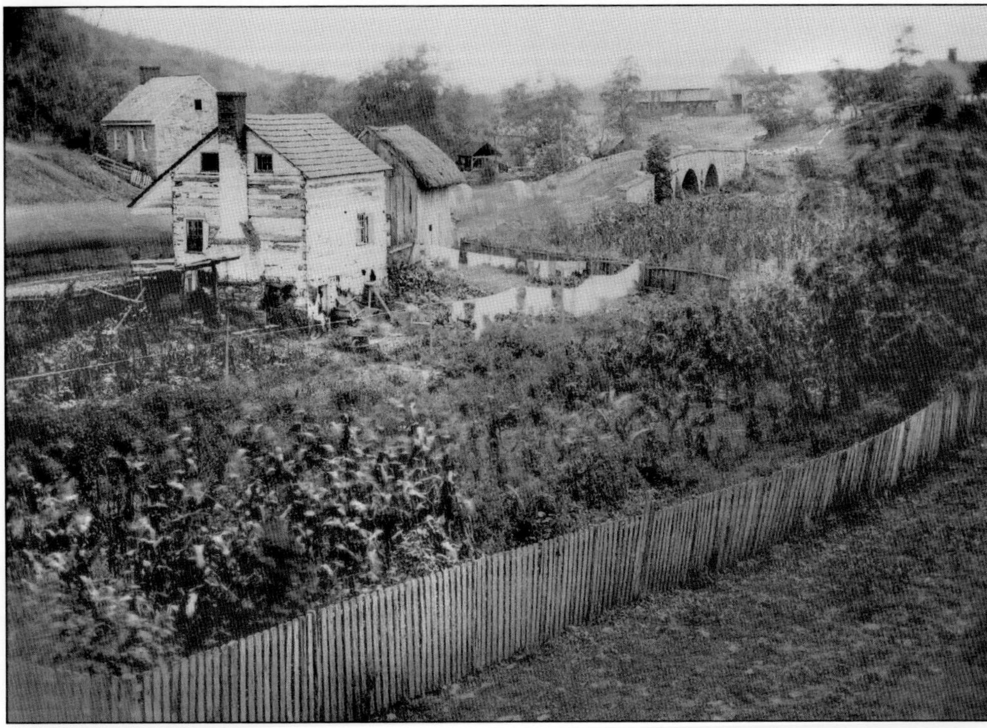

Looking toward Sharpsburg, Alexander Gardner took these photographs after the Battle of Antietam. The Middle Bridge is visible in both. The barn that still stands on Maryland Route 34 is also visible in both photographs. It is at the left of the picture with the covered wagons and in the middle background of the other photograph. The small building across the road and to the right of the thatched-roofed building is part of the mill. The covered wagons are heading toward Sharpsburg. The wagons appear, but very faintly, in the photograph with the tollhouse. The tollhouse at this time had whitewashed logs. Laundry is on the line, plants are upright in the garden, the fence is intact, and the property seems to have escaped damage from the battle that took place in its backyard. (Both, courtesy NPS/ANB.)

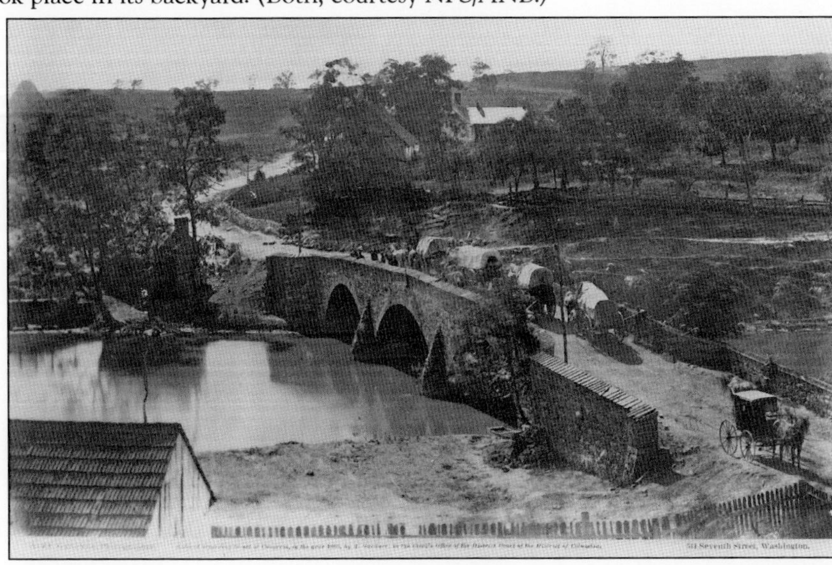

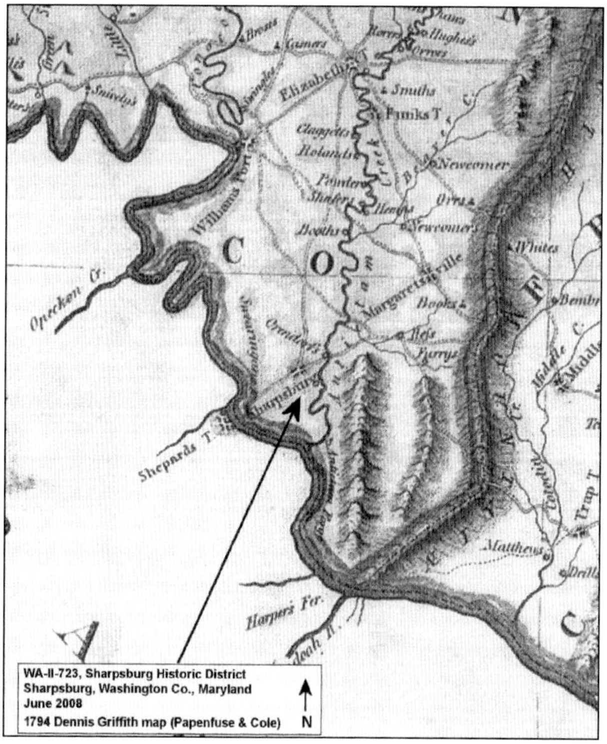

In 1794, all roads led to Sharpsburg. The road east from Sharpsburg leads to Hess's Mill on the Little Antietam Creek. The road north from Sharpsburg leads to Elizabeth Town (Hagerstown). The road west goes to Shepards Town via the Swearingen Ferry. A road from Sharpsburg to Margaretsville (Boonsboro) was not completed until 1825. (Courtesy Paula S. Reed and Associates, 1794 Dennis Griffith map.)

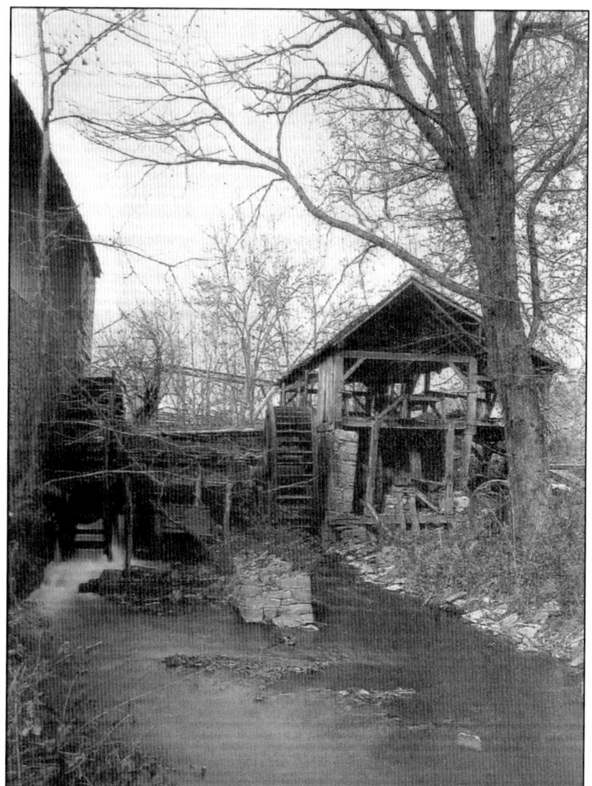

This photograph shows two wheels in the remains of the Orndorff Mill. It stood near what is now called the Porterstown Bridge on Maryland Route 34 east of Sharpsburg. Nothing of the mill buildings is still standing. Milling was a major industry in the 18th century, and towns often grew up around them. There were sawmills as well as gristmills or flour mills. (Courtesy SHS.)

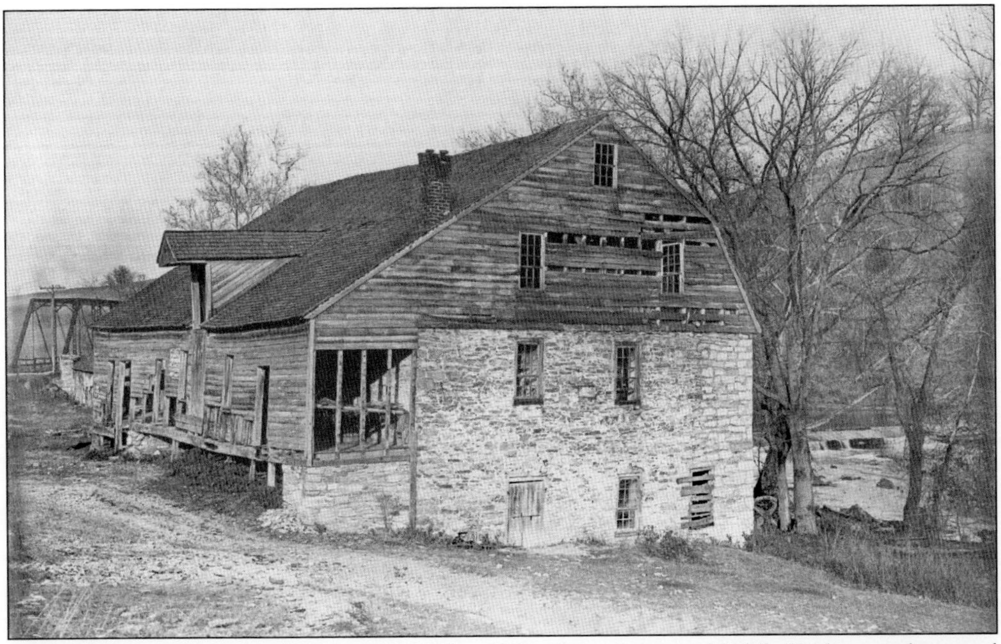

These photographs were taken sometime after 1889, when the stone Middle Bridge was destroyed by floodwaters. The metal bridge was its replacement. The building is deteriorating, with missing timbers, walls, and boarded-up windows. It was part of the gristmill first called the Orndorff Mill at one end of Hog Trough Road, said to date from 1795. That road, once used by farmers traveling to the mill to have grain ground, is now known as the Sunken Road or Bloody Lane. "C.O.M.O. 1782, Sept. 2" was carved on a stone in the mill. The initials were for Christian (sometimes reported as Christopher) and Mary Orndorff (sometimes written Orendorf). Orndorff's father-in-law was Jonathan Hager, founder of Hagerstown, Maryland. The mill was deeded to Jacob Mumma in 1796. By 1860, it was known as the Jacob A. Myers Mill. (Both, courtesy Bonnard J. Morgan Sr.)

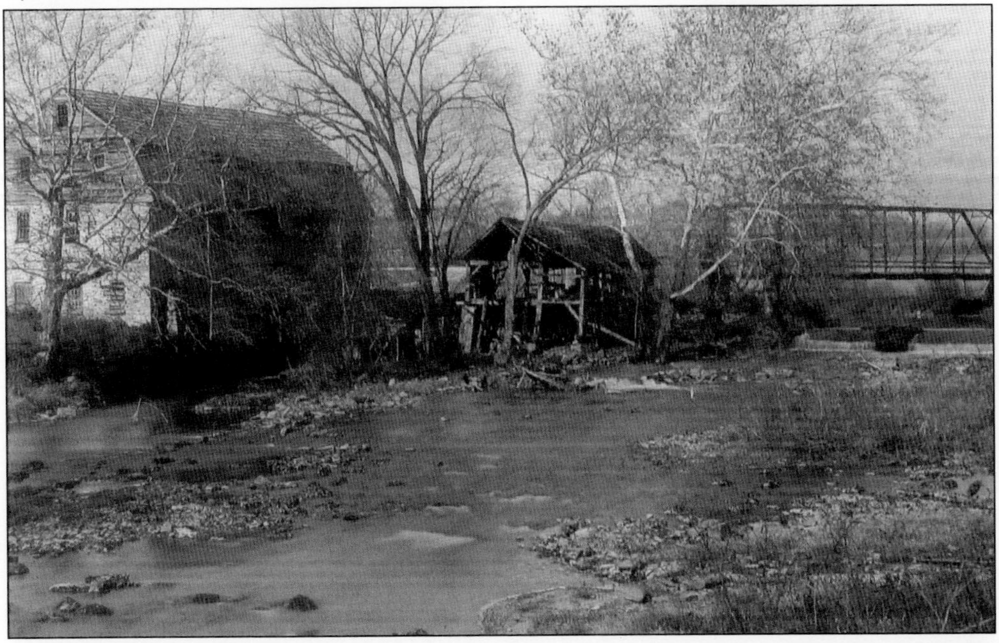

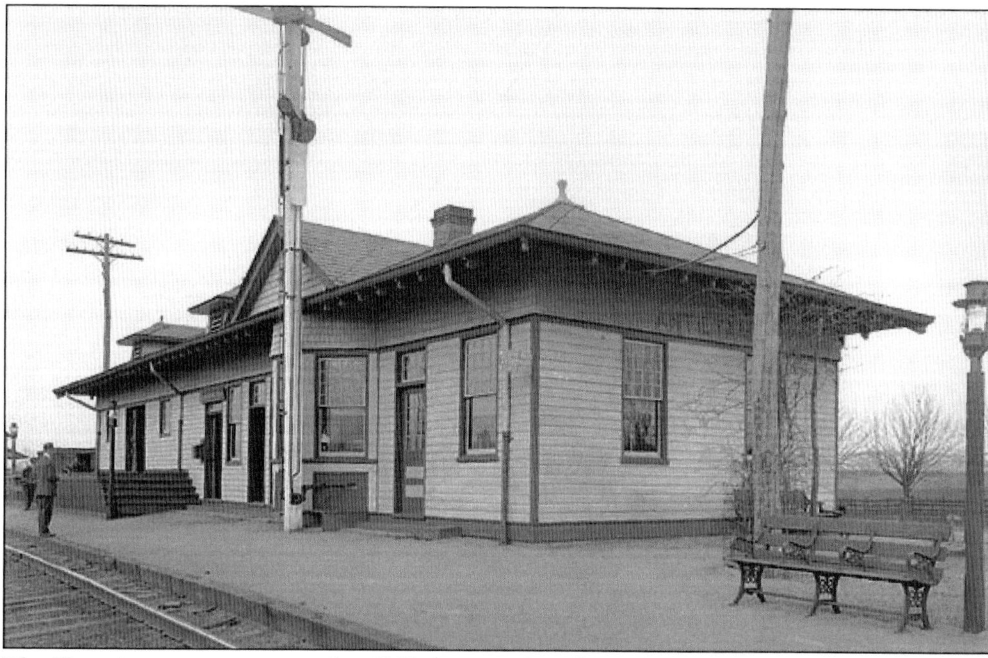

The Sharpsburg train station in this 1917 photograph is about six years old. It replaced the original 1880 station, a small frame structure that burned in 1910. The Shenandoah Valley Railroad changed the station's name to Antietam Station following a head-on collision caused by an operator's confusing of the words Sharpsburg and Shepherdstown. (Courtesy NPS/ANB.)

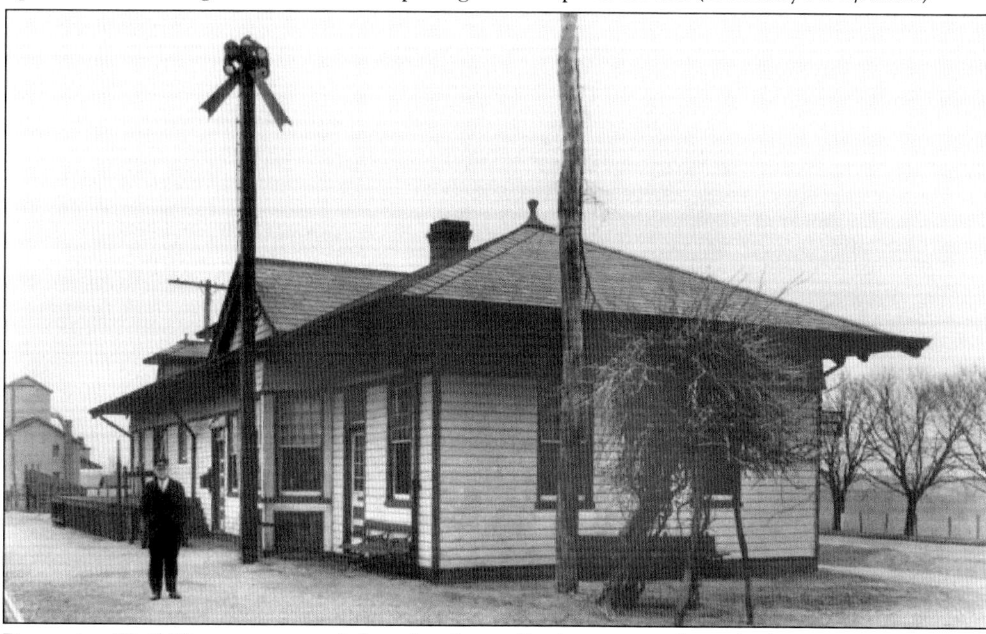

Returning Civil War veterans and their families walked into town from the location of the station shown in this 1933 photograph. It has two waiting rooms, a freight room, and the station agent's office with a large bay window trackside. The Norfolk and Western Railway closed the station in 1962. The trees along the roadside are some of the Norway maples on the Avenue of Trees, the main road from the train station into Sharpsburg. (Courtesy NPS/ANB.)

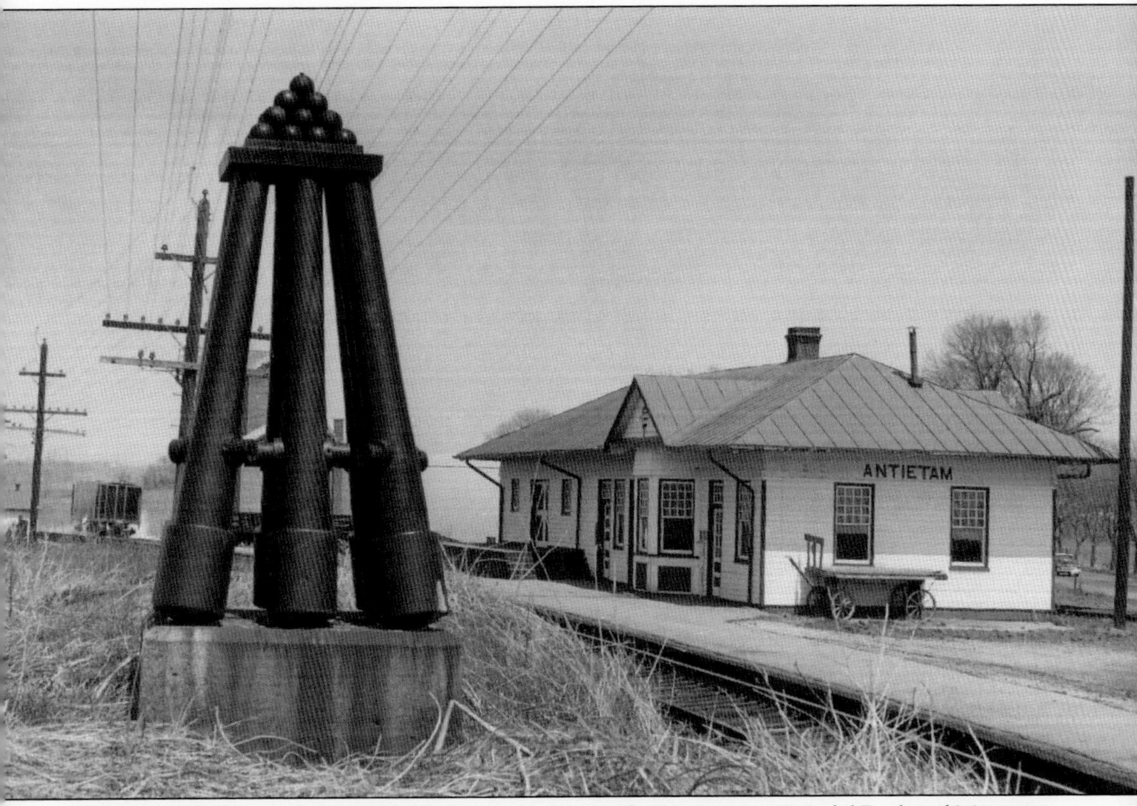

The Town of Sharpsburg leases this historic station to the Hagerstown Model Railroad Museum, Inc. The museum is restoring the station and constructing a large HO scale train layout in the former freight room of the station. The building was saved from demolition through the efforts of Washington County, Save Historic Antietam Foundation, and the Maryland Historical Trust. This 1959 photograph taken by A. K. McGraw shows the Norway maples above the roofline and a monument to the Battle of Antietam, as the North called the battle. The granite base of the monument is still in place and visible from Maryland Route 34; the cannon barrels and cannonballs were disassembled and moved to Antietam National Battlefield. When the station was closed and sold, it had to be moved from railroad property. In doing so, the buyer turned it 180 degrees; the large bay window now faces the road. (Courtesy WCFL/WMR.)

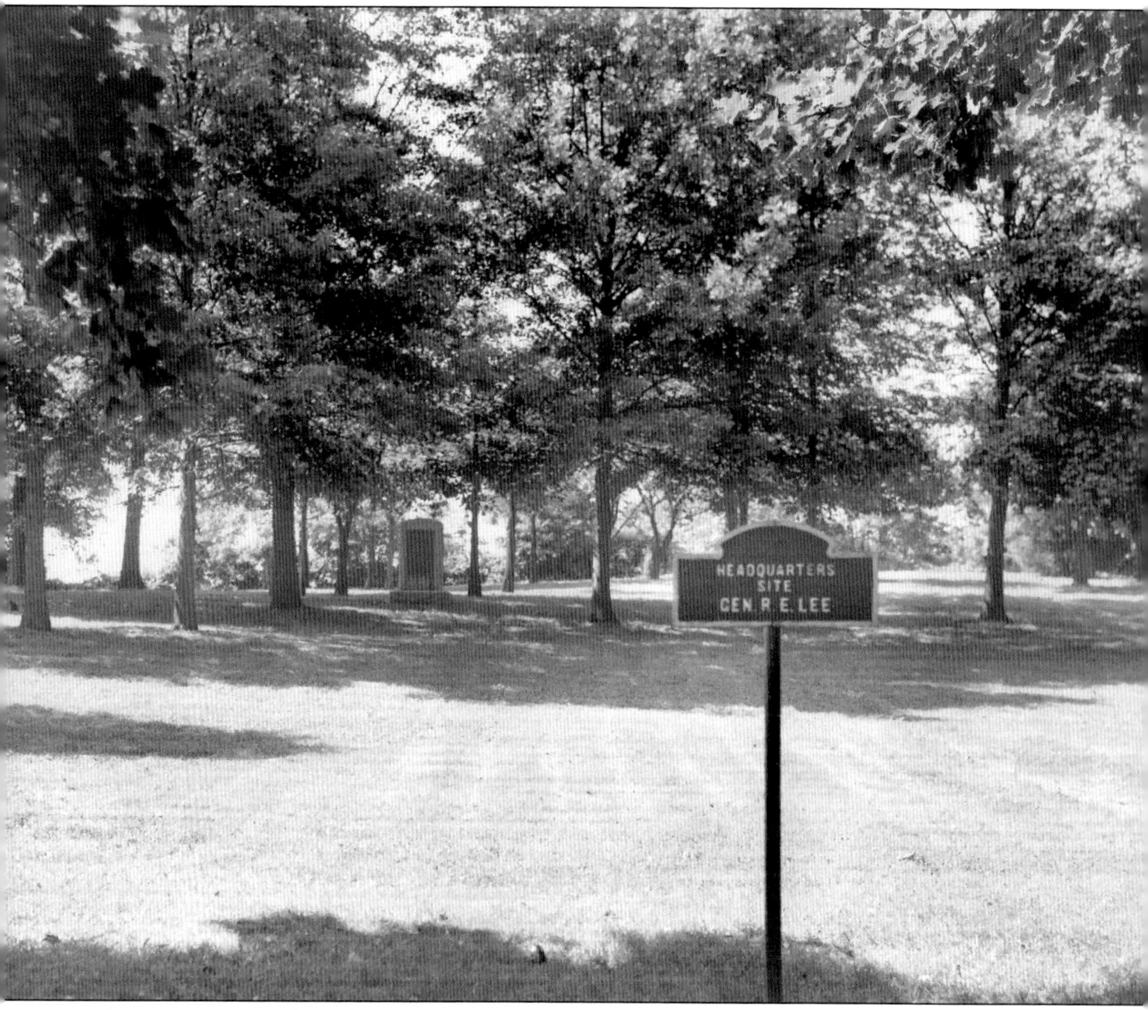

As visitors enter Sharpsburg on Maryland Route 34 from the west, they pass a small park-like area on their left. This stand of trees, known as the Town Woods in 1862, became the tent headquarters of Robert E. Lee. A small roadside marker identifies the park as "Headquarter site Gen. R. E. Lee." Standing in the middle of the lot is a monument of the Confederate States of America. The stone and its plaque are called the Sharpsburg-Lee Memorial. The plaque reads, "On this site in an oak grove from Sept. 15 to Sept. 18, 1862, stood the headquarters tent of General Robert E. Lee commanding the Confederate forces." The unveiling and dedication of the monument took place on Thursday, September 17, 1936, the 74th anniversary of the Battle of Sharpsburg, as the South called the it. The West Virginia Division of the United Daughters of the Confederacy erected the memorial. (Courtesy NPS/ANB.)

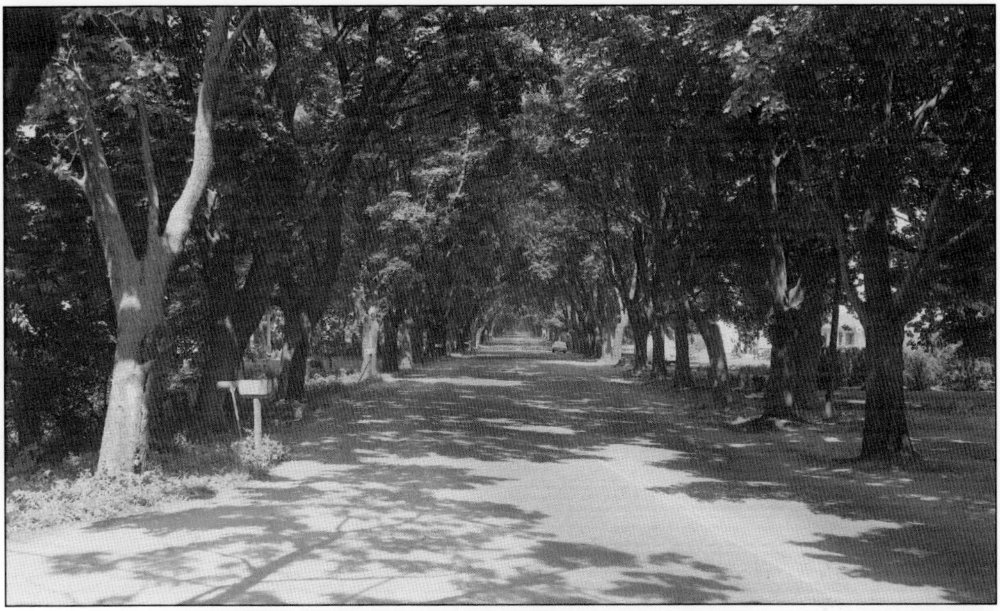

The walk from the Antietam Station west of Sharpsburg to the National Cemetery is 1.3 miles. Returning Civil War veterans collected money and bought Norway maple trees that the State of Maryland planted from the train station to the edge of town. In 1888, the trees were planted 30 feet apart in 8-foot-gravel walkways on both sides of the road, called McComas Avenue or Government Boulevard. Congressman Louis E. McComas was responsible for planting the trees. Norway maples have a life span of 100 years. These two photographs show the mature maples shading the road, as was intended, and the trees as they aged and lost large branches. Barron's *History of Sharpsburg* reports that by 1972 many of the trees had been removed. Replacement trees now line Main Street extended. (Above, courtesy WCHS, Raup photograph; below, courtesy WCFL/WMR.)

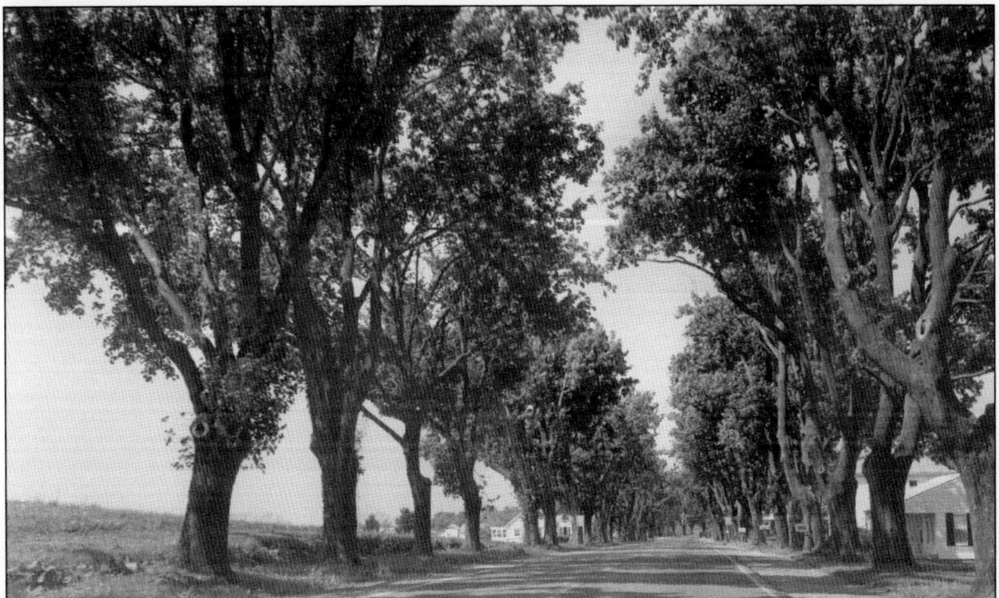

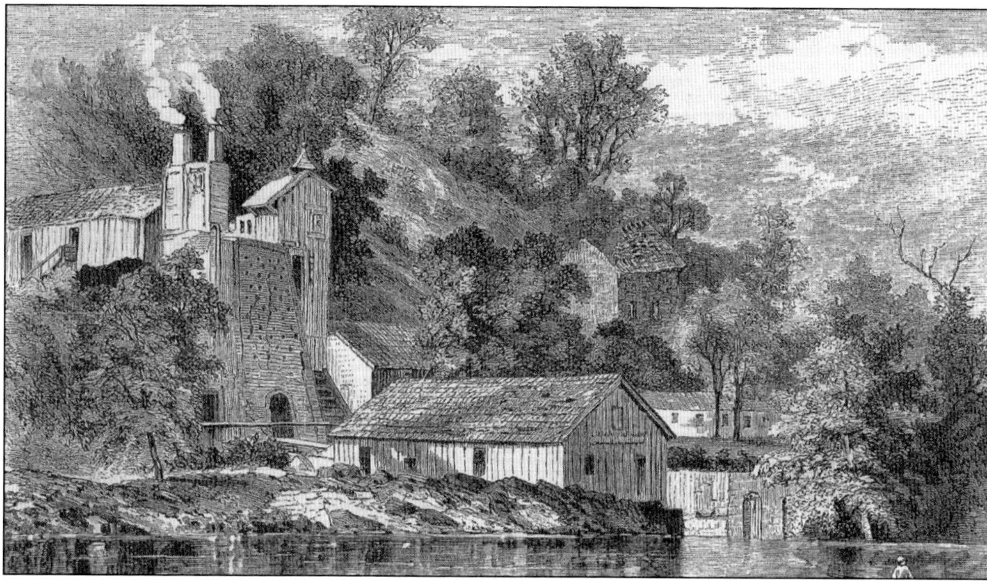

These two sketches show the John McPherson Brien's nail factory and rolling mill that operated on the Antietam Iron Works site. In the 1850s, about 200 white laborers and 60 slaves worked here producing 400 to 500 kegs of nails every week. Joseph Chapline Sr., one of the four founders of the ironworks, furnished land for the furnace in 1765. That company produced pig iron used in nearby forges. Following the Civil War, the Ahl family operated the works until 1880. The buildings were dismantled in 1891. All that remains are traces of the dam and millrace, a stone limekiln, and the building that included a store once run by Peter Otzelberger. (Above, courtesy WCFL/WMR; below, "Antietam Furnace" by Alfred R. Waud, Library of Congress.)

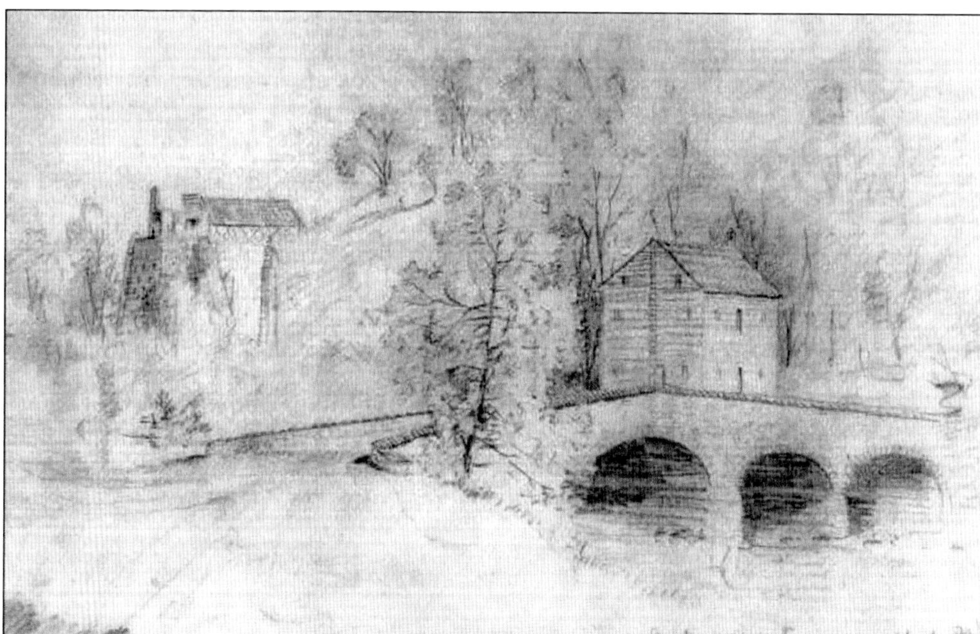

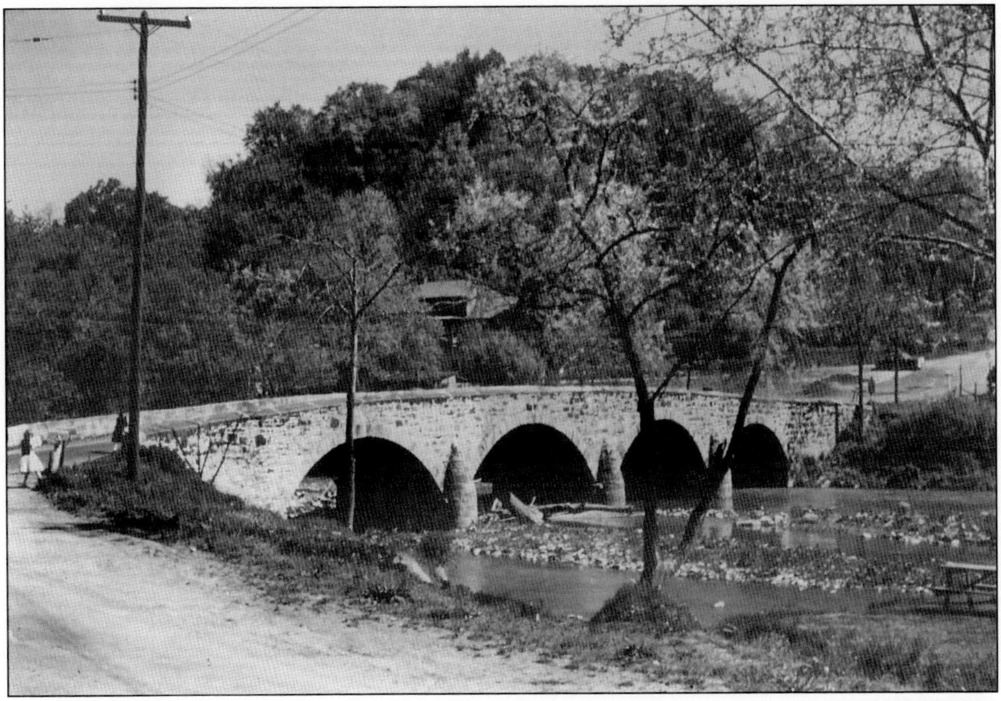

The Antietam Iron Works bridge is the only four-arch bridge on the Antietam Creek in Washington County. This 1957 photograph by Roy V. Chish is taken from the Harpers Ferry Road looking south. The sketch shows a view from creekside. The land around the bridge was acquired from the Catawba and Delaware tribes first by Israel Friend in 1727. A marker on Harpers Ferry Road near Limekiln Road explains the process of measuring the land deeded to Friend. Titled "An Indian Deed," it reads, "Israel Friend in 1727 secured a deed from the Indian chiefs of the Five Nations. Beginning 'at the mouth of the Andietum Creek thence up the Potomack River 200 shoots as fur as an arrow can be slung out of a bow' thence '100 shoots right back from the river' then 'squared till it intercedes with the creek.'" (Above, courtesy WCHS; below, sketch courtesy WCFL/WMR.)

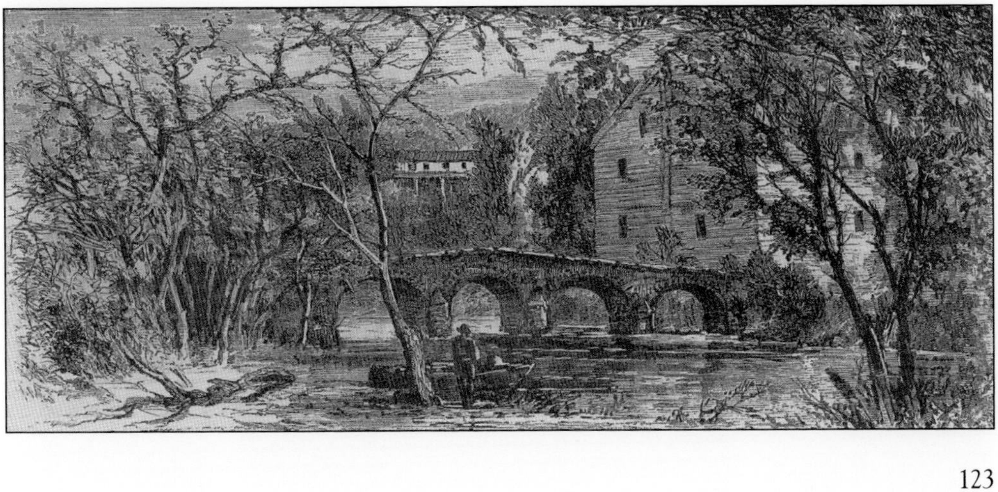

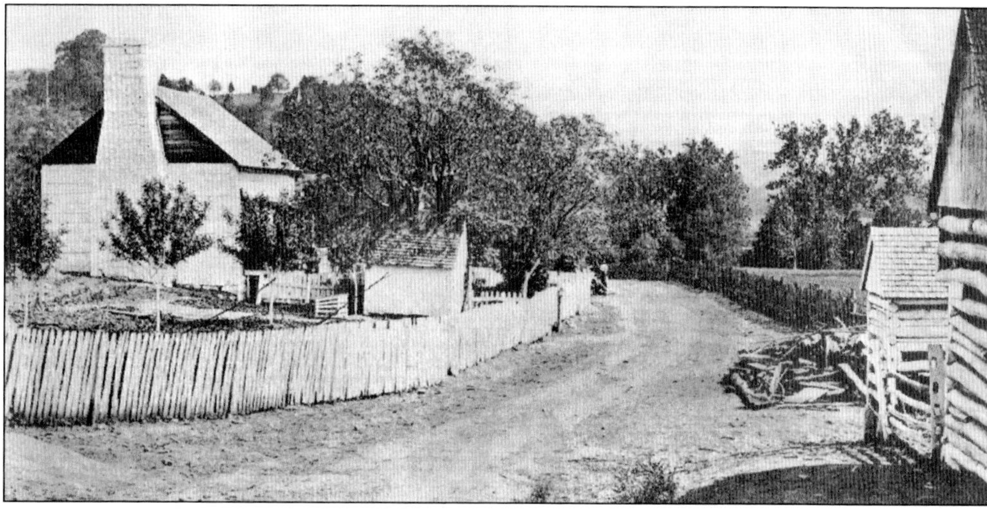

John Weaver's bridge is the only major component that survives at the site of the Antietam Iron Furnace and Antietam Village that grew up around the ironworks. The National Park Service now owns the large white house to the right of the bridge. About 20 other buildings dating from the 19th century still stand in the village. These two images of the village show elements also common in Sharpsburg, about 3 miles away. Clearly visible are log structures, whitewashed, and gardens enclosed by wooden fences. Employees and slaves of the ironworks, which later included a sawmill and a merchant gristmill, lived in the village and surrounding area. St. Paul's Episcopal Church served the village; there were three schools and a grocery store. The Asiatic cholera epidemic among the C&O Canal workers reached this area in the summer of 1832. Village residents are said to have helped bury many in an area near the village. (Both, courtesy WCHS.)

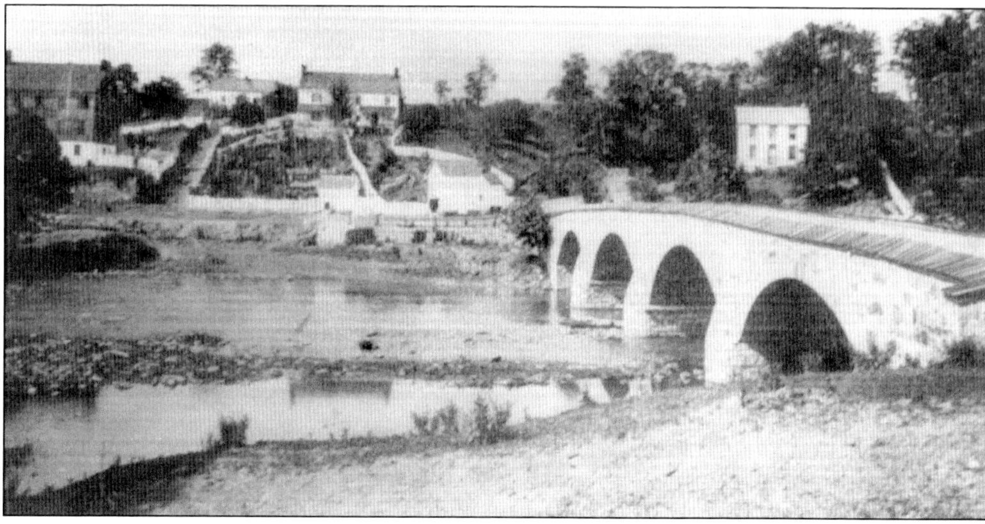

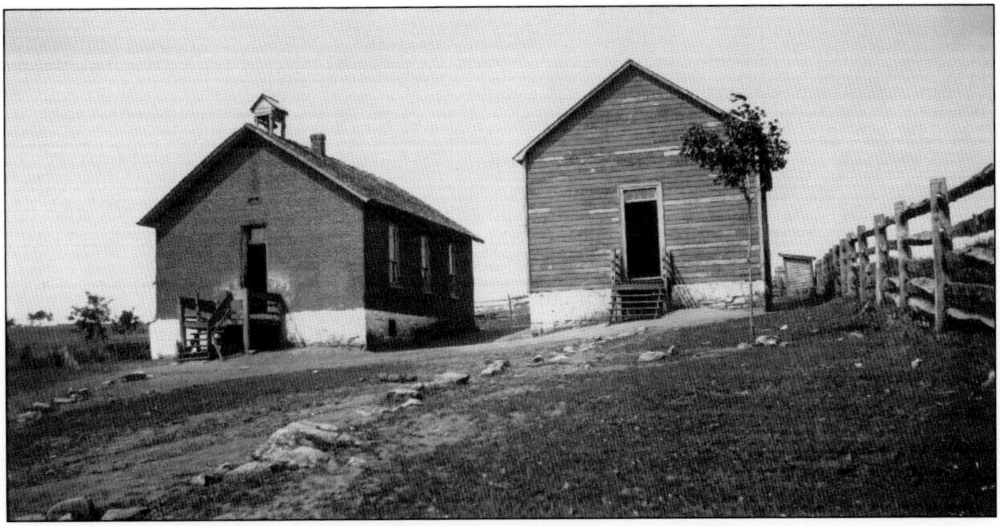

In 1910, George Bushey collected photographs of the 138 active schools in Washington County. Two of the schools recorded were the schools at Antietam Furnace or Antietam Iron Works. According to Barron's *History of Sharpsburg*, the ironworks ceased operation in 1880. Several hundred people had worked at the furnace and lived in the surrounding village. The furnace also had slave workers. The whole complex was sold in 1886 at a bankruptcy sale. Apparently the communities that grew up around the furnace remained, and their children had an opportunity for education. The brick school was for white children; the wooden building was for colored children. One outbuilding—a necessary, or outhouse—is visible behind the wooden building. A bell hangs in the tower of the brick school, whose front wall looks as if it was used to clean chalkboard erasers. (Both, courtesy WCFL/WMR.)

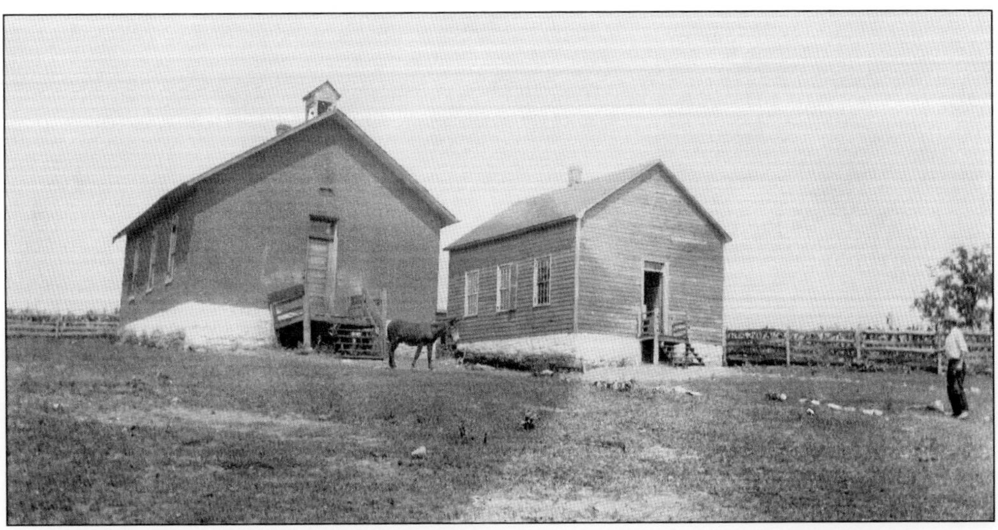

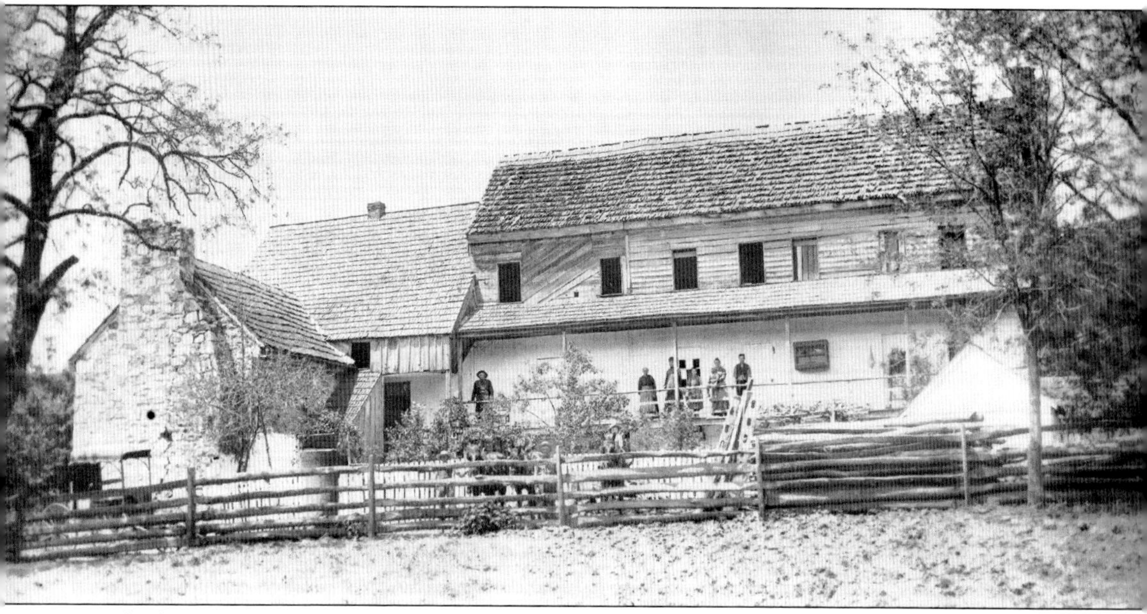

Belinda Springs was named after the owner's wife. Jacob Gardenhour (1764–1846) bought 153 acres on the Antietam Creek about a mile southeast of Sharpsburg in 1818 and created a fashionable resort and health spa. People came to "take the waters" and enjoy the setting and activities. The rates were $6 a week, $3 for a horse or servant. Water was sold to non-guests for $1 a barrel. Activities included horse racing, dancing, and theater. Visitors could take a boat from Harpers Ferry, West Virginia, on the Potomac to the Antietam Creek and the resort. They could also travel by stagecoach from Boonsboro. After a cholera epidemic swept the region, visitors and townspeople stopped going to Belinda Springs; the cottages and cabins fell into disrepair and ruin. Snavely and Lumm families later lived on the farm. The hotel pictured here was torn down in 1929. During the Battle of Antietam, Union troops crossed the creek at a ford near Belinda Springs, then owned by John Snavely. The crossing point is now called Snavely's Ford. (Courtesy Robert Brooks, M.D.)

BIBLIOGRAPHY

Antietam National Battlefield Historic Resource Study: Sharpsburg and the Battle of Antietam. Washington, D.C.: National Park Service, 2008.

Archives of Maryland. Maryland Hall of Records. www.msa.md.gov.

Barron, Lee and Barbara. *The History of Sharpsburg, Maryland.* n. p., 1972.

Ernst, Kathleen A. *Too Afraid to Cry.* Mechanicsburg, PA: Stackpole Books, 2007.

Hahn, Thomas F. *The C&O Canal Boatmen, 1892–1924.* Shepherdstown, WV: American Canal and Transportation Center, 1980.

———. *Towpath Guide to the C&O Canal.* Shepherdstown, WV: American Canal and Transportation Center, 1983.

Musser, Clifford S. *Two Hundred Years History of Shepherdstown.* Shepherdstown, WV: The Independent, 1931.

Paula S. Reed and Associates, Inc. "Sharpsburg Historic District." Hagerstown, MD: National Register Nomination, 2008.

Reilly, Oliver T. *Battlefield of Antietam.* n. p., 1906.

Schildt, John W. *Drums Along the Antietam.* Parsons, WV: McClain Printing Company, 2004.

The Churches of Sharpsburg Walking Tour. Sharpsburg, MD: Sharpsburg Historical Society, 2005.

The Stone Houses of Sharpsburg Walking Tour. Sharpsburg, MD: Sharpsburg Historical Society, 2005.

Unrau, Harlan D. *Historic Resource Study: Chesapeake and Ohio Canal.* Prepared by Karen M. Gray, Ph.D. Washington, D.C.: National Park Service, 2007.

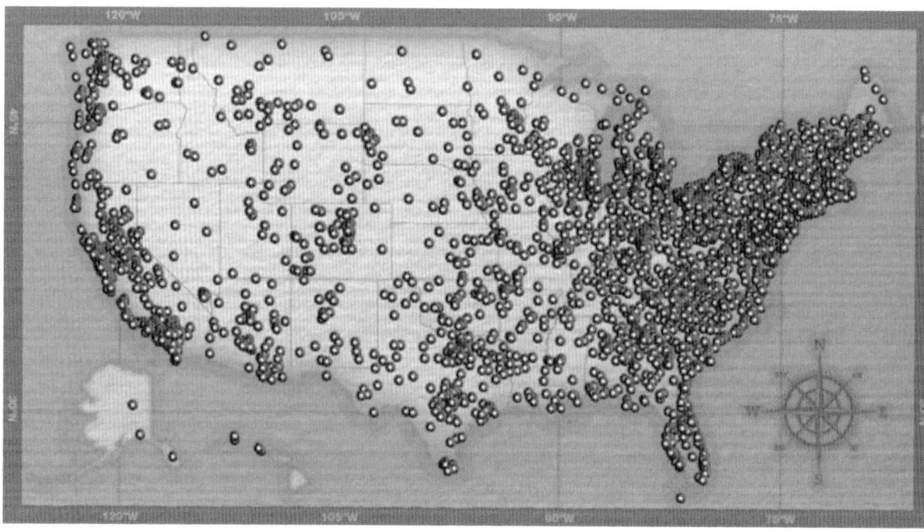